D0392862

Alaska's
<u>Southeast</u>

Alaska's Southeast

Touring the Inside Passage

Third Edition, Revised

by Sarah Eppenbach

A Voyager Book

The Globe Pequot Press

Chester, Connecticut

MANUFACTURED IN THE UNITED STATES OF AMERICA
FIRST EDITION PUBLISHED IN 1982
SECOND EDITION PUBLISHED IN 1985
SECOND PRINTING IN 1986

LIBRARY OF CONGRESS CATALOGING-IN-PUBLICATION DATA

Eppenbach, Sarah.
    Alaska's southeast.

    (A Voyager book)
    Bibliography: p.
    Includes index.
    1. Alaska—Description and travel—1981-
—Guide-books.   2. Inside Passage—Description and
travel—Guide-books.   I. Title.
F902.3.E66   1988   917.98'045   87-30218
ISBN 0-87106-658-0 (pbk.)

Book design by Judy Petry
Cover photograph, looking down the Gastineau Channel, near Juneau, by
    Tim Thompson.

Wherever you go and whatever you do in the outdoors, move at Nature's pace, seeking not to impose yourself but to lose yourself. If you must leave footprints, make them not with blindness but with care and awareness of the delicate balance around you. And if you must take souvenirs, take them not in your pockets but in your mind and spirit. In preservation lies the promise of renewal.

—the Publisher

Contents

Preface

My husband and I made our initial trip to Southeast Alaska in September of 1969. We sailed from Prince Rupert (where we saw the northern lights for the first time) on the Alaska ferry *Taku*, in the days when passengers on Alaska ferries were served by white-jacketed waiters in luxurious dining rooms. Alas, more practical heads have prevailed and the Alaska ferries have acquired a utilitarian image more in keeping with government service.

Nevertheless, in 1969 the ferries were close kin to cruise ships and we were enthralled with the blue and white vessels that transported Alaska's citizens "Outside" and home again with such style and grace. It is many years ago now, but I remember the sensation of steaming steadily northward, the pace never slackening or hastening, past vast island wildernesses and forested inlets, past corrugated glaciers and rude, rocky beaches, as we made our way from one isolated settlement to the next along the Inside Passage. I recall rising in darkness to watch the ship home in on a small crown of lights that was the sole evidence of human habitation on the horizon. This was our introduction to the staunch little town of Wrangell.

That first trip to Alaska was to get acquainted. When we reached Juneau we jumped on a plane and toured the rest of the state: north to Point Barrow, west to Nome, then down to Fairbanks, Anchorage, and the Kenai Peninsula. Every place we went we saw spectacular mountain and water views, but our hearts went out to the gray-green landscape of Southeast Alaska, with the great cloaking forests and endlessly branching waterways. We determined to come back one day and stay.

We moved to Southeast in 1971, in winter, with no idea what our future would be. In the days that followed, we moved from the best hotel in Juneau to the better and the not-so-good before my husband was offered a job as a research analyst with the treasury division of the Alaska Department of Revenue. Those were memorable times for anyone in the field of economics and investment theory. Alaska was already launched down the path to immense oil revenues, and treasury was just about the most exciting place in the world to be employed.

Some things are different now than they were when we first came to live in Juneau, but many more have stayed the same. Southeast Alaska is still a watercolor study of grays and greens and glacial blues. The passage north from Seattle or Prince Rupert remains one of the fine experiences in my life. The towns and villages continue to intrigue me, and the people there are the most energetic, personable, and generous of any I have encountered. The people may grow in number but they do not change in spirit. Those of us who live in Alaska are here because we want to be; we are at peace with ourselves to an extraordinary degree.

There are many people I would like to thank for their help with this book. Elizabeth Daugherty, former oceanography instructor at Juneau-Douglas High School and shipboard naturalist for the Alaska Marine Highway System, lent me her files of accumulated material which were an invaluable launching point, and helped very much along the way. Others to whom I turned repeatedly are R. N. De Armond, noted Juneau author and historian; Al Harris of the Forestry Sciences Laboratory of the U.S. Forest Service; Dave Zimmerman of the Southeast Regional Office of the Alaska Department of Fish and Game; and Neil Hagadorn, Regional Interpretive Specialist for the U.S. Forest Service. My good friends Judy Cooper and Rosemary Quast were characteristically generous with their time and considerable field knowledge on matters of Southeast birds and wild flowers. I never encountered a single person in any Southeast community who was not willing to help, and I am especially grateful to those staffing the visitor information offices who gave me such assistance. Finally, I must thank my husband, Larry, who took most of the photographs that appear in the book and who set aside many of his own projects to work on mine; and Deb Easter, my editor, who has been unflagging in her efforts to root out inconsistency in particular and lousy writing in general.

This book is dedicated to you, fellow traveler, whether your interests are in viewing trees and wild flowers; in fishing, camping, kayaking, climbing mountains, walking on glaciers, photographing wildlife, viewing totem poles, or simply sampling life in Southeast's towns and villages. I hope that your journey through the Inside Passage will be as filled with wonder and adventure as ours was some twenty years ago, and that you will return again and again to savor Alaska's Southeast.

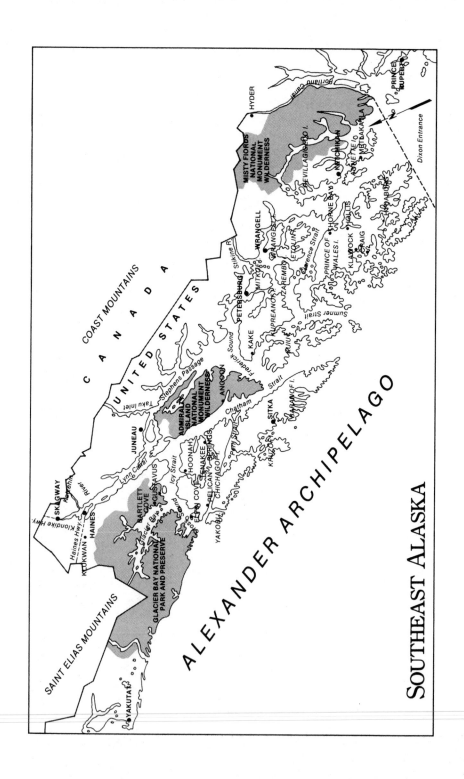

SOUTHEAST ALASKA

ALEXANDER ARCHIPELAGO

SAINT ELIAS MOUNTAINS

COAST MOUNTAINS

CANADA

UNITED STATES

GLACIER BAY NATIONAL PARK AND PRESERVE

ADMIRALTY ISLAND NATIONAL MONUMENT WILDERNESS

MISTY FIORDS NATIONAL MONUMENT WILDERNESS

YAKUTAT

SKAGWAY

HAINES

KLUKWAN

BARTLETT COVE

GUSTAVUS

ELFIN COVE

HOONAH

PELICAN

TENAKEE SPRINGS

CHICHAGOF

JUNEAU

SITKA

ANGOON

KAKE

PETERSBURG

WRANGELL

HYDER

KETCHIKAN

METLAKATLA

CRAIG

KLAWOCK

HOLLIS

THORNE BAY

PRINCE RUPERT

Klondike Hwy.

Haines Hwy.

Klehini River

Chilkat River

Lynn Canal

Taku Inlet

Stephens Passage

Icy Strait

Glacier Bay

YAKOBI

KRUZOF

BARANOF I.

Chatham Strait

Peril Strait

Frederick Sound

KUPREANOF I.

ZAREMBO I.

MITKOF I.

Stikine R.

Wrangell

ETOLIN I.

Clarence Strait

PRINCE OF WALES I.

REVILLAGIGEDO I.

ANNETTE I.

GRAVINA I.

DUKE I.

Sumner Strait

Portland Canal

Behm Canal

Dixon Entrance

Southeast Traveler Basics

There are 10 million acres of forest in Southeast Alaska; 1,000 islands, 10,000 miles of shoreline, 50 to 70 major glaciers, 25,000 brown bear, 15,000 bald eagles, and 66,000 people. The people have caused a blight here or there upon the land, but on the whole have had little visible effect. When you visit this land of ice blue glaciers and forested islands, you will look upon a part of the earth that has changed remarkably little in the past one thousand years. The green water fjords that you cruise along appeared just the same to the Tlingit and Haida Indians who first settled along these shores. Now, as then, stands of giant spruce and hemlock reach toward the mountain peaks, while thickets of wild berries run rampant over the land.

We of the twentieth century, contemplating matters from the womb-like comfort of our heated living rooms, think of Southeast Alaska as a cold, wet forbidding place, but the early Native residents knew it for what it truly is: a hospitable land. Southeast might even be called a perfect land for aboriginal inhabitants. The climate was temperate—yes, *temperate*. The rain forest provided an environment that was pleasantly cool most of the time and seldom so cold, even in winter, that a fire and some animal skins could not provide adequate warmth within the walls of a planked enclosure.

The forest and the sea provided all the food that could be wanted, and it was not difficult to gather. The Tlingit and Haida Indians did not wear themselves out running through the woods with bow and arrow in order to eat: they went down to the mouth of the salmon stream and harvested the required amount of fish. For a change of pace, they sent a line down to the bottom and brought up a halibut. Or a snapper. Or a crab. When they wanted fruit they had their choice of salmonberries, blueberries, straw- berries, nagoonberries, crowberries, cloudberries, thimbleberries, cran- berries, or currants. Almost every patch of land in Southeast Alaska yields one type of berry or another.

The land provided food, shelter, fuel, and transportation. There were no lions, tigers, or crocodiles to prey on helpless humans, not a single poi- sonous snake or insect. There was only the occasional grizzly or the icy water that could snatch a precious life in minutes.

Southeast Alaska is still a hospitable land. Those of us lucky enough to live along this forested coast know that the land continues to provide food, fuel, shelter, and spiritual solace in generous portions. The cold, clear waterways are not only beautiful to gaze upon, they still provide the only certain link from one community to the next. Water is our lifeline. There is not a single thriving community in Southeast Alaska today, from the capital city of Juneau to the smallest hamlets of Tenakee Springs or Elfin Cove, that does not face the water.

The waterfront atmosphere enjoyed by all Inside Passage towns is a unique aspect of Southeast Alaska. There are few places in the world where the toot of a ferryboat heralds an important event, but in Southeast Alaska an entire population relies upon this gentle means of transport for supplies, mail, and transportation. An automobile takes you only about thirty miles in most Southeast communities. There is only one road south of Haines or Skagway to connect with the outside world, and that's at Hyder, a community of 75 at the head of the Portland Canal. The water is our highway. You will find the real Southeast Alaska down at the docks, where fishing boats are unloading salmon, freighters are onloading lumber, ferries and cruise ships are off-loading passengers, and tugs and barges are delivering refrigerators and mobile homes to a grateful population.

WHEN TO GO

No matter when you make your trip, you probably will not be able to escape some of the soggy weather that keeps Southeast Alaska so deliciously green. There is no dry season in Southeast. Statistically speak- ing, May and June are the sunniest months of the year and October the wettest, but picking the right time to travel in Southeast is a little like bet- ting on horses—you can study the racing forms all you like, but you still need a measure of luck. Traveling in May gives you the added advantage of beating the crowds, but May is still early spring in Southeast Alaska with temperatures in the fifties and below. Many areas will still be emerg-

Eaglecrest ski area near Juneau offers superb downhill and cross-country skiing with no lift lines. (Mark Kelley)

ing from the winter snow cover, and the scenery will not be at its prime. For most people, June is the best choice, followed by July and August.

More and more visitors are venturing into Southeast in winter for a less conventional view of the country. The obvious disadvantages to this scheme are the temperature and the fact that many local exhibits, shows, and excursions (including Glacier Bay) will be unavailable. Cruise ships do not travel the Inside Passage in winter, so you must fly or take the Alaska state ferry. Winter sports enthusiasts find Southeast at its best in this season, though, when the mountains are sculpted whiteness and the open muskegs are transformed into vast, sparkling playgrounds made for snowshoes and cross-country skis. Eaglecrest ski area in Juneau provides superb downhill skiing for all skill levels (with no lift lines). Winter is also the time to view the world's largest gathering of bald eagles at the Chilkat Bald Eagle Preserve near Haines, to see the various Southeast communities in their everyday dress, and to take advantage of lower fares and guaranteed staterooms on Alaska state ferries.

WHAT TO BRING AND WEAR

Southeast Alaska is a casual place, where formal dress has little practicality. The important factor for residents and visitors alike is comfort. For most occasions this boils down to warmth and dryness, because Southeast Alaska is wet. Southeast Alaska can also be cold, and wet plus cold makes an unpleasant and sometimes dangerous combination. You should not underestimate the effect of cool weather. Even if you are traveling to Southeast in midsummer, the usual temperature is only in the fifties or sixties. You will not enjoy walking about and sight-seeing, especially in a drizzle, unless you are adequately dressed.

Whatever time of year you visit, your most important article of clothing will be something to keep you warm: either a warm coat or jacket that you wear over something of moderate weight; or a warm shirt, vest, or sweater that you wear under a lighter coat. Alaskans swear by wool to keep in the warmth and keep out the wind. For men, a wool Pendleton shirt is a good choice for any season. The addition of a light down or polyester vest and a waterproof parka, windbreaker, or raincoat will keep you warm and dry under any circumstances. A cotton shirt topped with a heavy wool sweater and the windbreaker or raincoat would be another good choice. For women, the same is true. Whether you prefer to dress in blue jeans, trousers, or skirts, you will appreciate something wool or downy on top, followed by a windbreaker or raincoat.

Gloves and hats are a good idea, even in the summer. You will appreciate them on board ship as well as in port. A woolly hat to pull down over the ears when the wind blows and some warm mittens will add at least an hour to your sight-seeing stamina. You might also consider bringing a lightweight set of long underwear. Even if you do not plan to hike, camp, boat, fish, or generally be outdoors, a thin layer of cotton or silk under your clothes will help cut the chill. Now available in an array of colors, fabrics, and styles, long underwear has made a quantum leap from the bulky woolens of yesterday.

For staying dry, consider bringing a thin rain poncho that you can fold up and carry in your pocket or purse when the sun comes out. These ponchos have deep hoods to keep your head dry, and come in all sorts of inviting colors. You can't go wrong with a folding umbrella, either. A raincoat with a warm, zip-in lining works well in this climate as an alternative to the ponchos or plastic raincoat over a warm coat.

Footgear is always a difficulty in wet climates. If the day happens to be dry you have no problem, but walking around with wet feet is a disaster. Southeasterners often solve the problem with a pair of rubber moccasins. Rubber on the bottom and leather on top, these lightweight, slip-on boot/shoes provide excellent traction for the steep or slippery spots on shore and on the deck of your ship. (All of the major outfitters make these now.) Light overshoes are an alternative for men. If you are the sporty type or intend to do a lot of walking or hiking, wear your hiking boots. You will not be out of place anywhere in Southeast Alaska.

If you really want to fit into the Alaska scene, this is the standard equipment for southeasterners of either sex. On the feet: hiking boots, rubber boots or moccasins, or athletic shoes. On the legs: jeans. On top: a halibut shirt, which is a heavy, long-sleeved, wool shirt-jacket, sometimes with an extra wool flap over the shoulders (guaranteed to keep out the rain, even if you are a halibut fisherman). Over it all: a parka, waterproof and windproof, with hood. On the back: a light day pack for your belongings. You might want to consider a daypack for your trip, especially if you are planning to get off the beaten path. The pack can carry your lunch, your camera, your extra film, wallet, tickets, and traveler's checks, leaving your hands free to take pictures, read maps, and carry purchases.

I think you would enjoy having a small pair of binoculars during your trip up the Inside Passage. Cruising along the quiet waterways, you will want to have a closer look at eagles, whales, fishing boats, logging operations, navigational markers—so many things. Very compact but powerful binoculars are available that are easy to tuck into your bag. While you are about it, tuck in some insect repellent and sunscreen. When the sun does come out in the summer, it is very bright because the air is so clear. You can suddenly find yourself with a nice burn, especially if you are out on the water.

USING THE FERRIES OR "BLUE CANOES"

The Alaska Marine Highway System has been in official operation since 1963 when the motor vessels *Malaspina*, *Taku*, and *Matanuska* came on line—the first of the popular "Blue Canoes." Each of the blue-hulled ships was outfitted to carry 108 cars and 500 passengers on the regular

THE SOUTHEAST FLEET

NAME OF VESSEL	SPEED	LENGTH	PASSENGERS	VEHICLES	STATEROOMS
Columbia	19.0 knots	418 feet	970	180	91
Malaspina	16.5 knots	408 feet	750	120	86
Matanuska	16.5 knots	408 feet	750	120	112
Taku	16.0 knots	352 feet	500	105	44
Aurora	14.5 knots	235 feet	250	47	—
LeConte	14.5 knots	235 feet	250	47	—
Chilkat	10.5 knots	100 feet	79	15	—

Southeasterners rush to the solarium deck when the sun comes out. Sleeping bags replace lounge chairs at night.

service between Prince Rupert and Haines. Today the Southeast fleet has expanded to four main-line ferries (as above plus the flagship *Columbia*) and three smaller ferries (the *Aurora, LeConte,* and *Chilkat*).

Two of the original vessels have been lengthened by more than fifty feet to accommodate 750 passengers and 120 vehicles. The main-line service runs year-round between Seattle or Prince Rupert and all of the major towns in Southeast Alaska, including Ketchikan, Wrangell, Petersburg, Sitka, Juneau, Haines, and Skagway. The smaller vessels fill in the gaps with short-distance hauls to the smaller communities of Metlakatla, Hollis, Kake, Angoon, Hoonah, Tenakee Springs, Pelican, and Stewart/Hyder (summer only) off the main route. All of the vessels carry automobiles (including campers and trailers) as well as passengers.

The main-line vessels operate just like regular passenger ships except that transportation, and not luxury, is their aim. They have comfortable staterooms, deck chairs, movies, video games, observation lounges, cocktail bars and dining rooms. The meals on most of the ferries are self-service, and the food is adequate but definitely so-so. The *Columbia,* however, offers both table service and cafeteria meals. Fares—reasonable at any time of year—are discounted still further during the off-season (roughly October through April). Also during this period, senior citizens and the handicapped can travel free between Alaskan ports (you still pay for staterooms, meals, and vehicles)—in other words, anywhere on the system except to or from Seattle, Prince Rupert, and Stewart/Hyder.

If you do not want to pay for a stateroom, you can doze in a reclining chair or spread your sleeping bag on the floor. (You cannot sleep in your vehicle as the car deck is off limits between ports.) All of the four larger ships are equipped with a heated, glassed-in solarium on the top deck, an ideal spot for sleeping out-of-doors without getting wet. Coin lockers and public shower rooms are available, too, and you can even rent a towel. None of the three smaller ferries has staterooms. Overnight passengers stretch out in the lounge chairs, the solarium (except on the *Chilkat*, which has none), or on the floor. You are welcome to bring your own food aboard any of the Alaska ferries, but cooking is not permitted.

You can design your whole trip around the state ferry system if you are willing to plan in advance. You can leave for Alaska from either Seattle or Prince Rupert and stop at any port along the way to Skagway, and back. You do not have to make the entire trip at one time. You can get off at each town for as long as you like and resume your trek on another ferry—providing you have made reservations if you have a vehicle or want a stateroom. With judicious planning, however, you can schedule your travels so that you make virtually every leg of the trip in the daytime, and do not need a stateroom at all. In this case, foot passengers will need reservations for passage only if traveling during a heavy traffic period such as the weekend of the Southeast State Fair in Haines in August, or the Little Norway Festival in Petersburg in May. In summer, U.S. Forest Service interpreters are on board the main-line ferries to point out sights along the route and enhance your enjoyment of Alaska's scenic wilderness.

You can also use the little vessels to make side trips from the major

Ferries link towns along the Inside Passage. Smaller vessels like the Aurora *serve communities off the main line.*

communities and investigate what most tourists miss. You can take the *Aurora* from Ketchikan to Prince of Wales Island, for example, and explore for days. There are several hotels and lodges where you can stay on the island. Take a day trip to Metlakatla; you can go over and back from Ketchikan in one day. Go to Tenakee Springs and spend a few restful hours in the hot sulfur baths, or go to Angoon on Admiralty Island and watch the tide boil through the narrow entrance of Kootznahoo Inlet.

You can take your car or camper on the ferry, but should you? I would recommend against it, unless you particularly want to camp out, or unless you intend to get off at Skagway or Haines to connect up with the Alaska Highway for the trip to Interior Alaska or down to the Lower 48. Once arrived in each town, you will probably want to do most of your exploring on foot. If you decide to do some sight-seeing outside of the city center, you can always rent a car or hire a taxi.

It is decidedly more expensive to take a car, and you will spend precious time waiting in ferry lines—especially if you plan to get off and on

Approximate Mileage and Sailing Time Between Ports
Alaska Marine Highway System

PORTS	SAILING TIME	STATUTE MILES
Seattle to Ketchikan	40 hours	750
Prince Rupert to Ketchikan	6 hours	103
Ketchikan to Wrangell	5 hours, 30 minutes	100
Wrangell to Petersburg	3 hours	47
Petersburg to Juneau (Auke Bay Terminal)	7 hours, 30 minutes	138
Juneau (Auke Bay Terminal) to Haines	4 hours, 15 minutes	77
Haines to Skagway	1 hour	17
Petersburg to Sitka	10 hours	177
Sitka to Juneau (Auke Bay Terminal)	8 hours, 30 minutes	150

at several communities. My most relaxed and rewarding trips have been on foot.

Reservations for peak season travel present something of a Catch 22. Summer sailings from Seattle are so popular that you need to reserve early, but the summer sailing schedule does not come out until December. The Alaska Marine Highway reservations office has recently changed its policy and will now accept written requests for reservations at any time, but since the schedule will not be available yet, you will have to give the approximate dates you want to travel. Telephone requests are accepted also as of the first working day in January. On that date, written and telephone requests are processed simultaneously, written ones in the order received. Because telephone lines are usually jammed, your best chance is to send in your written request well before 1 January.

Ideally, you should begin planning your trip a year in advance by writing for current schedule and tariff information. Even though the schedule will be out of date for your trip, you can get an idea of the itinerary you want to work out. Then, as far in advance as possible, put in your written request for reservations. Keep in mind that ships departing from Prince Rupert are usually less booked than those leaving from Seattle, and southward-bound ferries are usually less booked than those heading north. Try to be flexible in your planning and provide the reservations office with several alternative dates. For current schedules and reservations write *Alaska Marine Highway, P.O. Box R, Juneau, Alaska, 99811.* Telephone *(907) 465-3941/42;* or *toll free (800) 642-0066.*

BEFORE YOU GO

Depending upon your interests, you may want to write for advance information from various state, federal, or community agencies. A useful first step when planning your trip is to write for a copy of the Alaska Division of Tourism's *Alaska Vacation Planner.* This free color publication describes all of the communities of Southeast Alaska (and other regions of the state, too) and provides more than sixteen hundred listings of hotels, campgrounds, sight-seeing opportunities, charter services, and the like. Included are addresses for local Chambers of Commerce and visitors' centers, state and national parks, national monuments, and other government offices, so you can write directly with your questions. Write *Alaska State Division of Tourism, P.O. Box E, Juneau, Alaska, 99811.* Another excellent planning guide is available free from the Southeast Alaska Tourism Council *(P.O. Box 20710, Juneau, Alaska, 99802).* I have used these booklets extensively to plan my own travels around Southeast Alaska and found them accurate and indispensible.

IF YOU WANT TO HUNT OR FISH

If you plan to hunt or fish, you should consult directly with the Alaska Department of Fish and Game for regulations concerning the particular quarry you have in mind. Write *Public Communications Section, Alaska Department of Fish and Game, Box 3-2000, Juneau, Alaska, 99802.* In general, a fishing license is required for anyone sixteen years or older fishing in fresh or salt water. For nonresidents of Alaska, three types of license are available: a one-year license (thirty-six dollars), fourteen-day license (twenty dollars), and three-day license (ten dollars). Licenses are available at most sporting-goods stores in Alaska.

Hunting licenses and appropriate tags are required for nonresidents of any age. Fees are sixty dollars for a one-year license, or ninety-six dollars for a one-year combination hunting and sport-fishing license. Tag fees, seasons, and bag limits vary with the species, so check with the Fish and Game Department in advance. Those wishing to hunt brown bear or Dall sheep must be accompanied by either a registered guide or a relative within the second degree of kindred who is an Alaska resident and over nineteen. ("Within the second degree of kindred" means blood relatives who are parents, grandparents, sisters, brothers, children, or grand-children.) This rule is strictly interpreted and enforced. Visitors from other countries should check with the Fish and Game Department for special regulations pertaining to them. A list of registered guides is available for five dollars from the *Department of Commerce and Economic Development, Division of Occupational Licensing, P.O. Box D-LIC, Juneau, Alaska, 99811.*

IF YOU WANT TO CAMP

You can camp anywhere in the Tongass National Forest (which covers much of the Southeast) unless you see a sign specifically prohibiting it. In only a few places is camping prohibited (at archaeological sites, for ex-ample), which is one of the unique features of Southeast Alaska. No per-mit is necessary to camp or to build a fire, but you should be cautious about fires even in the rain forest. Many serious fires have been caused by campers who mistakenly thought the rain would put out their campfires for them. Not so: use the same precautions you would camping anyplace else. Also be extremely wary of bear anywhere in the Tongass. Do not camp on known bear paths and do not leave food in or near your tent. For advice about camping and hiking in bear country, write for the pamphlet *The Bears and You* from the Alaska Department of Fish and Game.

There is a U.S. Forest Service office in almost every community along the Inside Passage. Staff members are glad to recommend places to camp, hike, or otherwise enjoy the national forest. Before striking out into the wilderness, it is a good idea to call or visit the local Forest Service office to ask their advice and let them know your plans. There are also federal, state, or city campgrounds in virtually every community along the Inside Passage. Consult your *Alaska Vacation Planner* for information about specific sites, or write to the appropriate Chamber of Commerce or visitors' bureau.

For a true wilderness adventure and an incredible bargain to boot,

The king salmon lures many an angler to Southeast Alaska. (Alaska Department of Fish and Game)

consider renting a U.S. Forest Service recreational cabin. There are over 150 from which to choose in the Tongass. All are located in remote areas: along saltwater inlets, for example, or freshwater lakes. Many are accessible only by chartered floatplane. The cabins are made of wood and are suitably rustic. All have a wood-burning or diesel stove, as well as wooden bunks, and a table. Firewood is provided but not stove oil. Lakeside cabins are supposed to be equipped with a skiff and oars, but you should not depend upon either. For other equipment and food, you are on your own. In fact you are on your own, period, once the floatplane leaves, so plan carefully. The cost for the cabin is only fifteen dollars per night for your entire party, but you can count on spending two hundred to three hundred dollars for your round-trip transportation from the nearest town. Cabins can be reserved up to 180 days in advance for a maximum stay of seven nights (in summer). For a map showing cabin locations and other information write *Public Affairs Office, U.S. Forest Service, P.O. Box 21628, Juneau, Alaska, 99802.*

A FEW MISCONCEPTIONS

Before getting started on the Inside Passage, this is an opportunity to clear up some common misconceptions about this southernmost region of Alaska.

ARE THERE ANY IGLOOS IN SOUTHEAST ALASKA?

No, and there are not any igloos in northern Alaska, either. Igloos belong in the realm of children's stories and adventure tales. They are not a real part of Alaska. It is true that the Eskimos of the northern part of the state sometimes build temporary shelters out of snow if they are out hunting or fishing, or get caught in the wild in a storm. But they have never been a permanent form of housing for any Alaska Natives, much less those of the Southeast forests.

ARE THERE POLAR BEARS IN SOUTHEAST ALASKA?

No again. Polar bears are creatures of the Arctic, far to the north of Southeast Alaska. There are two other species of bear that inhabit Southeast, however: the black bear and its larger cousin the brown bear or grizzly.

ARE THERE ESKIMOS IN SOUTHEAST ALASKA?

Eskimos are not indigenous to the region. The Native groups that originally inhabited Southeast Alaska are Tlingit and Haida Indians. The Tsimshian, another group of Indians, migrated to Southeast in the recent past. Most Eskimo groups live in the northwest and Arctic corners of Alaska. The Chugach Eskimos, however, live not far from Southeast, in the Cook Inlet and Prince William Sound area.

ISN'T IT UNCOMFORTABLE TO LIVE IN ALASKA IN THE WINTER?

Not really. The winters in Southeast Alaska are not nearly as severe as winters in the Midwest or the East Coast of the continental United States. The snowfall is heavy, but the temperature remains moderate. The average winter temperature throughout Southeast is a modest thirty-three degrees. Winters are a long time passing, though. Spring is not here to stay until the end of May.

WILL I SEE A LOT OF WILDLIFE ALONG THE INSIDE PASSAGE?

Not as much as you would probably like, unless you get outside of the major towns and into the more remote areas of Southeast. If you are traveling in your own boat and anchoring in isolated coves, you will likely see plenty of wild animals. If you are cruising the Inside Passage by tour ship or ferry, you will certainly see bald eagles—more, in fact, than you can imagine. You will also see lots of other birdlife, from ducks to Steller's jays. You will almost certainly see humpback whales and other marine mammals, although they may be in the distance. You may see some Sitka black-tailed deer and possibly a bear, but you will be lucky indeed to see a moose or a wolf.

CAN I USE U.S. CURRENCY AND POSTAGE STAMPS IN ALASKA?

Of course you can. As the forty-ninth state, Alaska has the usual rights and privileges.

WHAT TIME IS IT?

Alaskans are a little confused about this question, too. As of October 1983, all of Alaska is encompassed within two time zones instead of four. Southeast Alaska, along with most of the rest of the state, now operates on Alaska Standard Time (Alaska Daylight Time in summer), which is one hour west of Pacific Standard Time.

The Lay
of the Land

If you look at a map of Alaska, you will see that the Southeast region consists of a narrow strip of coast wedged between the Pacific Ocean and the Canadian border and a multitude of sizable islands that lie offshore. The rest of Alaska is positioned far to the north in a distinctly separate chunk. The awkward shape of the state has been likened to that of a frying pan, which is why Southeast Alaska is frequently called the Panhandle.

Most of Southeast Alaska, whether island or mainland coast, is covered with either permanent snow and ice (10 percent) or with dense rain forest of spruce and hemlock (45 percent). The only exceptions are the alpine zones above tree level that are snow-free in summer, the marshy estuaries, and the river valleys that cut through the mountains to the sea.

THE PANHANDLE

The Panhandle extends from Dixon Entrance, which separates the Queen Charlotte Islands that lie in Canadian territory from their Alaska counterparts, to Icy Cape, on the western edge of Malaspina Glacier—a distance of some six hundred miles. The mainland strip averages 120 miles across and is bounded by the Coast Mountains and the border between the United States and Canada that follows the line of the mountain peaks. These Coast Mountains are actually part of the Pacific Mountain System

Glaciers flow out of ice fields high in the Coast Mountains. (Tourism Collection, Alaska Historical Library)

that continues along the coast to the north to take in the Saint Elias Mountains behind Yakutat, the Chugach Mountains that border Prince William Sound, the Kenai Mountains that extend southward from Anchorage, the Kodiak Mountains on Kodiak Island, and the Aleutian Range. In total, this mountain system wraps 1,000 miles around the Pacific Coast. In Southeast, the most rugged of the Coast Mountains are those of the Fairweather Range, which forms the western edge of Glacier Bay, separating the national park and preserve from the Pacific Ocean. Mount Fairweather rises to 15,300 feet, the highest mountain in Southeast Alaska.

The coastal mountains extend into the Pacific Ocean to form a complex arrangement of mountainous islands called the Alexander Archipelago. Close to one thousand in number, these islands constitute a major portion of the land mass of Southeast Alaska and contain four of the major communities in the area (Ketchikan, Wrangell, Petersburg, and Sitka) and most of the smaller ones as well. Several of the islands are more than 1,000 square miles in area. The largest is Prince of Wales Island, across Clarence Strait from Ketchikan, with 2,770 square miles.

Separating the islands from the mainland and one another is a veinlike system of waterways that have come to be known as the Inside Passage. Many of the waterways are fjords—narrow, sheer-sided troughs that were scraped out by advancing glaciers thousands of years ago and subsequently flooded by the sea. These inlets are deep—frequently more than four hundred feet—and remarkably straight. The Inside Passage has served as a transportation and communication network since human beings first settled in Southeast Alaska. Even today, there is no road system to connect the communities along the Panhandle, and the waterways have taken the place of highways. As a result, the island communities of Southeast Alaska are no more isolated than those on the mainland.

The rugged face of Southeast Alaska was carved during the Great Ice Age one million years ago. During this era, the Pleistocene, thick plates of ice covered all of the Panhandle except the very tops of the highest mountains and extended miles out into the Pacific Ocean. Glaciers flowed down the natural drainage courses in the Coast Mountains, scouring the trenches into deep, narrow channels as they moved. When the Ice Age ended some ten to fifteen thousand years ago, Southeast was frozen in place. As the climate warmed, the ice receded and ocean water flooded into the glacial trenches to form the fjords we see today. There followed other periods of cooler climate when the glaciers surged forward once again. The most recent was the Little Ice Age that culminated in the seventeenth and eighteenth centuries. Today most of the glaciers continue to retreat, but a few are offering some surprises, as we shall see.

GLACIER FACTS

A glacier is an accumulation of snow and ice that continually flows from a mountain ice field toward sea level. Glaciers are formed when successive snowfalls pile up, creating pressure on the bottom layers. Gradually, the pressure causes the snow on the bottom to undergo a structural change into an extremely dense form of ice called glacier ice, a process that may take several years. Once the ice begins to accumulate, gravity causes the mass to move downhill. Glaciers usually take the path of least resistance, following stream beds or other natural channels down the mountainside. As they move, they scrape along the surface of the earth, picking up rocks and other sediment on the way. The ice and the debris carve a deep U-shaped valley as they proceed down the mountain. If they advance far enough, they will eventually reach the sea and become tidewater glaciers that break off, or calve, directly into salt water. Southeast Alaska is one of only three places in the world where tidewater glaciers exist. (They also are found in Scandinavia and Chile.) Other glaciers, called hanging glaciers, spill out of icy basins high up on valley walls and tumble toward the valley floor.

Glaciers are in a constant state of flux because of increases or decreases in precipitation and temperature. Minor changes can cause significant buildup or reduction in the accumulation of snow on the glacier. When the buildup of glacier ice is greater than the amount lost to melting or calving at the terminus, the glacier will gain ground and is said to advance. If the reverse is true and the ice melts faster than new ice accumulates, the glacier will lose ground and is said to retreat. Some glaciers are simply in a state of equilibrium, the new snowpack roughly equaling the degree of loss. Glaciers can stay in a state of equilibrium for years. Regardless of whether a particular glacier is advancing, retreating, or in a state of equilibrium, the ice continues to flow down the mountain. Only the total length of the glacier is affected.

The surface of a glacier is broken by deep cracks that develop as the mass moves downhill. It also accumulates a dark layer of dirt and rocks and other debris that falls from the valley walls. This sediment, called a lateral moraine, usually occurs in two distinct dark stripes, one on each side of the glacier. When two valley glaciers come together to form one, the inner stripes merge to become one medial moraine that can be seen in the middle of the new super-glacier. On some glaciers, these dark stripes of sediment are very distinct.

Glaciers are not blue, although they certainly look blue, especially where a new wedge of ice has just calved from the face. What looks like lapis lazuli is actually a light trick: the molecules of ice absorb all of the colors of the spectrum except for blue, which is reflected back. The blue color is noticeably more intense on overcast days.

Glaciers exist only in areas that provide the heavy snowfall needed to accumulate into glacier ice. Southeast Alaska is such a place. Most of the glaciers in Southeast are born out of two massive ice fields in the Coast Mountains: the Stikine Ice Field and the Juneau Ice Field. The Stikine Ice Field, which starts in the mountains behind Wrangell, has spawned at least a dozen sizable glaciers, many of which can be seen from the water. The best known is the Le Conte Glacier that empties into salt water at the head of Le Conte Bay, between Wrangell and Petersburg. The Le Conte is the southernmost tidewater glacier in North America. Although the glacier is pretty much in a state of equilibrium, it, like all glaciers, continues to flow downward into the sea and discharges icebergs into the bay. You can view this glacier from excursion vessels leaving from either Wrangell or Petersburg (there is no road access).

The Juneau Ice Field consists of more than one thousand square miles of ice sprawling back of Juneau, over the border into Canada, and north nearly to Skagway. The ice field has produced more than thirty glaciers, the most prominent of which is the Mendenhall. The Mendenhall Glacier is approximately twelve miles long and one and one-half miles wide at the

Icebergs from the Le Conte Glacier wash up near the Stikine River.
(John Matthews)

face, terminating in a deep lake. The glacier is in a slow retreat, backing up fewer than one hundred feet per year.

The Mendenhall is the most accessible glacier in America. It is reached by road from the main highway north of Juneau and a splendid view can be had even from the parking lot near the face of the glacier. The U.S. Forest Service maintains trails to the flanks of the glacier, and a self-guided nature walk illustrates features of the terrain where the ice has recently retreated.

The other glaciers emanating from the Juneau Ice Field that are visible from either the highway north of Juneau or from the water include Lemon Creek Glacier, Herbert Glacier, and Eagle Glacier. None of these glaciers descends to tidewater. While these and the other glaciers from the Juneau Ice Field are retreating, one is definitely on the move. The Taku Glacier, on the north side of Taku Inlet (south of Juneau) is advancing at a steady clip. Presently reaching thirty miles in length, this glacier is the largest from the Juneau Ice Field.

The sixteen tidewater glaciers of Glacier Bay National Park and Preserve course out of the massive Saint Elias Mountains. Two hundred years ago, when Captain George Vancouver visited the area while exploring for Great Britain, Glacier Bay did not exist as we know it today because it was filled with ice. The various glaciers that flow into the bay have retreated at a remarkable rate, to the extent that the bay presently measures sixty miles long. Today, the Johns Hopkins and Grand Pacific glaciers on the west arm of the bay are slowly advancing; the others in the area are stabilized or retreating.

Traveling up Glacier Bay is like taking a trip back in time: the farther you proceed toward the active glaciers at the head of the bay, the more primitive the plant forms become. A retreating glacier leaves behind a deposit of rock and other sediment that was scraped along its advancing path. This deposit, called glacial till, is composed chiefly of ground-up rock with little or no organic content. Thus the soil left by a retreating glacier is not very productive, and only limited organisms such as lichens and mosses are able to establish themselves. With time, however, such low-growing pioneer plants as dwarf fireweed and dryas gain a foothold and begin improving the soil for other species. Next come low shrubs and broadleaf trees such as willow and alder, which improve the soil still further. Last to take root are the evergreens that develop into the common spruce and hemlock forest of Southeast Alaska. At present the forest is established only at the entrance to Glacier Bay where the land has been ice-free the longest.

No discussion of glaciers would be complete without mentioning the ice worm. The ice worm, or glacier worm, is a variety of earthworm that lives in the glacier ice. It is small, measuring not more than an inch, and colored black. The ice worm lives off the algae that grows on the glacier, or on other organic matter that falls onto the ice. These strange creatures were first noted in Alaska on the Muir Glacier in 1887, but they are rarely seen. This species is the only earthworm known to inhabit snow and ice.

THE WEATHER FORECAST

Contrary to popular opinion, Southeast Alaska has a mild climate: moderate in winter and cool in summer. (Compare the average winter temperature of thirty-three degrees to that of Chicago or New York, and you will have to agree.) This maritime climate is primarily the result of Southeast's proximity to the sea, which is a warming influence in winter when the water is warmer than the air, and a cooling influence in summer when the air is warmer than the water. Regardless of the season, the ocean pumps quantities of moisture into the air, providing water for clouds, rain, or snow. In winter, the dense cloud cover acts as a layer of insulation to retain the heat generated by the land and water. In summer the effect is reversed and the clouds insulate the cool landmass from the sun's rays.

The temperature varies little from one Southeast community to another. The average year-round temperature is forty degrees, with the coldest weather usually in January and the warmest in July. Besides being moderate, the temperature is also quite constant in Southeast, normally varying fewer than ten degrees in the course of the day. In winter, temperatures range from the high teens to the low forties. In summer, the midfifties to the midsixties is the norm, although the thermometer can soar to the eighties on a sunny day.

Extreme temperatures can occur in winter as well. The prevailing winds are light southeasterlies, but once in awhile they blow out of Interior Canada, across the ice fields of the Coast Mountains, and rush down the passes and glacier valleys to the coast. These vicious winds, occurring a couple of times each winter, are worthy of every epithet that has ever been associated with the frozen north. They gust to one hundred miles an hour and more, and are always associated with clear, cold conditions. In Juneau, the bitter winter winds are known as Taku winds, and when the Takus blow, you have no choice but to take cover and hope you do not have to go out. The worst part about Taku conditions is that it looks so inviting outside—between gusts, that is.

While temperatures vary little from place to place, precipitation varies quite a lot. Southeast Alaska is basically a rain forest, averaging more than 100 inches of rain and snow a year. The southern third of the Panhandle is rainier than the rest. Ketchikan usually takes credit for being the "liquid sunshine" capital of the state with an average yearly precipitation of 152 inches, but the record is actually held by Little Port Walter near the southeast tip of Baranof Island at 221 inches of precipitation a year. To the north, things are a bit drier: 106 inches in Petersburg, 70 in Juneau, and only 26 in Skagway. In winter, most of this precipitation falls as snow. In the northern part of the Panhandle, much of the snow stays on the ground and accumulates, even at sea level. In the mountains, Southeast is able to produce more than 200 inches of snow a year, which is what keeps the glaciers on the move.

What this translates to for Southeastern residents is a predominance of cool, moist days with overcast skies. June is usually the driest month and October the wettest. The winters are not at all unpleasant, with moderate temperatures and lots of snow for skiing and sledding, but they are *long*. Winter in Southeast starts at the end of October and is not gone until the end of May.

What drives most southeasterners "Outside" for periodic respites is the same gray cloud that seems to hang overhead for weeks at a time. When the cloud moves on, however, and the sun comes out, the beauty of the lush, green forests and the snowcapped mountains quickly erases all unpleasant memories of endless gray days and winters that endure through spring.

THE WATERS

Alaska is a land of enormous tides and Southeast is no exception. The height of the tide increases as it moves over the continental shelf and squeezes up the narrow passages of the Alexander Archipelago. At maximum high, the tide reaches 20.9 feet in Skagway at the far northern limit of Lynn Canal, and falls to a maximum low of −4.0. In Juneau, the range is from a maximum high of 20.6 feet to a low of −4.0. At Sitka the tidal range is more moderate, from 12.5 feet to −2.6. There are two high tides and two low tides within every twenty-four-hour period.

The effect of the large tides is to cause powerful currents as the tide ebbs and flows through the tight waterways. In Wrangell Narrows south of Petersburg, and Sergius Narrows en route to Sitka—two of the most famous stretches of water along the Inside Passage—the current has been clocked at more than eight miles an hour. If you are traveling in a small boat, especially a canoe or kayak, the tidal currents can prove dangerous. Always check the tide table before starting through a narrow channel and talk with local residents about the conditions. Make the passage when the tide is slack—either high or low—and not on the change. If you are camping, the effect of the tidal change can be an unexpected soaking if you are parked too near the waterline. Again, a thorough session with the correct tide table for the particular region is in order. Tide tables are available at most sporting-goods shops in Southeast.

The temperature of the water kills. Even though the coastal waters are warmed by the Japanese current that keeps Southeast ports ice-free in winter, the water is too cold to support human life for more than a few minutes. The surface temperature of the water varies from place to place but the range is typically as follows: winter, 42.5 to 45 degrees; spring, 45 to 47 degrees; summer, 55 to 57 degrees; fall, 45 to 47 degrees. The difference between winter and summer temperatures is not much.

When a human being is immersed in these waters, the body heat is lost into the water, causing a condition known as hypothermia, or subnormal body temperature. If the body temperature drops far enough, the person becomes unconscious and death will follow. Survival time in the water varies according to the size, shape, physical condition, and mental attitude of the victim, but the table on the following page shows the approximate survival time of a human being immersed in the ocean. When the *Prisendam* caught fire in October, 1980, and the passengers and crew were evacuated into lifeboats to wait twenty-two hours before rescue, the water temperature in the Gulf of Alaska was probably about forty-six degrees. These people were very lucky indeed.

The point here is not to alarm you about conditions in Southeast Alaska, but simply to make you aware that the cool climate can turn a normal situation into a dangerous situation in a hurry. Be cautious whenever

SURVIVAL TIME

WATER TEMPERATURE (FAHRENHEIT)	EXHAUSTION OR UNCONSCIOUSNESS	EXPECTED TIME OF SURVIVAL
32.5 degrees	15 minutes	15 to 45 minutes
32.5 to 40 degrees	15 to 30 minutes	30 to 90 minutes
40 to 50 degrees	30 to 60 minutes	1 to 3 hours
50 to 60 degrees	1 to 2 hours	1 to 6 hours
60 to 70 degrees	2 to 7 hours	2 to 40 hours
70 to 80 degrees	3 to 12 hours	3 hours plus (indefinite)

you are facing the elements, whether you are boating, hiking, skiing, fishing, or simply walking around on the docks.

EVERLASTING DAYS AND NIGHTS

Southeast Alaska is far enough north to enjoy the midnight sun effect of the Arctic. Not to the same extent, of course—the sun does not sink below the horizon for months at a time—only below the perpetual cloud cover. In the course of the year, Southeast communities enjoy from seven to eighteen and one-half hours in daylight. In the summer, however, most of the remaining five and one-half hours are in twilight, so the useful daylight is actually some twenty-two hours. If you step outside at midnight on a clear night in midsummer, you can read a newspaper in the available light without straining. On the longest day of the year, the sun rises at 4:05 A.M. (daylight time) in Ketchikan, 3:51 A.M. in Juneau, and 3:43 A.M. in Skagway; and sets at 9:32 P.M., 10:09 P.M., and 10:23 P.M. respectively.

In winter, the opposite conditions prevail. On the shortest day of the year, the sun rises at 8:12 A.M. in Ketchikan, 8:46 A.M. in Juneau, and 8:58 A.M. in Skagway; to set at 3:18 P.M., 3:07 P.M., and 3:01 P.M. respectively. It is dark when you go to work in the morning and dark again when you come home.

The number of daylight hours is reflected in the activities of Southeast residents. In summer when there is light virtually all of the time, southeasterners go off to the office and put in a full eight hours, then go home and reroof the house or take the boat out fishing for another eight hours, and never think a thing about it, no matter what the weather. Staying indoors is the last thing on anyone's mind. Parents despair over getting their children to sleep at night. In the winter months, the typical southeasterner stumbles off to work in the dark and stumbles home again to hole up in front of the fire like a mole. Shoveling snow and, on decent days, skiing are about the only activities that induce an adult southeasterner to go out of doors in winter. Early to bed and sleep as long as possible are the watchwords for winter, and spring, such as it is, cannot come too soon.

Southeast Past to Present

Fifteen thousand years ago, the watery trail now known as the Inside Passage was locked in an icy embrace. Glaciers flowed down the ten-thousand-foot peaks and scoured the valleys below. As the land warmed, the ocean waters gradually thawed. Rivers sprang from melting glaciers and coursed across the land, carrying a succession of unknown peoples who lingered along the coast as many as nine thousand years ago. Eventually—perhaps some fifteen hundred years ago—groups of Tlingit Indians followed the waterways out of Interior Alaska and Canada and into the lush coastal forests of Southeast Alaska where they made their home.

The Tlingit lived comfortably off the land. They gathered in small villages along the coast where they could harvest the resources that the sea and land placed within their reach. They fished for salmon and halibut, collected seaweed from the beach, and picked the blueberries, salmonberries, and nagoonberries that grew wild along the Southeast shore. They learned to use the forest cedar and spruce for shelter, tools, and complex works of art.

The Tlingit traveled the length of their six-hundred-mile domain by wooden canoe. Occasionally they contacted the Haida Indians who lived to the south of them or the Athapaskans who ranged across Interior Alaska to the north. Life was good and the Tlingit peoples prospered and increased. By the middle of the eighteenth century, the Southeast Alaska coastline was one of the most heavily populated regions north of Mexico.

No white man had yet set foot upon the shore.

On the day that the first sailing ship appeared off the Southeast coast, according to one Tlingit tradition, the villagers had sent several boys to the beach to see if the wild celery shoots had reached the height that meant the seaweed was ready to harvest. The boys came running back with the news that a huge white Thunderbird—in Tlingit mythology, a powerful spirit that created thunder by beating his enormous wings and lightning by blinking his eyes—was approaching from the sea. Most of the villagers fled. Those who stayed behind watched as the Thunderbird folded his wings and white men came ashore for the first time in Southeast Alaska.

At that moment, life along the Inside Passage was irrevocably changed. The future of Southeast Alaska would be governed by the harvesting of resources as first furs, then gold, fish, timber, and even the ice itself brought wave after wave of fortune hunters into the coastal wilderness.

FIRST CONTACT

The men who rowed ashore from the white "thunderbird" might have come from the *Saint Paul*, one of two Russian ships that set out on an exploratory expedition under the command of Vitus Bering in 1741. The North Pacific coast was an unknown entity in the 1700s. European expeditions had unraveled the mysteries of much of the rest of North America (the English had been settled in Hudson's Bay since 1670 and the Spanish were on the California coast), but the northern region had remained obscure. In 1725 the Russian czar Peter the Great had sent Bering on a preliminary voyage to find out what lay to the east of Russia: were the continents of Asia and North America one and the same, or were they separate? Sailing from the mouth of the Kamchatka River in Siberia, Bering passed through what would come to be called Bering Strait and northward into the Arctic Ocean, concluding that the continents were indeed separate. On his second voyage, in 1741, Bering left with two ships: the *Saint Peter*, under his own command, and the *Saint Paul*, captained by Alexei Chirikof. Fifteen days out, they became separated and never caught sight of each other again.

Chirikof, in the *Saint Paul*, was the first to glimpse the North American continent. He sighted high wooded mountains near Cape Addington off the west coast of Prince of Wales Island on 15 July 1741. Two days later he anchored in a bay (possibly where Sitka is located today) and sent an armed party ashore. When the men failed to return, a second landing party went to investigate. They did not return either. On the day after that, two parties of Tlingit paddled out to the ship in canoes, shouted something that the Russians of course could not understand, and went back to shore. Having no other landing boats at his disposal, Chirikof turned back to Russia without learning the fate of his men.

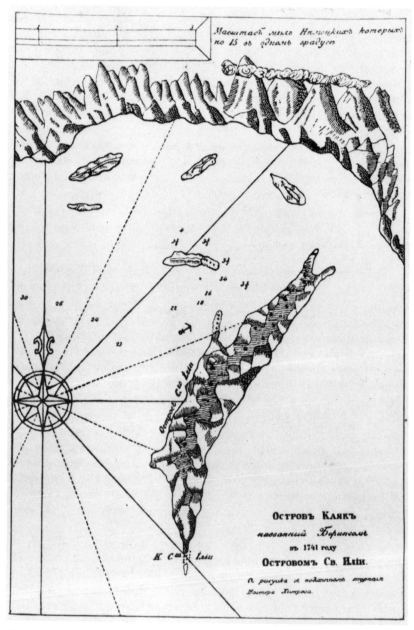

A 1741 Russian map shows Kayak Island and cloud-capped mountains. (Centennial Collection, Alaska Historical Library)

Bering, meanwhile, proceeded in the same east-by-northeast direction and sighted eighteen-thousand-foot Mount Saint Elias near Yakutat. Anchoring near Kayak Island at the eastern edge of Prince William Sound, he sent two parties ashore to investigate the area and replenish the water supply. The shore parties found a few deserted Native dwellings made of logs and rough planks, some underground storehouses, and signs of a recent cooking fire. They took away several household items, such as a child's clay rattle, bundles of dried fish, and a wooden box, and left some of their own possessions in exchange, among them reportedly some tobacco, clay pipes, cloth, and an iron kettle. (This must have caused quite a sensation when the rightful inhabitants returned.)

One of the members of the shore expedition was the naturalist Georg Wilhelm Steller. In the short time that Bering allowed him to remain ashore, Steller collected specimens of plants and birds that were not native to Europe or Asia, among them a most important find: a dark blue jay with a high head crest known to be an inhabitant of North America. Steller realized that this bird—now called the Steller's jay—was proof that the new land was part of the North American continent and separate from Asia.

Bering, anxious about the deteriorating weather, turned the *Saint Peter* for Kamchatka as soon as the water casks were full, but encountered a massive storm in the Aleutians that drove the ship hundreds of miles off course. After battling the Aleutian weather throughout late summer and fall, he made a landing on one of the Commander Islands (west of the Aleutian chain) in November. The crew scraped pits in the bank of a ravine for shelter, collected driftwood for a roof, and settled in to try to survive the winter, keeping themselves warm with pelts from blue foxes and other animals that were plentiful around the island. The *Saint Peter* was blown ashore and they salvaged what they could from the wreck. Bering died in December, like so many of his crew a victim of exhaustion, exposure, and scurvy, the scourge of early seafarers.

When spring came, the survivors built a forty-foot craft from the wreckage of the *Saint Peter* and reached home port in little more than two weeks. Among their baggage were nine hundred sea otter pelts that had been collected during the stay in the Commander Islands. Richly colored, glossy, and luxurious, the pelts fetched astonishingly high prices from Chinese merchants and before long the first wave of Russian fur traders set off to find the mysterious fur-rich lands to the east and their small marine inhabitant, the sea otter.

THE EUROPEAN EXPLORERS

In the years following the return of the Bering expedition, word trickled through the courts of Europe that the Russians had discovered a great land in the North Pacific that was rich in furs and possibly other treasures as well. A progression of exploratory voyages was soon underway to find this land, and to find the Northwest Passage between the Pacific and Atlantic oceans that rumors persistently claimed to exist. Between 1774 and 1800, sailing ships from Spain, Britain, France, Russia, and America glided among the misty waterways of Southeast Alaska. Some of them reached tentatively northward along the Gulf of Alaska to Prince William Sound and Cook Inlet, then passed through the Aleutian Chain to the Bering Sea and proceeded into the Arctic. Eventually all came to the same conclusion: if the Northwest Passage lay in that direction, it would not be usable anyway. (It took until 1837 to prove that there was a passageway from the Arctic Ocean to the Atlantic, but so clogged with ice for much of the year that it was of little practical use.)

The early explorers bartered with the local Natives they encountered along their route, paving the way for the trading vessels that would soon follow. Besides the coveted furs, the sea captains brought out of Alaska the first examples of Southeast Alaska Native art and culture, and detailed sketches of Native villages. These items—woven blankets and baskets, carved wooden feast dishes, fishing equipment, and household tools, for example—are valuable today for the glimpse they give us of the Tlingit and Haida peoples at the time of their initial contact with European culture. Among the legacies of the explorers were the place names they gave to many of the landforms in Southeast Alaska.

Juan Pérez was the first of the international boating community to follow the Russians into Alaska, sailing from Spain in the *Santiago* in 1774. With holdings in Mexico and California, the Spanish were in an excellent position to continue their explorations northward along the Pacific coast. Pérez proceeded far enough to sight Prince of Wales Island, which he named Santa Maria Magdalena. The following year he returned with two ships. He turned back because of a storm before reaching Alaska, but Lieutenant Juan Francisco de la Bodega y Quadra in the second vessel sighted Mount Edgecumbe at Sitka before scurvy forced him to retreat. On the way home he entered and named Bucareli Bay on the outside coast of Prince of Wales Island.

English sea captain James Cook reached Southeast in 1778 on the third of his remarkable explorations to the Pacific (the first two had taken him to New Zealand, Australia, and the Antarctic). In the ships *Resolution* and *Discovery*, he sighted and named Mount Edgecumbe off Sitka and Mount Fairweather off the Gulf of Alaska, and continued along the coast to the north until he was stopped by the Arctic ice. He then headed south to winter in the Hawaiian Islands, preparatory to continuing the search for the Northwest Passage the following summer, but was killed there in a dispute with the Natives.

The French explorations were carried out by Jean François Galaup de

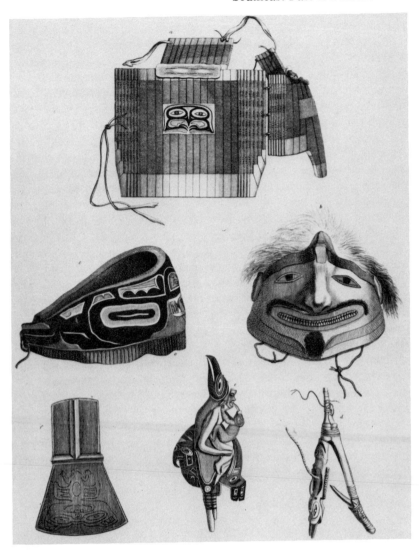

These Tlingit artifacts were sketched during a Russian voyage in 1805. (Centennial Collection, Alaska Historical Library)

la Pérouse in the ships *Astrolabe* and *Boussole*. La Pérouse arrived in Southeast in June of 1786. He sighted Mount Saint Elias and anchored for some days at Lituya Bay (south of Yakutat), surveying the inlet and trading with the local Tlingit. The trip ended in disaster when two of the survey boats were swept into the breakers at the entrance to the bay and all hands lost. La Pérouse left Alaska after the catastrophe and journeyed to the Kamchatka Peninsula where he arranged for his journals to be sent on to Paris, which was a good idea because when he turned south again the *Astrolabe* and *Boussole* vanished in the southern oceans.

The British returned to Alaska in 1793. Captain George Vancouver sailed from England with instructions to verify Cook's findings and make one more search for the Northwest Passage. Cook's voyages had pretty much convinced the British government that no practical waterway existed north of latitude 60° (to the north or west of the Gulf of Alaska), but rumors persisted that the elusive passage lay to the south of latitude 60° (i.e., in Southeast Alaska). Vancouver was also charged with charting the coast from the Columbia River to Cook Inlet. Having served with Cook on the last voyage, he was no stranger to the territory.

Vancouver's ships, the *Discovery* and *Chatham*, arrived in Southeast Alaska in July of 1793. Throughout that summer, he and his four-man survey teams worked along the inlets and passageways of the Alexander Archipelago. They ran south in the fall to winter in the Hawaiian Islands, returned the following summer, and mapped their way south from Cook Inlet. When they left for England in August 1794 (arriving the following year), Vancouver took with him a set of charts so accurate that they were used for years after Alaska became a U.S. possession. Vancouver also provided a good many of the names for geographical features we use today (among them Chatham Strait, which he named for English statesman William Pitt Chatham, the Earl of Chatham, and Lynn Canal, which he named for his birthplace, King's Lynn, in Norfolk), and proved conclusively that there was no usable passage through North America between the Pacific and the Atlantic below or above latitude 60°. Besides successfully completing his mission, Vancouver accumulated a remarkable safety record. During the four and one-half years that the expedition was gone from England, the *Discovery* lost only six men out of a crew of one hundred: five through accidents and one from disease. The *Chatham* did not lose a single man.

THE RUSSIAN OCCUPATION

When the survivors of the *Saint Peter* staggered back to Saint Petersburg with their souvenir pelts of lustrous sea otter that fetched fabulous prices from Chinese traders, they touched off a fur stampede to the North Pacific. The onslaught consisted mainly of *promyshlenniki*—gangs of toughs who moved through the mountains of Russia, conquering villages and forcing villagers to pay a tribute in furs to the czar. The *promyshlenniki* had reached the coast of Kamchatka by the time of Bering's expedition, and when they saw the rich furs coming in from the unknown waters to the east, they recognized an unparalleled opportunity for profit.

The *promyshlenniki* built boats out of anything they could find and set

The unassuming sea otter caused a fur stampede to the North Pacific. (Centennial Collection, Alaska Historical Library)

out for the Commander Islands where Bering's party had been ship-wrecked. The *promyshlenniki* were mountain men, not seamen, and many were swamped at sea in their unseaworthy crafts, but those who managed to complete the trip found their dreams come true—acres of sea otter available for the picking. The Russian opportunists gradually worked their way along the Commander Islands and onto the Aleutian chain, harvesting the sea otter as they went. They met little resistance from the Aleuts who lived on the Aleutian Islands and who were gentle and unwar-like by nature. Before long the standard practice was to take the Aleut women and children hostage and force the Aleut men to hunt sea otter. In their lithe skin kayaks, which the Russians called *bidarka*, the Aleuts were much more efficient hunters than the Russians were anyway.

KODIAK COLONY

Inevitably, the Russian expeditions had to travel farther and farther from Kamchatka as the hunting grounds were depleted, and the excursions became more costly. The fur traders gradually banded together in small companies to make the trips economical. In 1783, a merchant named Grigor Shelikof decided to establish a permanent hunting base on the Aleutian Islands that would make the fur-gathering business more efficient still. That summer Shelikof, his wife Natalie, and a small party of settlers founded the first Russian colony in Alaska on the southeast part of Kodiak

Island. The Russians soon had a working settlement with houses, offices, and outbuildings. They organized the local Native population into work parties to hunt sea otter, gather food, and perform other menial tasks. The idea worked tolerably well and the storehouses filled up with furs. Shelikof's company was the forerunner of the Russian-American Company, which would ultimately be granted a royal charter with exclusive rights to all trade and properties in Alaska.

By 1790, Shelikof had concluded he needed someone to manage the Alaska colony for him. Alexander Baranof was a natural organizer, gutsy and efficient, and experienced in trading with Siberian Natives. When at last he arrived at Kodiak, after a shipwreck in the Aleutians, he set about trying to improve conditions in the settlement. Sea otter were growing scarce and supplies, which had to be shipped out from Russia, were constantly running out. There was also the increasingly serious problem of trying to prevent traders from other countries, now familiar with the Alaska coast, from encroaching upon the Russian position. Baranof began to scout around for a better location for the colony.

SAINT ARCHANGEL MICHAEL

A small agricultural settlement was established at Yakutat in 1795, but Baranof's choice for a new headquarters was a natural harbor on the outside coast of Baranof Island. In April of 1799, a convoy of Russians and Aleuts crossed the Gulf of Alaska to the new site in Southeast Alaska. Baranof negotiated with the chief of the local Tlingit Indians for land on which to build a fort. The site was on the harbor about six miles north of the present town of Sitka. The Russians and a detachment of Aleuts stayed to start the building, while the rest of the Aleut hunters went back to Kodiak with instructions to hunt along the way. Two days after their departure they had rounded the northern shore of the island and were camped on the beach when they ate a meal of purple-black mussels that grew there in great profusion. Many of the Aleuts became violently ill and more than one hundred died—the first known case of paralytic shellfish poisoning in Southeast Alaska. From this event, the body of water became known as Pogibshii, the Russian word for deadly, and has come down to us as Peril Strait.

The Russians quickly completed a two-story barracks and various outbuildings, all enclosed within a wooden stockade. Baranof named the new settlement Saint Archangel Michael. The Russian outpost was simply a foothold in the midst of what had become an international trading center on traditional Tlingit ground. French, Spanish, British, and Yankee vessels had visited Sitka Sound for years. They traded cloth, beads, blankets, metal, and anything else they could get the Tlingit to take as payment for the profitable furs they had come to find. During the 1790s, twenty to thirty trading ships a year anchored at various harbors along the northern coast. Sooner or later, some of the sea captains found two other items that the local Indians would readily accept in exchange for furs: alcohol and arms.

The Sitka Indians tolerated the Russian settlement, but became increasingly angry about the way the Russians treated them, especially their women, and they got into wrangles with the Aleuts over the skins. The situation became volatile. When Baranof left on a trip back to Kodiak three years after founding the Sitka settlement, he gave strict instructions to avoid giving offense to the Tlingit and to be continually on the alert.

On Sunday, 20 June 1802, most of the Russians and Aleuts were away from the fort hunting, fishing, or picking berries in the woods when the Tlingit attacked. Wearing their fierce-looking wooden helmets and armed with guns and spears, the warriors emerged from the forest where they had been hiding and quickly overran the stockade. The Russians resisted the attack, but almost all were killed or captured. A few of those in the woods escaped to the water and were rescued by English and American boats anchored in the Sound. The Tlingit burned the buildings and the post was completely destroyed.

RETAKING SITKA

Baranof immediately made preparations to retake the Sitka outpost. In the summer of 1804, a second convoy left Kodiak for Sitka Sound. This time the party was made up of some 400 *bidarkas* carrying 800 Aleuts, plus two small sailing ships with 120 Russians. The expedition stopped at Yakutat to pick up an additional two vessels that Baranof had commissioned for the attack. When they arrived at Baranof Island, they found the frigate *Neva* had arrived from Kodiak to assist.

The Tlingit retreated to a stronghold when the Russians began their cannon assault. The Russians landed 150 men on the beach, but were repulsed with 10 killed and 26 wounded, including Baranof who took a shot in the arm. After several days of alternating negotiations and bombardment, the Tlingit quietly abandoned their fort during the night and slipped away to Chichagof Island to the north. Baranof ordered the Tlingit stronghold burned. He built a new stockade with houses, storehouses and other buildings within, calling the settlement New Archangel.

For the Tlingit, the hero of the occasion was the young chief Katlean, who led the battle against the Russians, fighting fiercely hand-to-hand and, tradition has it, swinging at his enemies with a mighty hammer. Remarkably, Katlean's raven-shaped helmet can be seen today in the Sheldon Jackson Museum in Sitka. (At Sitka National Historic Park, the actual battle site, you can see a film about the contest and the Russian settlement at Sitka.)

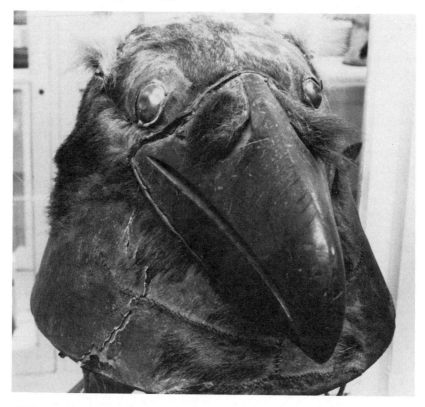

Katlean's Raven helmet, legacy of the 1804 battle, is on display in the Sheldon Jackson Museum.

NEW ARCHANGEL

The year after retaking Sitka, the Russians had completed eight new buildings and cleared ground for gardens and livestock. The Tlingit had not been a particular problem. Baranof had concluded a treaty with part of the tribe and while others remained hostile, relations had improved to the point that the Indians were invited to the settlement occasionally for feasting and presents. The main worry was food. Why Baranof thought the food situation would be improved by a move to Sitka is a good question, for the climate was cool and damp, the Russian settlers were not farmers by trade or inclination, the soil was unproductive, and the crops were not a success. Baranof developed a penchant for buying ships with cargoes intact from Americans who happened into port.

The Sitka Indians were invited to return to the area in 1821. In the intervening years they had caused periodic trouble for the colonists by interfering with the Aleut hunting parties, and Baranof thought it wiser to let them return to their ancestral home. Also, the Russians needed them to provide game and fish for their larders. The Indians settled around the Russian fort. They outnumbered the Russians, and the colonists were in constant fear of another uprising, but an uneasy truce prevailed.

In 1834, the Russians established a second outpost in Southeast Alaska. Redoubt Saint Dionysius was built to prevent the British Hudson's Bay Company, a fierce competitor for the Native fur trade, from using the Stikine River to gain access to the fur-rich Interior. The post was placed close to the mouth of the Stikine, at today's Wrangell.

The 1840s were the height of development for the colonists at New Archangel. The physical plant had grown to include a governor's residence atop Castle Hill, a clubhouse for lower officials, barracks and other housing, a library, an observatory, churches, a hospital, an arsenal, a wharf, and three schools, including an academy that trained students in surveying, navigation, engraving and accounting; a finishing school for young ladies, and a theological seminary. There were shipyards that built steam vessels, a forge that fabricated plow blades and spades for Spanish farmers in California, and a foundry, sawmill, flour mill, and fish saltery. New Archangel was not only the center of commerce for the twenty-four Russian settlements that then existed in Alaska, the town was the largest port on the entire North Pacific coast. In the days when San Francisco was still a muddy hole in the Pacific, Sitka was a haven of culture for trading vessels from all over the world.

In the 1850s, a new industry was born: ice. Enterprising capitalists discovered that lake ice from Southeast Alaska could be packed in sawdust deep in a ship's hold and arrive in San Francisco intact. Over the next decade, tons of ice were sawed from freshwater lakes at both Sitka and Kodiak and shipped south. Fish and lumber were sent south, too, for sale in California, Mexico, and Hawaii. Other ships came north to be repaired in Sitka's well-equipped shipyards. On occasion there were fifteen vessels in the harbor at once, loading and unloading wares.

THE RUSSIANS OPT OUT

At length, Russia's expenses of maintaining the Alaska colonies began to outweigh the benefits. The fur trade diminished to almost nothing as the supply of pelts grew scarce. Provisioning remained a constant headache, as did the difficulties of maintaining a political presence so far from the mother country. Treaties had fixed the boundary between Russian-America and Canada in 1824 and 1825, but both British and American traders were pushing past the Russian boundaries into the Alaska Interior. Renewal of the Russian-American Company charter was in question, too. The Russian government had proposed to renew the charter for a twenty-year term beginning in 1862, but company officials were not pleased with new conditions that would exempt Aleuts and all other Alaska Natives from forced labor and allow them to participate in other industries.

The Russian government had never really intended to occupy Alaska. The settlements had come about through the fur traders and then the Russian-American Company which had represented the government's interests there while they gathered in the rich harvest of Alaska resources. If the company was no longer interested in governing the new settlements, the government was not particularly interested either. The czar decided to give up the Alaska colonies. The question was, to whom? Both Britain and America were likely prospects. The czar opted to have the United States as Russia's neighbor instead of England, their enemy in the Crimean War.

The treaty of purchase was concluded by U.S. Secretary of State William Seward on 30 March 1867, and ratified that May. The purchase price was $7.2 million. The boundaries between the new possession and Canada would be the same as were agreed upon in the 1824–1825 treaties between Russia and Great Britain, with the lower extreme fixed at 54°40′ north latitude and then following the natural boundaries of the Portland Canal and the Coast Mountains before turning due north at Mount Saint Elias.

At Sitka, the Russian flag was exchanged for the American on 18 October 1867. The Russians were promised citizenship rights in the new American territory, but most went home to Russia. The Aleuts went back to their native islands, and the Tlingit Indians were left to wonder what new indignities this new development would bring.

RACING FOR GOLD

Thousands of miles to the south of New Archangel—now called Sitka—gold had been struck near Sacramento, California, and the gold rush was under way. Prospectors fanned across California, exploring the creek beds and mountain canyons for gold. The search took them northward through Oregon and Washington and on into Canada and its bordering neighbor, Alaska.

In 1858, a discovery was made on Canada's Fraser River and thousands of prospectors surged into this area. Three years later, in 1861, came the first strike to affect Alaska. A Hudson's Bay Company trader named Buck Choquette found gold on the upper Stikine River in Canada at a spot that came to be known as Buck's Bar. Prospectors flocked to Southeast Alaska to get to the new Stikine strike. Their destination was Wrangell, at the mouth of the Stikine in Russian territory. William Moore, an enterprising riverboat captain, was running a steamer upriver to the strike site with cargoes of optimistic prospectors.

Exhaustion was the only certainty about the Klondike rush for gold.
(P.E. Larss Collection, Alaska Historical Library)

THE CASSIAR

In 1873, word of a huge, new strike in Canada brought another wave of opportunists up the Stikine on their way to the Cassiar gold fields in the Interior. This time Wrangell ballooned from a quiet outpost to a booming tent city of fifteen thousand. Captain Moore was on the scene again to move prospectors and their gear upriver where they could pack the two hundred-odd miles to the diggings. Other steamers, both British and American, carried passengers and goods as well. At the end of the prospecting season, everybody came downriver to Wrangell to patronize the stores, saloons, dance halls and other boomtown delights. At the time, Wrangell—now a U.S. town—was the busiest place in Alaska.

Prospectors picked around in both Canada and Alaska, searching for that next big strike. The first find in Alaska came in 1870 at Windham Bay on the mainland, sixty-five miles south of Juneau. Forty thousand dollars in gold is said to have been taken from the placers in that region. Gold mining was carried out near Sitka shortly thereafter and, in 1880, ore samples from Silver Bow Basin on Gastineau Channel led to the founding of Juneau, Douglas, and Treadwell and, ultimately, the largest gold-mining operation in the world.

But the biggest gold strike was yet to come. The gold trail led onward to a region close to Canada's western border called the Klondike. At its center was the boomtown of Dawson on the Yukon River. The route to the gold fields lay through Southeast Alaska and the migration of men and equipment was one of the greatest in history.

KLONDIKE MADNESS

The Klondike story began in August of 1896 when George Washington Carmack and his two Indian companions, Skookum Jim and Tagish Charlie, found gold on a tributary of the Klondike River in the Yukon Territory of Canada. That winter, rumor had it that rich gold deposits had been found in the Yukon, and a few prospectors working nearby managed to get into the area by spring. On 17 July 1897, headlines in the *Seattle Post-Intelligencer* screamed that the steamer *Portland* was on her way with a "ton of gold" from the Klondike.

All through that summer and the fall, prospectors stampeded to the

Those that reached Dawson had good prospects and a lot of panning to do. (P.E. Larss Collection, Alaska Historical Library)

Prospectors trudge to the summit of Chilkoot Pass in 1898. (P.E. Larss Collection, Alaska Historical Library)

Klondike and the fields of gold. There were at least seven ways to get into the Klondike, and not one of them was easy. Predictably, the safest route was the longest: the all water route that led from Seattle to the port of Saint Michael on the far western coast of Alaska. From there prospectors would enter the Yukon River where it exited into the Bering Sea and follow along the nearly two thousand miles to Dawson. All of the other possibilities involved a combination of water and land travel. There was the White Pass Trail that left from Skagway at the head of Lynn Canal, and the shorter, but steeper, Chilkoot Pass from nearby Dyea. Both exited in a system of treacherous waterways that led to the Yukon and Dawson. Or there was the Dalton Trail from Haines, that also led to the Yukon headwaters; the old Stikine River route; the Edmonton route through Canada; and finally the gruesome climb over Valdez Glacier and into the Interior river systems from Prince William Sound.

The most popular routes were the White Pass and Chilkoot trails. In the summer of 1897, Dyea, at the foot of the Chilkoot Trail, consisted of a trading post and a couple of saloons. At Skagway, there was a log cabin that had been put up by a homesteader by the name of . . . Captain William Moore. Now there was a man with vision. Overnight Dyea and Skagway turned into typical boomtowns as some twenty-five thousand people prepared to pack up the trails with the required year's worth of provisions during the first year of the rush. On the other side of the Coast Mountains in Canada the trails came together at Lake Bennett. Twenty-thousand would-be prospectors camped around the lake that spring of '98, constructing boats to carry them downstream to the Yukon. As soon as the ice gave way on the lakes, seven thousand boats headed downriver on the next leg of the journey. By midsummer, eighteen thousand people had arrived at Dawson. By summer's end, many had started for home—broke. Others went on down the Yukon to the next big strike in 1899. The place was Nome where, rumor had it, there was gold on the beach, just waiting to be picked up.

When Salmon Was King

Simultaneous with the gold strikes in Canada and Alaska, a new industry was launched: salmon. The first salmon canneries were built in 1878 at the Native village of Klawock, on Prince of Wales Island, and at Sitka. The canneries spread like wildfire up and down the Southeast coast until there was at least one cannery in virtually every nook and cranny from Haines to Ketchikan. Ketchikan grew from an Indian summer fishing camp to first a salmon saltery in 1883 and a cannery in 1887. The next year the nearby Loring Cannery was finished. Prince of Wales Island developed other canneries at Craig, Kasaan, and other sites. Three canneries were started near Haines in the 1880s. Wrangell got one in 1887 and a second in 1889. In 1900 the town of Petersburg was born with a salmon cannery and an equally lucrative halibut industry that kept the fishermen occupied over the winter.

Southeast waters were choked with salmon and Ketchikan was at the center—the "Salmon Capital of the World"—with more than a dozen canneries operating in the 1930s. During the peak years, the Ketchikan district alone packed more than two million cases a year. The piper had to be paid, however, and the years of overfishing took their course in the 1940s. Today the empty, sagging remnants of the great cannery buildings can be seen in many quiet Southeast coves; picturesque, but forlorn reminders of plentiful days gone by.

One result of the decline in the salmon runs has been the development of aquaculture. Fish hatcheries were introduced in Alaska around 1900 when the salmon stocks were first becoming depleted, but most projects were busts. Research and experimentation have since led to successful techniques for rearing salmon. The Alaska Department of Fish and Game built several hatcheries during the 1970s, and a dozen or more private, nonprofit hatcheries are operating or under construction in Southeast as well. Millions of dollars worth of hatchery-reared salmon are harvested in the fisheries every year. The industry is still in the formative stage. The hatch-

In the late 1800s, Southeast's supply of salmon seemed limitless.
(H.G. Barley Collection, Alaska Historical Library)

eries are expected to show greater and greater return as they reach capacity.

Two of the oldest hatcheries in Southeast are also the most accessible to view. Sheldon Jackson College in Sitka was the first to set up an aquaculture program geared to educational training. The hatchery, situated near the Sheldon Jackson Museum, releases up to fifteen million pink and chum salmon and two hundred thousand coho a year. Ketchikan's Deer Mountain Hatchery is operated by the Alaska Department of Fish and Game. Built in 1954 on Ketchikan Creek, the hatchery can produce three hundred thousand salmon and ten thousand steelhead trout every year. Deer Mountain Hatchery is included on the city's walking tour and is probably the best opportunity in Southeast to view aquaculture in action.

CASHING IN THE FOREST

The wood products industry has backed up the Southeast economy since Russian times. The Russian-American Company harvested the local timber for shipbuilding and for fuel. (Evidence of their clear-cutting practice can still be seen around Sitka today.) They also operated sawmills and exported lumber to faraway markets in South America and China.

After the U.S. purchase of Alaska, additional sawmills were constructed to provide lumber for packing boxes to ship out the cans of Southeast salmon. The industry was in an awkward situation in the early years of U.S. ownership, however, because there was no civil government in Alaska to regulate ownership of the land being logged. The situation was clarified somewhat in 1884 when Congress passed the Organic Act, providing machinery for the regulation and administration of government in Alaska according to the laws of Oregon. In 1907, the federal government created the sixteen-million-acre Tongass National Forest—the largest national forest in the United States (since expanded to seventeen million acres)—incorporating most of the timber in the Alexander Archipelago. Now that the forest was managed by the U.S. Forest Service, which could hold timber sales, private timber companies were able to get into business.

During World War I, Sitka spruce was in demand for building fighter planes because of its strength and light weight. Mills at Craig and Ketchikan cut spruce for the war effort and supplied lumber for local fishing and mining operations. The demand for spruce reappeared during World War II for the same reason. The Alaska Spruce Log Program called for one

Rafted logs await milling at the Tsimshian village of Metlakatla on Annette Island.

hundred million board feet of timber to be cut annually from Prince of Wales Island. The logs were tied into enormous oceangoing rafts called "Davis Rafts," 280 feet long by 60 feet wide and 30 feet deep, that were towed to Puget Sound mills. In the 1950s, the forest industry passed the declining salmon industry for the first time. The annual timber harvest in Southeast doubled and doubled again as pulp mills were constructed at Ketchikan and Sitka.

In recent years the Alaska Native Land Claims Settlement Act has added a new dimension to the timber industry in Southeast as Alaska Native corporations have received title to lands they have selected out of the Tongass National Forest. Their final land selections will total some 550,000 to 600,000 acres, many of them on prime logging land. Several corporations are already entering the logging business and exporting timber to Japan.

Today forest products remains one of the major industries in Southeast Alaska. Pulp mills continue to operate in Ketchikan and Sitka and there are sawmills at several other communities. In 1980 Congress prescribed that the level of timber harvest from the Tongass could equal four and one-half billion board feet over the decade, and approximately two million acres of the commercial forest are scheduled for harvest over the next one hundred years.

SHORT-LIVED VENTURES

Over the years numerous other ventures have stirred the economy in various locales, but they have been short-lived. Whaling was one of the industries that touched Southeast Alaska briefly. In 1880, Northwest Trading Company of Portland, Oregon, built a shore-based whaling station on Killisnoo Island opposite the Tlingit village of Angoon. The company harvested whales from local waters and reduced the carcasses to oil, bone meal, and fertilizer. A second company started a whaling station on the southeast tip of Admiralty in 1907, and a third set up shop at Port Armstrong on the Southern end of Baranof Island. This operation was the longest-lived, but all had shut down by 1923.

The Killisnoo plant, however, turned to another resource that proved profitable for several more years: *herring*. In 1882, the whaling station was converted to a herring reduction plant to process the plentiful, small, oily fish into fish meal. Quite a market developed for the meal, first as fertilizer and then as a food additive for livestock and poultry. Herring oil—a second product—was valued as a superior industrial oil for manufacturing such varied products as leather, cosmetics, and ink. Eventually seventeen herring reduction plants were operating in Southeast Alaska, processing millions of pounds of herring a year. The industry gradually declined as the herring were fished out and the last plant closed in 1966. Herring also figured in food industries. Herring salteries had operated on a small scale at least since 1894. The 1920s saw a great demand for salted and pickled herring, but this industry declined as competition appeared from the East Coast and foreign producers. Commercial production ended in 1953. Today's limited herring industry consists of two products: bait, which is processed whole and frozen, and roe, which in Southeast Alaska is taken from the fish before spawning, salted, and exported to Japan as a delicacy.

Copper provided a fleeting boom in the Ketchikan area. Copper claims had been located on Prince of Wales Island as early as 1867, and mining was under way on both sides of the island by 1900. The boomtowns of Coppermount and Hadley grew up around the copper industry. High costs and depleted ores closed down the smelters by 1908, and the copper-mining industry faded away—taking Coppermount and Hadley with it. Marble provided a flurry of activity in the same region in 1912 when the Vermont Marble Company began quarrying at Tokeen on Marble Island, off the west coast of Prince of Wales. The white Tokeen marble was used in many buildings in the Pacific Northwest, including the Alaska Capitol at Juneau. The industry folded when the Depression cut into the building market.

Another industry that swept Southeast for a time was fox farming. Furs brought high prices during the 1920s, and some bright entrepreneur realized that the little, tree-studded islands in Southeast Alaska would make ideal fox pens. Food would be easy to come by in the form of scraps from the many nearby salmon canneries and the water perimeter would prevent the foxes from escaping. The U.S Forest Service leased the islands for as little as twenty-five dollars per year. One or two pair of blue fox—which provided pretty, sooty brown pelts with bluish hairs beneath—could stock the entire farm in just a few years. Many fox farms operated in the Tongass in the 1920s, but by the mid-1930s the price of furs had dropped again and the foxes were left to run wild.

SOUTHEAST TODAY

With the exception of gold, which is still plentiful, but prohibitively expensive to extract in most cases, the economy of Southeast Alaska today is based upon the same industries that operated a hundred years ago: fish and forest. Two new industries top the list, however. The tourism industry was born in Southeast Alaska soon after the great naturalist John Muir visited the country for the first time in 1879. Muir landed in Wrangell and canoed into Glacier Bay with his Presbyterian missionary friend Hall Young. Muir's accounts of the ice-locked wilderness were so inspiring that steamship companies began to offer summer tours up the Inside Passage. The first was the steamer *Idaho*, which came north in 1883. On board was a twenty-seven-year-old journalist named Eliza Ruhamah Scidmore, whose

The City of Topeka *rides at anchor while tourists step ashore at Glacier Bay in 1895. (Alaska Historical Library)*

descriptions of the voyage appeared in national newspapers and magazines and later in a guidebook to Alaska. The tourism industry was launched.

The early steamships were oases of comfort with carpeted lounges, crystal chandeliers, starched linens, and superior food. The ships stopped at all of the mining towns and cannery sites along their route to deliver supplies, which was entertaining to the passengers. By 1889, five thousand tourists a year were making the trip up the Inside Passage. The practice continues today, but the number of visitors who pass along the same route has swelled to a quarter of a million a year.

The number-one employer in Southeast Alaska today is government. Roughly one-third of the Southeast work force earn their annual wages from federal, state, or local government. The greatest number of government employees is, of course, in Juneau, which has been the capital of Alaska since 1906. In Juneau, one out of every two working people is an employee of either state, federal, or local government.

SOUTHEAST HISTORY IN BRIEF

1741	Alexei Chirikof, sailing for Russia with the Bering expedition, makes the first recorded sighting of Alaska 15 July 1741. Two landing parties go ashore, possibly near Sitka, but fail to return. Vitus Bering anchors at Kayak Island. Shore parties inspect deserted Native dwellings and collect several household items.
1774	Spanish explorer Juan Pérez sights Prince of Wales Island.
1775	Spanish explorer Bodega y Quadra sights Mount Edgecumbe.
1778	Captain James Cook visits Southeast Alaska on his third voyage of exploration in the Pacific for England.
1783	Russian merchant Grigor Shelikof establishes a Russian settlement on Kodiak Island.
1786	La Pérouse sights Mount Saint Elias and surveys Lituya Bay for France.
1793-1794	Captain George Vancouver charts the Alexander Archipelago for England.
1795	Russians establish a small agricultural settlement at Yakutat.
1799	Russians settle at Old Sitka.
1802	Sitka Tlingit attack and destroy the Russian post.
1804	Russians retake Sitka and build a new fort at the present site.
1825	Treaties fix boundaries between Russian-America and Canada.
1834	Russians establish Redoubt Saint Dionysius at Wrangell.
1839	British lease mainland coast from Russia; Redoubt Saint Dionysius passes into British hands as Fort Stikine.
1861	Buck Choquette discovers gold on the upper Stikine River in Canada; prospectors flock to Wrangell.
1867	United States purchases Alaska from Russia.
1873	Wrangell balloons to fifteen thousand people with a new gold strike in the Canadian Cassiar.
1877	First mission school in Alaska opens at Wrangell.
1878	First salmon canneries in Alaska built at Klawock and Sitka.
1879	S. Hall Young founds a Presbyterian mission at Haines.

1880	Joe Juneau and Richard Harris find gold on the Gastineau Channel and stake the townsite of Juneau.
1880	First Southeast whaling station begins operation on Killisnoo Island.
1882	U.S. Navy vessels shell and burn village of Angoon.
1883	Steamer *Idaho* brings tourists up the Inside Passage.
1884	Congress passes Organic Act providing minimum framework for administering government in Alaska.
1887	Father William Duncan and Tsimshian followers found Metlakatla on Annette Island.
1896	George Washington Carmack, Skookum Jim, and Tagish Charlie strike gold in Yukon Territory, precipitating a rush to the Klondike.
1897	Skagway takes shape as a tent city of ten thousand people.
1897	Peter Buschmann homesteads along Wrangell Narrows to found Petersburg.
1898	Porcupine becomes the center of a rich gold-mining district.
1900	White Pass and Yukon Route is completed from Skagway to Whitehorse.
1900	Copper mining booms on Prince of Wales Island.
1903	U.S. Army constructs Fort William H. Seward at Port Chilkoot, Haines.
1906	Capital of Alaska transferred from Sitka to Juneau.
1907	New sixteen-million-acre Tongass National Forest is largest in the United States.
1912	Alaska is granted territorial status.
1912	Marble quarries begin production on Marble Island.
1913	First territorial legislature's first law gives women the right to vote.
1917	Cave-in floods all Treadwell mines except one.
1925	Glacier Bay is proclaimed a national monument.
1941	Sitka hosts thirty thousand military personnel with an army base and naval air station.
1943	Haines Highway links Haines with the Alaska Highway.

1944   Closure of the Alaska-Juneau Mill ends hard-rock mining in Juneau.

1948   Steve Homer initiates ferry service between Haines, Skagway, and Juneau.

1959   Alaska achieves statehood.

1963   First vessels of the Alaska Marine Highway fleet come on line.

1971   Alaska Native Land Claims Settlement Act awards Southeast Native corporations 550,000 to 600,000 acres of land.

1978   Klondike Highway connects Skagway with the Carcross and the Alaska Highway.

1978   Presidential Proclamation designates Misty Fiords and Admiralty Island national monuments to be managed by the Forest Service.

1980   Alaska Lands bill reaffirms national monument status for Misty Fiords and Admiralty Island and designates these areas and twelve others as wilderness. Wilderness lands within the Tongass National Forest now equal 5.5 million acres.

1982   Alaskans rescind vote to move state capital from Juneau to Willow.

Southeast's Native Heritage

Many thousands of years ago when the North Pacific Ocean was still in the grip of the Great Ice Age, groups of human beings wandered out of Asia and Siberia, across the bridge of land that is now the Bering Sea, and into Alaska and northern Canada. As the glaciers withdrew and the great rivers were freed of ice, these peoples and their descendants were able to range throughout the Canadian and Alaskan Interior and southward to California and Mexico.

Among these early wanderers were the ancestors of all of Alaska's Native peoples: the Eskimos of the Arctic coast, the Aleuts of the Aleutian Chain, the Athapaskan Indians of the Interior region, and the Tlingit, Haida, and Tsimshian Indians of Southeast Alaska. Over the next several thousand years, these different groups settled into their own geographic regions and developed distinct and complex cultures. Historians have estimated that at the time of the first recorded European voyage to Alaska in 1741, the total Native population numbered 60,000 to 80,000 people, of which perhaps 10,000 were located in Southeast. Today's total Native population is approximately 64,000. The Southeast groups number about 13,000 people.

FIRST INHABITANTS

The coastal Indians of Southeast gradually migrated out of Interior

Canada, following the river valleys through the Coast Mountains until they reached the saltwater shore. The Tlingit ('klink-et) settled into villages along a six-hundred-mile stretch of coast between Yakutat Bay and the Portland Canal (now the southern boundary of Alaska). They also inhabited several of the islands of the Alexander Archipelago. The Haida ('hy-dah) established themselves to the south of them on the coast of British Columbia and on the Queen Charlotte Islands. Later, in the late seventeenth or early eighteenth centuries, they extended their range farther north and took over the southern end of Prince of Wales Island in Alaska from the Tlingit.

The Tsimshian ('sim-shee-anne) are a case apart in that they did not settle in Southeast until twenty years after the Alaska Purchase and even then were isolated from the mainstream of Southeast Native society. Their people originally lived along the Nass and Skeena rivers in British Columbia, some relocating near the Hudson's Bay Company trading post at Port Simpson in the 1830s. In 1857, a twenty-one-year-old missionary, William Duncan, arrived in Canada to educate the Tsimshian in the ways of the Church of England. He founded a church there, but decided that liquor and other unhealthy activities around the post were leading his flock astray. Duncan and his followers left the community and returned to original Tsimshian lands to establish a new model village called Metlakatla.

In 1881, Duncan had a falling out with his church leaders and was dismissed from the missionary society. The U.S. government gave him permission to relocate his community on Annette Island in Southeast Alaska. Duncan moved to Annette with 825 Tsimshian in 1887 and built a new town that they named New Metlakatla. Like the old village, the new Metlakatla community was designed to be self-sufficient and self-contained. Duncan encouraged his followers to break from the past and pursue a new life-style in wooden frame houses and well-laid-out streets. The community continues today as a part of the self-governing Annette Island Indian Reserve.

SEAGOING CULTURE

The Tlingit and Haida Indians were able to live well on their coastal land and islands. The climate was moderate, and the constant precipitation favored the lush rain forests that provided them with most of their wants. They built permanent villages along riverbanks or on protected coves or inlets facing the sea, and in summer moved to temporary fishing camps that were convenient to the salmon supply.

They developed into expert seamen. In their cedar canoes, they traveled throughout their watery realm, harvesting the sea's resources, visiting allied communities, and trading or warring with other Native groups. The

Haida were the unquestioned masters of canoe building. Red cedar, the preferred wood for dugout canoes, was more plentiful in the southern region where they lived, and they were known up and down the Northwest coast for their large, well-built, beautifully decorated craft. A Haida sea-going canoe could easily measure seventy feet in length and carry fifty to sixty men. (The early European explorers frequently found their vessels overshadowed by the Indian canoes.) The Tlingit and Haida regularly canoed down the coast of British Columbia to Puget Sound, some seven hundred miles away.

HOUSING

The traditional Native houses were shared by several families. They were constructed of rough cedar planking set horizontally and notched at the corners. There was a low doorway, but no windows, and a bare earth floor. An opening at the top let out smoke from the central fire pit that served for both cooking and heating. Around the perimeter of the house was a raised wooden platform for seating during the day and sleeping at night. Sometimes there were two of these platforms, one above the other. The platforms were also used to store wooden boxes, sleeping mats, blankets, clothing, weapons, hunting and fishing gear, and other belongings. Dried fish, meat, and other foodstuffs hung from the ceiling.

With no ventilation except the smoke hole, these houses were fairly aromatic affairs. The early traders who observed some of these dwellings before they were adulterated with European goods and ideas reported themselves much bothered by the darkness and acrid smoke that permeated the interior. The visitors were invariably either too hot or too cold, depending upon their distance from the fire.

There are five replicas of Native community houses in Southeast today, four of which are convenient to view. The latter include houses at Haines (Port Chilkoot), Wrangell (Chief Shakes Island), and Ketchikan (Saxman and Totem Bight). The fifth replica, at Kasaan on Prince of Wales Island, will be outside your itinerary unless you are traveling in your own boat. A replica of an interior is displayed at the Alaska State Museum in Juneau.

FOOD GATHERING

Food was plentiful and varied along the Northwest coast. The primary staple was fish: salmon, halibut, herring, trout, and a small, oily member of the smelt family called eulachon ('hoo-li-gan). If eating fish grew tiresome, the forests were generous with bears and deer, and mountain goats were available for the price of a climb. There were birds of all types, and bird eggs. In addition to fish, the sea provided several types of seaweed, seals, the occasional whale, and all manner of shellfish. The land produced wild rhubarb, wild peas, wild rice, and nearly every imaginable form of berry. If necessary, even the hemlock forest could be eaten. With the bark peeled away, the soft cambium layer beneath could be scraped off, cooked, and consumed.

Not surprisingly, the Tlingit and Haida Indians were superb fishermen. The early European explorers quickly discovered, to their astonishment, that the Natives could fish circles around them, even with their "primitive" gear of wood and bone. In fact, the Indian fishing equipment, while fabricated from natural materials, was fine-tuned for efficiency. Nets were fashioned out of twined cedar bark or spun nettle fibers, and lines were made from spruce roots, cedar bark, or kelp stems. Fishing methods depended upon the quarry. Salmon were speared, netted, or trapped. Herring and eulachon were netted or brailed out of the water with long-handled rakes.

Probably the most ingenious fishing device was for halibut. The traditional halibut set consisted of a wooden hook with a stone or bone barb (later metal, fashioned from nails), a stone weight to hold it down because halibut are bottom dwellers, and a line leading to the surface with an inflated seal bladder or wooden float at the end to mark the location of the set. Two men in a canoe could watch over several halibut sets at once. The hooks were baited with squid or octopus, lowered into position, and left to do their work. When a halibut took the bait, the surface float would bob

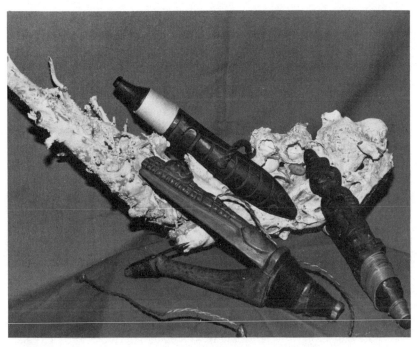

Carved wooden halibut hooks in the Wrangell Museum show the beauty that accompanied an efficient design.

and jerk, signaling the fishermen to paddle over and haul the fish aboard.

The genius of the operation lay in the hooks, which were designed to discriminate between halibut and other bottom fish. Halibut are peculiar creatures. When they are juveniles they look like any other fish, but very soon one of their eyes migrates across to join the other so that both eyes are on one side of the head. Then the fish turn over so that the two eyes are uppermost and spend the rest of their days swimming on their sides. As a result, the halibut's mouth opens side to side rather than up and down like a salmon's. Thus halibut hooks were built in the shape of a V. The halibut, with its sideways mouth, could slip between the arms of the V to take the bait when other fish could not.

Besides being of efficient design, the Tlingit and Haida halibut hooks were objects of great beauty. The unbarbed arm of the V was carved in the figure of an animal or human. The carvings were evidently significant to the matter of catching halibut. Perhaps they represented spirits that were called upon to assist the fishing effort, or perhaps they simply attracted the halibut's eye. Whatever the reason, wooden halibut hooks are truly a form of art. The wooden floats that marked the lines also were carved into shapes, usually of animals or birds. Almost all of the museums in Southeast Alaska have carved halibut hooks and other Native fishing gear on display.

Most fish was smoked or dried for preservation. The eulachon, however, was valued most for its oil. The flesh of this small fish is so oily that a dried eulachon can be lighted like a candle, hence the nickname "candlefish." Southeast Alaska Natives considered eulachon oil a desirable addition to any meal. They used it as a dipping sauce and mixed it with berries and other foods to preserve them over the winter. To obtain the oil, the fish was allowed to decompose for several days and was then boiled in water. Most of the oil collected on the surface of the water where it could easily be skimmed off. The remainder was obtained by pressing the cooked fish in a basket. In the old days, eulachon oil was frequently stored in the long, hollow kelp stems that are plentiful in Southeast waters.

The Tlingit and Haida were not the only Alaska Natives to enjoy the oil: so much eulachon oil was traded to the Athapaskans that the trade routes to the Interior became known as the "grease trails." Dieticians now know that eulachon oil is rich in iodine and vitamins and was important to the Native diet. Non-Natives usually find the oil unpleasantly strong tasting, but, even today, eulachon oil is a precious, if increasingly rare, commodity among Southeast Natives.

Until the Europeans came, Southeast Natives had no iron except the few bits that drifted ashore from distant shipwrecks, and no pottery. Their cooking vessels consisted of wooden boxes and tightly woven baskets. They placed water and the food to be cooked in a basket or box and dropped in stones that had been heated in the fire. Sometimes the Indians also used hot stones for pit cooking, similar to East Coast clambakes, wrapping or layering fish with seaweed or leaves.

SOCIAL STRUCTURE

The Southeast coastal Natives observed a rigid social structure that emphasized kinship lines. The concept of lineage permeated every aspect of their lives, but for those of us on the outside looking in, its primary manifestation was in art. It is thanks to this strong adhesion to kinship that we can admire today the great totem poles, the beaded blankets, the carved serving dishes, and all of the other items, both ceremonial and quotidian, that have been marked with the animal crests denoting family line.

EAGLE AND RAVEN

As you travel throughout Southeast Alaska and observe the artifacts of Tlingit and Haida culture, you will quickly notice that the dominant motifs are Eagle and Raven. Every individual in Tlingit or Haida society was (and still is) born into one of two great social divisions, known as Eagles and Ravens (northern Tlingit use Wolf interchangeably with Eagle). These two groups are called moieties or phratries—anthropological terms meaning tribal subdivisions. Tlingit and Haida societies are matrilineal, so each child automatically assumes the moiety of the mother, but must marry into the opposite moiety. Thus we have one Eagle and one Raven in every set of parents, with all of the children belonging to the mother's group.

KINSHIP CLANS

Both Eagle and Raven moieties are subdivided into several kinship clans that identify themselves by totems: animal names and crests that were adopted long ago because they had special significance for the groups they represent. For example, Frog and Beaver are common clans of the Raven moiety; while Grizzly Bear, Killer Whale, and Wolf are Eagle clans. Clans represent specific lineages, like branches of a family tree, that theoretically could be traced back to the time of their migration to and throughout Southeast Alaska. Thus, each individual is born into one moiety and one clan, for example Eagle and Killer Whale, both according to the mother's group.

Traditionally, clans controlled such property rights as were acknowledged by the coastal Indians. They owned the right to use specific salmon streams, berry patches, hunting grounds, and house sites; as well as the right to employ the clan crest and other designs, songs, dances and names. The head of each clan was an important and powerful chief whose responsibility was to look after the clan and its property and act as spokesman.

HOUSE GROUPS

Clans were further subdivided into as many house groups as were necessary to accommodate all of the clan members and their families in a particular village. The community house was the minimum political and social unit in all Southeast Native societies, and all houses were ranked according to prestige and importance. The head of the most important house in a village was automatically the village chief. Within each house lived various families and individuals of like clan and moiety. Each house had a name, usually relating to one of the clan's totemic crests or to a physical feature of the structure. Dog Salmon House, House of Many Levels, and House with Sand All Around would be examples.

KWANS

So far we have moieties, kinship clans, and house groups—all irrespective of geographical location. Because of intermarriages between clans, however, the same clan might have houses in several different villages, and each village was made up of at least two and usually several different clans, all of which vied to be most important. Historically, the Tlingit, the largest of the Native groups, were arranged into several different geographical groups called kwans. The exact number of kwans in Southeast Alaska that existed at the time of the first contact with Europeans is uncertain, but seems to have been at least thirteen. The kwans took their names from a prominent river or bay in their region. Each contained a number of permanent villages.

Tlingit kwans were fairly tight-knit groups. They stuck together as a political unit and earned reputations befitting their actions. The Chilkat Tlingit, for example—the Chilkat-kwan—from the Klukwan area were reputed to be fierce and warlike, and the most powerful of all the kwans. Their principal village of Klukwan, on the Chilkat River north of Haines, is still one of the most important Tlingit villages in Southeast. The Chilkat controlled the mountain passes that lead to the Interior, traded with the Interior Athapaskans, and were known up and down the coast for their skill at weaving the famed Chilkat blankets from the hair of mountain goats. Other well-known kwans included the Stikines, near Wrangell, who controlled the river trade that passed up the Stikine River to Interior Canada, and the Sitka Tlingit.

CLASS

Superimposed upon the fabric of moiety, clan, house group, and kwan was the fundamental question of social class. Southeast Native society ranked all individuals into roughly three classes: nobility, including clan chiefs and their heirs and families; commoners, who comprised the majority of the population; and slaves, who were born into servitude, purchased from neighboring groups, or captured in raids on other villages. Social status was of the utmost importance to Southeast Natives. Rank could always be improved through the acquisition of wealth and prestige, the pursuit of which was a continuous and passionate undertaking.

THE POTLATCH

The various Tlingit and Haida groups did not live in isolation, but traveled around Southeast and beyond on trading missions or social visits. Sometimes they went to war against other groups to capture slaves or property, or to avenge a past slight. Occasionally they journeyed to another village to attend a potlatch, which was a party thrown by a clan chief on some meritorious occasion (perhaps to erect a totem pole, celebrate a marriage, dedicate a new house, or perform memorial rites) for the purpose of bringing honor to himself, his house, and his clan.

In the old days, a potlatch could go on for weeks with feasting, singing, dancing, and storytelling. Gift-giving was an important aspect of the potlatch, and the esteem of the potlatch chief was measured by the amount of wealth that he distributed to his guests. Clans saved for years to accumulate the wealth necessary to throw a potlatch, and often the rise in status was about the only thing they had left when it was over. It was more than enough, however, because an astute potlatch host could expect to get everything back—with interest—by the time the necessary reciprocal potlatches had been held.

Summer was the time for trading. The coastal Tlingit followed the Stikine, Taku, and Chilkat river systems into the mountains to trade with the Interior Athapaskans. They exchanged eulachon oil for such items as durable moose and caribou hides, then went south to barter these things plus thick Chilkat blankets for the superior cedar canoes of the Haida. When the Hudson's Bay Company established a trading post in British Columbia in 1831, the Tlingit and Haida ventured even farther for the chance to trade furs for manufactured goods such as iron tools and cooking utensils, cloth blankets, beads and buttons, rifles, tobacco, sugar, molasses, and flour.

THE RAVEN CYCLE AND OTHER MYTHS

The Southeast Coast Indians enjoyed a rich tradition of stories and myths, passed down orally from one generation to the next, that helped to explain the natural phenomena that surrounded their forested home. They did not practice any organized religion, but tried to stay on the right side of the various spirits that inhabited the earth in the form of animals, fish, trees, water, winds, and other natural elements. They did have a shaman among them whose job was to interpret spirit signs and, in his role as healer, to intercede with the supernatural beings on behalf of the sick.

The most important myths involve Raven, who winged his way into the mythology of many Indian cultures, both inside Alaska and out. This is not surprising when you consider that ravens are some of the most distinctive residents of the coastal forests. In Tlingit mythology, there are actually two Ravens: Yehl, the Great Raven, also called Nass Raven, is the creator figure. From his home above the Nass River (at the southern border of Southeast Alaska), which the Tlingit believe to be their original homeland, he controlled the sun, the moon, and the stars.

Scamp Raven, his grandson, is known as the trickster, and most of the Raven stories pertain to him and his usually comical adventures. It was Scamp Raven, however, who manufactured the earth out of mud and rocks, and then stole the sun, moon, and stars away from Nass Raven so that the world would have light. He also acquired fire, got the tides under control, painted birds their various colors, and accomplished many other feats. Scamp Raven is a much-beloved character. He has a rather coarse sense of humor and something of a mean streak; he loves to play tricks on people. He is basically lazy and a glutton, which are endearing characteristics to human beings with similar faults. His stories have always made good telling and, even today, anyone who knows these tales can get a chuckle when recalling some escapade in the career of Scamp Raven.

Raven stories were a favorite topic of illustration for totem poles. They differed in detail from place to place, but the main story line is fairly consistent. So that you will know what they are about when you see these poles on your travels through Southeast, here are very abbreviated versions of some of the best-known tales.

"How Raven Stole the Stars, the Moon, and the Sun"

All of the light in the world was kept by a man (Nass Raven) who lived at the head of the Nass River. He kept the light hidden in various boxes and bundles inside his house and guarded them closely. Scamp Raven wanted some light for the world and he thought and thought how to go about getting the light away from the man on Nass River. The man had a beautiful daughter, but she always had her slaves with her so Raven was not able to approach. Finally he thought of turning himself into a hemlock needle and slipping into her glass of water. She swallowed the needle and then grew large with child, which is how Scamp Raven happened to be born into the household.

The girl's father loved the baby dearly and gave him everything he asked for. One day the baby cried and cried and simply would not be comforted until his grandfather reluctantly let him play with the bag of stars. Raven rolled the bundle around and around on the floor and when he was positioned beneath the smoke hole in the roof, quickly untied it. All of the stars flew out the smoke hole and escaped into the heavens.

Raven's grandfather was extremely cross about losing his precious stars, but when again the baby cried and cried, he relented a second time and gave him the moon to play with. The same thing happened and the moon took its place in the sky. When Raven finally got hold of the box of daylight, he flew with it up the smoke hole and enjoyed his new world full of light.

"HOW RAVEN STOLE WATER"

In the beginning there were no lakes, no streams, and no rivers; no water anywhere except at Petrel's house where there was a natural spring. Raven wanted water for the world and he thought and thought of a way to get some of that water from Petrel.

Raven went to visit Petrel, who was reasonably courteous but very suspicious. He would not let Raven anywhere near the spring. In desperation, Raven invited himself to spend the night at Petrel's house, but still he was not able to approach the spring. The next morning he got up very early and found a pile of dog excrement that he smeared over the poor sleeping Petrel and his blankets. Then he woke Petrel up and, with a great show of commiseration, pointed out that the unfortunate bird had dirtied himself in the night. Petrel, humiliated, went off to bathe. Raven took the opportunity to drink as much water as he could and then escaped out the smoke hole.

As he flew, Raven spat out the water in his beak and the Nass, the Stikine, the Chilkat, the Taku, and the Alsek—all the great rivers of Southeast Alaska—took shape beneath him. Little drops fell here and there as well, forming the smaller salmon streams.

"RAVEN AND TIDEWOMAN"

Tidewoman, or Tidewatcher, lived high on a cliff where she controlled the tide. Raven decided that she kept the tide too high and people could not gather enough food on the beach. He vowed to do something about that. He went down to the water and gathered some sea urchins, then approached Tidewoman and asked her to lower the tide. When she refused, he pricked her bottom with a sea urchin spine. "Ouch!" she cried, and she let the tide down just a little bit. Raven stuck her with another sea urchin spine. "Oh! Ouch!" she cried. "Please don't stick me anymore!" The tide receded a little farther. Raven stuck more spines in her bottom until Tidewoman promised to make the tides rise and fall every day so that the people could collect the food they needed.

"Raven and the Daughters of the Fog"

Raven created the salmon streams when he stole the water from Petrel, but unfortunately, the salmon refused to go up them and the people could not catch the fish to eat. One day when Raven was wondering what to do about this he noticed a fine-looking woman sitting beside one of the streams. He decided to place her at the head of the stream so that all the salmon would rush upstream to look at her. This worked just fine, and now all of the salmon travel up the streams every fall to see the beautiful women, the Daughters of the Fog, who live there.

Other Tales

Both Tlingit and Haida mythology includes the giant Thunderbird that was responsible for lightning and thunder. The Thunderbird had enormous wings and a large curved beak. He lived on a mountaintop and when he was hungry flew down to the sea, and returned with a whale in his talons. The thunder was caused by his great wings beating the air, and lightning flashed from his eyes when he blinked.

One Raven story explains why something does not exist, in this case "Why There Is No Large River Near Sitka." According to this tale, Raven alighted one day near Sitka in a place that he thought would make a fine river. The tide was out and there were clams all over the beach. As Raven walked about to get the lay of the land, the clams kept squirting, making so much noise that Raven could not hear himself think. "Stop squirting, you clams!" he yelled, becoming increasingly irate, but the clams paid no attention. Next Raven picked some blueberries and stuffed them down the necks of the clams, but that did no good either. Finally he flew away in a huff, vowing not to make a river there after all.

This last Raven story about "How Raven Lost His Beak" makes a gentle point about laziness at Raven's expense. It concerns Scamp Raven who was hungry one day and looking for an easy meal. He noticed some men fishing for halibut and decided to make his dinner from the bait on their hooks. For a long while he succeeded at this and was feeling very pleased with his cleverness when he caught his beak on one of the hooks. Raven could not get free and his beak came completely off.

The fishermen took home the curious object they had brought up on their halibut hook. That night, Raven turned himself into human form, wrapped himself with a blanket to cover the hole in his face, and went to their house. He asked to examine the object they had found, pretending he might be able to identify it. When they showed him the beak, Raven clapped it back on his face and flew away.

ART AND ARTIFACTS

The bounty provided by the coastal waters and forests left the Tlingit and Haida with plenty of time for other pursuits. One of them was art, which they managed to integrate into virtually every aspect of their daily lives. There is a fine line between producing a utilitarian object such as a basket or a wooden bowl that is beautiful for its workmanship and design, and making a functional object beautiful by enhancing it with decorative design. The Southeast Indians did both, and some of the most delightful art objects in museums today were created for everyday use. The Tlingit and Haida also used their sophisticated design sense to create objects that were strictly ceremonial, such as totem poles; or strictly decorative, such as carved metal bracelets. Fortunately for us, most of these art forms have undergone a revival in recent years and are still practiced today.

Men were the artists and artisans in traditional Tlingit and Haida culture, with one exception: basketry was women's work. The other deviation from this pattern was the weaving of Chilkat blankets. Women performed the actual weaving, but the men created the pattern boards that the women followed to make the design.

BASKETRY

Two types of basket were woven in Southeast Alaska: cedar bark baskets made from the stringy inner bark of the cedar tree, and spruce root baskets. The latter were the most difficult, requiring long years of practice and immense skill, not just in the weaving, but in preparing the materials as well. First the roots had to be collected; the smaller roots were preferred. These were roasted in the fire so that their outer covering could be removed by pulling the roots through a forked stick. Then each root was split into still smaller strands with the aid of a long thumbnail. The smooth and shiny outer portion was set aside for the part of the design that would show, and the inner layer used for the rest of the weaving.

Spruce root baskets could be woven watertight. Before contact with other civilizations brought pottery and iron vessels, baskets were used extensively to carry water and for cooking. Special needs called for special shapes. Very small baskets were designed to be carried around the neck when berrying, so that both hands were free to pick the fruit. When full, the small basket was upended into a larger basket borne on the back, which was in turn emptied into an even larger model for transporting the berries back to camp. Sometimes the Indians wove extremely large, flat, floppy baskets that they placed beneath the bushes to catch the berries as they

Years of practice were required to weave a spruce root or cedar bark basket. (Alaska State Museum, Alfred A. Blaker)

fell. The Indian women of the northern Panhandle were known for their skill at weaving this type of basket. Their baskets were so finely woven and flexible that they could be folded and stored for the winter.

To decorate their baskets, the women bleached or dyed tall grasses and overlaid the woven spruce roots with patterns of stripes, zigzags, or other geometric designs. Natural dyes have become very popular in recent years, but the coastal Natives had nothing else. For a black pattern, they buried the grass in black mud or steeped it in a solution of hemlock bark. Yellow dye could be made from moss, blue from a solution of urine and copper ore, red from urine that had stood in an alder dish.

Spruce root was also used for weaving hats. The ordinary Native hat was roughly lampshade-shaped, made of coarser roots, and left undecorated. Wealthy and important people wore larger hats that were more finely woven and decorated with a painted crest design. The weaver's talent was put to the test with the potlatch hats worn by clan chiefs on ceremonial occasions. The potlatch hat was one of the most important symbols of Southeast Indian society. They also were decorated with painted crests, but their distinguishing feature was a series of flat cylinders stacked one on top of the other to form a topknot over the crown. These potlatch rings signified the number of potlatches that the wearer had given during his lifetime and thus symbolized his status in Tlingit or Haida society.

There are many fine examples of cedar bark and spruce root basketry

The rings on top of ceremonial potlatch hats indicated the status of the wearer. (Alaska State Museum, Alfred A. Blaker)

in the museum collections of Southeast Alaska, especially the Alaska State Museum in Juneau, Sheldon Jackson Museum in Sitka, and the Tongass Historical Society Museum in Ketchikan. A few baskets are being produced today and can sometimes be purchased in local gift shops, but they are very expensive. You can expect to pay up to two hundred to three hundred dollars for a three-inch specimen. Not many of the modern generation have yet learned this highly specialized skill, however.

BENTWOOD BOXES

Another speciality of Southeast Alaska and other Northwest Coast Indians was bentwood boxes. Bentwood boxes were essentially all-purpose boxes, used for storage, packing, carrying, or cooking. What made them special was the method used to construct them. The boxes were formed out of a single plank of cedar that was folded or bent in three places and joined at the fourth corner. A bottom was added, and sometimes a removable top, and the finished box adorned with carved or painted designs.

To make a bentwood box, the plank of wood first had to be chiseled or adzed to the correct thickness. Then the side that would form the interior of the box was routed out where the three bends would be placed. The board was steamed until it could be bent to the correct box shape, and the ends were joined together with wooden pegs or spruce root stitching. In later years, iron nails were used, too.

Bentwood boxes are remarkable for their ingenious construction and their simple beauty. The bending of the wood results in half-round corners that are pleasing to the eye, and the spruce root stitches are practically invisible. When you see these boxes in museums, be sure to look for the seamed corner and notice how cleverly the ends are joined. (The coastal Natives used spruce root stitching to mend their wooden canoes, too.)

CHILKAT BLANKETS

Many people consider Chilkat blankets the crowning glory of Tlingit art. These stunning shawl-shaped robes combined a most difficult weaving task with the most complex design, bordering on the abstract, of any Southeast Native artifact. "Blanket" is really a misnomer. The Chilkat blanket, like other blankets decorated with buttons or beads, was never used for sleeping or warmth, but draped over the shoulders as a ceremonial mantle or dance robe. A good dancer can work the blanket so that the long bottom fringe creates a wonderful image of motion. If you are fortunate enough to attend a Native dance performance (such as the Chilkat Dancers of Haines), you will see authentic Chilkat blankets in action.

The blanket was made from the hair of mountain goat. The wool was spun by hand (traditionally between the palm of the hand and thigh, like Cuban cigars). For added strength, the yarn of the warp (the up-and-down part of the weave that is fixed, as opposed to the weft, which is woven horizontally in and out), was wound around a strand of cedar bark. If you look closely at one of these blankets, you can spot the reddish brown bark in the fringe that hangs from the bottom of the blanket.

Women were the weavers of Chilkat blankets. The yarn was worked with the fingers—not shuttles—on a simple, upright frame, following a pattern board drawn by one of the male artists of the village. The colors of the intricate design were black, yellow, and a mossy blue-green, set against the cream background of the natural goat hair. To obtain the colors, the wool was dyed in various concoctions similar to those used to dye grass for decorating baskets. Black usually came from hemlock bark, yellow from a type of moss, and blue-green from urine and copper.

The art of weaving the Chilkat blanket was not limited to the Chilkat

The shawl-shaped Chilkat blankets are the highest expression of Tlingit art. (Jorgen Svendsen)

Tlingit, but they were considered the true masters of the craft. In part, this was because the goat wool was more easily available to them in their northern villages than to some of the other Tlingit groups. The original art form is thought to have originated with the Tsimshian peoples who used a similar technique to create a different type of robe. It is not known when the present style of blanket was first developed, but Captain Cook acquired geometrically styled goat hair robes that may represent the early stages of the art form when he visited the Northwest Coast in 1778. The blankets have always been coveted by Southeast Natives as objects of beauty and status. They signified wealth and were very valuable trade items.

The Sheldon Museum in Haines has the most informative display about weaving the Chilkat blankets. The exhibit includes a pattern board, the raw materials, and a partially completed blanket. The best closeup opportunities for examining Chilkat blankets are at the Sitka National Historical Park Visitors' Center, the Tongass Historical Society Museum in Ketchikan, and the lobby of the Sealaska Plaza in Juneau.

Button blankets came into use after traders introduced plain woolen blankets into Southeast Alaska late in the eighteenth century. The Indians adapted the blankets for ceremonial use by decorating them with red trade cloth and bits of abalone shell. Commercially manufactured buttons, glass beads, and sequins were added to the crest designs when they became available.

TOTEM POLES

Totem poles are undoubtedly the most recognized and least understood of all art objects in Southeast Native heritage. Some of the false impression has been created by the grotesque and gaudily painted poles in curio shops that seem to symbolize some mysterious religion or primitive Native rite. All of this is false. In fact, traditional Haida and Tlingit poles were never worshiped as religious objects, and they were not gaudy at all. They were, for the most part, bare cedar with painted accents of the typical Southeast Alaska palette: black, red, and blue-green. As the poles aged, they were allowed to return gracefully to their natural state, never being touched up or restored, so that in time they sprouted bits of grass and a woolly moss blanket. In later years, when the art form was in danger of being lost, efforts were made to retrieve and rehabilitate the best of these poles.

Many people, upon seeing a particular totem pole, will ask what it "says." What is the story carved in the pole? For many poles, there is no story at all. For others, the answer can be given only by the carver or the person who commissioned the pole. Totem poles were carved and erected for several different purposes or occasions. None of them involved worship in any sense; they were not religious objects. Some of them were memorial poles that were erected to honor an important individual upon his death. Many memorial poles were comparatively simple: a plain shaft topped by a crest figure representing the individual's clan. The crest figure might be Eagle, Raven, or one of the other totems such as Bear, Beaver, or Frog. Some early poles were mortuary poles, which were similar to memorial poles except that a niche was carved in the back of the pole to contain the ashes of the deceased.

Sometimes poles were carved to commemorate a particular event, such as the building of a new house, the giving of a potlatch, or an occasion of even more widespread significance. One of the best known poles in Southeast, the Lincoln Totem pole, was commissioned by a Tongass Island chief about 1883 to commemorate his clan's first sighting of a white man many years before. The carver evidently used a likeness of Abraham Lincoln as a model for the figure of the white man at the top of the pole, which is why the pole has come to be called the Lincoln Totem pole. The pole is

The Lincoln totem, carved about 1883, is an uncanny likeness of the president. (R.N. De Armond)

more properly known as the Proud Raven pole from the Raven crest that was carved at the base. The original carving, very weathered but bearing an extraordinary resemblance to the president, is in the State Museum in Juneau, and a replica at Saxman Totem Park in Ketchikan. A last type, rare, was the ridicule pole, which was erected to shame publicly a family or individual who had failed to pay a debt or otherwise broken a trust. When the debt was paid, the pole was taken down. The Three Frogs totem on Shakes Island in Wrangell is a copy of a famous ridicule pole from the Wrangell area.

Regardless of the type of pole, the dramatic carvings on the column served to remind the Native viewers of events, people, and legends out of their past. With no written language, this was a significant contribution. Totem poles are "story poles" only in the sense that the figures carved on them acted as symbols or memory aids to remind the storyteller of the principal characters and events he was relating.

Totem poles were carved by artists commissioned by the clan chief. The chief decided what figures he wanted on the pole and the artist executed the design. Red cedar was the preferred wood, although yellow cedar (Alaska cedar) was acceptable in the north where red cedar was not available. The Haida, especially, who had very large trees at their disposal, frequently hollowed out the back of the log to reduce weight and guard against splitting. The artist was left with a half-round shell approximately ten inches thick on which to carve his designs. (Be sure to look at the backs of totem poles, too.) The artist shaped the figures on the pole by chipping off small, uniform bites of wood with an adze. The Southeast Natives looked upon a fine-textured, evenly adzed pole as a true indication of the carver's skill.

The next step was paint, which was applied sparingly. The artists did not begin painting the entire surface of the pole until commercial paints became readily available. In the old days, the paint was a version of egg tempura using pulverized salmon eggs for a binding medium. Soot, graphite, or charcoal ground and mixed with the salmon eggs produced black paint. Red was made from red ochre, and the blue-green came from copper sulfide.

Originally, wood-carving tools were polished stone, bone, or shell, but trade with the Europeans brought sharp iron blades that cut through the cedar like butter. The metal blades enabled carvers to create larger and more complex designs, culminating in totem poles up to sixty-five feet tall. Most of the poles now seen in Southeast Alaska were carved in the latter half of the nineteenth century when trade with Europeans and Americans had brought considerable wealth to local Native groups and touched off a renaissance of Native carving.

Once erected, totem poles were generally not taken down (except for ridicule poles), even if the villagers moved to a new site. The poles were simply abandoned. Most of the totem parks around Southeast today stem from the 1930s when the Civilian Conservation Corps, working in conjunction with the U.S. Forest Service, undertook to collect old poles from abandoned sites and restore them to public view. Over the course of the project, more than one hundred totem poles were either restored, duplicated, or carved from memory and placed in parks around Southeast. Three community houses were replicated as well.

The most extensive collections are at the Sitka National Historic Park, and at Ketchikan, at Totem Bight to the north of town or Saxman Totem Park to the south. If you have to choose, Sitka has the most dramatic display because the poles are spaced along a beautiful path within the Tongass National Forest. There is an exhibit center where you can watch carvers and other craftspeople work and see a film about the history of Sitka and the Tlingit culture. In Ketchikan, the Totem Bight site is preferable for the spectacular setting overlooking Tongass Narrows. The totem poles are arranged in a clearing above the beach, and the park includes one of the three replicated community houses.

The other great collections of poles are at the villages of Hydaburg, Kasaan, and Klawock on Prince of Wales Island. Kasaan is the site of the second replicated community house, and the Klawock park contains some of the best examples of mortuary and memorial poles in existence. There are also many single poles to be seen as you walk around Southeast towns. In Wrangell there are several poles and the third Civilian Conservation Corps community house on Chief Shakes Island. Haines has many poles on view, too, thanks to the Indian Arts Center at Port Chilkoot. Alaska's tallest totem pole, rising to 132 feet, six inches, stands in the village of Kake on Kupreanof Island. The pole was carved in the 1970s at the Indian Arts Center.

OTHER CARVING

The Tlingit and Haida carvers—in those days always men, but no more—were kept busy. Besides bentwood boxes and totem poles, many other utilitarian and ceremonial objects were decoratively carved with clan crests or other significant totemic designs. The posts supporting the house roof beams frequently were patterned in designs that celebrated the history of the clan. There were elaborate wooden serving dishes for special feasts, "grease dishes" to hold eulachon or seal oil, enormous sheep horn spoons with handles carved of black goat horn, dance rattles shaped like birds, and ceremonial wooden hats with the crest animals carved on top. Intricate dance masks, some with moving parts that the wearer controlled by strings, represented birds, animals, or spirits. You will see some of these fantastic masks in use if you have the opportunity to watch the Cape Fox Dancers in Saxman or Chilkat Dancers in Haines. Otherwise, all of these objects—and

A totem pole merges with the woodland setting at Sitka National Historic Park.

more—are displayed in museums throughout Southeast Alaska.

In the early 1800s, the Haida developed a new art form: argillite carving. Argillite is a black shalestone that was discovered around 1820 on the Queen Charlotte Islands. The Haida artists found that the new substance could be carved and polished to a high luster that the traders frequenting the Northwest coast found attractive. The Natives began carving boxes and ceremonial dishes from argillite, sometimes adding decoration of ivory, abalone shell, or operculum to the traditional crest designs. Miniature totem poles of argillite were a later development that proved profitable in the tourist trade. Haida argillite carving is considered one of the highest art forms of the Northwest Coast. Especially fine argillite displays are found at the Museum of Northern British Columbia in Prince Rupert and Sheldon Jackson Museum in Sitka.

BASIC COMPONENTS OF TOTEMIC DESIGN

Almost every object in Southeast Native life, whether ceremonial or strictly utilitarian, was adorned by a design. Sometimes the design was carved into the wood of the object, and sometimes it was painted on top. The designs were generally of a totemic nature, meaning that they represented the clan totems, or crests. The crests served to signify ownership of the object and they engendered a sense of pride, in much the same way that a coat of arms created pride and allegiance in medieval Europe. Perhaps more than anything else, they turned plain household implements into objects of beauty and delight. Looking at an exquisitely carved halibut

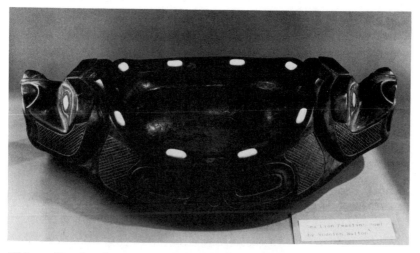

This sea lion feasting bowl, from the Sheldon Jackson Museum, is a fine example of the carver's art.

hook or a perfectly proportioned dish, in the shape of a seal, for example, it is easy to believe that these early artists worked primarily out of love for the materials, their tools, and the designs they were creating. Surely they felt great joy in filling their workaday world with beautiful objects.

Tlingit and Haida designs may all look the same to you at first—you will not be able to distinguish one totem from the next. In time, though, when you get accustomed to picking out the identifying characteristics, you will be able to sort many of them out, which will add enormously to your pleasure in viewing Native art.

If you want to learn more about totemic design, I strongly recommend Hilary Stewart's *Looking at Indian Art of the Northwest Coast* (University of Washington Press). The author breaks down the elements of totemic design into understandable bits, with wonderfully explicit illustrations.

THE TOTEMS

Whether painted on canoes or spruce root hats, or carved into the soft cedar of totem poles or storage chests, Native designs consist of the same basic totemic motifs. Only the format differs according to the shape of the object. The basic crest figures are most easily recognized in three-dimensional form as they appear on totem poles. Whether the carving is Tlingit, Haida, or Tsimshian, there are certain distinguishing features that you can look for in each crest animal. Usually the identifying characteristic is a particular body part, but a characteristic pose or an object frequently associated with that animal may be part of the design convention as well.

Raven is probably the most important design figure because he appears so frequently, either as one of the two major totems or in his mythological guise. Either way, Raven is usually portrayed as birdlike with wings. His distinguishing feature is a long, straight beak.

Eagle is the other major totem. His beak is shorter than Raven's and curved downward. Frequently he is shown with large claws. Occasionally you will see a double-headed eagle, such as the one on the totem pole in front of the Pioneers' Home in Sitka. This does not represent the Eagle crest, but the Russians in Alaska.

Bear is an important family crest. He is usually sitting on his haunches, in the attitude of a begging dog. He has upright ears, prominent teeth, large nostrils, and no tail. Sometimes a bear represents not a clan crest but a story, such as "Kats and His Bear Wife." This popular Tlingit legend tells of Kats, whose life was saved by a female grizzly bear that appeared to him in human form. Kats and the bear woman lived together as man and wife, but he was killed by their cub children.

Beaver is similar to Bear in overall shape and begging-dog attitude, but he has very large front teeth for gnawing. He also has a distinctive paddle-shaped tail that frequently is turned up in front of him and decorated with

Grizzly Bear

Double-headed Eagle

Raven

Beaver

Frog

Wolf

cross-hatching. Beaver sometimes holds a stick between his front paws.

Wolf often assumes the begging-dog pose, with these differences from Bear or Beaver: a pointed snout, pointed ears, and a long tail. Sometimes his tongue hangs out of his mouth.

Frog generally looks exactly like a frog, with a large, toothless mouth; short, little legs; and a squat body, sometimes with spots.

Killer Whale is the easiest totem to identify. Look for a blunt head, sometimes with prominent teeth, a forked tail, and a circular blowhole. The most recognizable feature, however, is the tall dorsal fin that protrudes from his back. Usually Killer Whale is placed vertically on the totem pole, head down, but sometimes he rides crosswise on top.

Halibut is not seen as frequently as some of the other totems, but is eminently recognizable with close-set eyes that are off-center, mouth to one side, and flatfish body.

Humans are occasionally portrayed on totem poles as figures from legends or notable events. They can be distinguished from animals by their ears, which are located on the side of the head instead of the top. White men are commonly given beards, clothes, and curly hair. Native women have lip ornaments called labrets, which were popular in former days. Haida poles are frequently topped by one or two human figures wearing tall potlatch hats. They are the "watchmen" on the lookout for enemies.

Killer Whale

Halibut

White man

APPLIED DESIGNS

The same techniques for carving animal designs onto a log could be applied to other surfaces and shapes, such as wooden serving vessels. A bowl could be shaped like a halibut, for example, with a broad tail at one end, a head with two offset eyes and crooked mouth at the other end, and the body hollowed out to form the cavity. Or a grease dish made to hold seal oil could be formed in the shape of a seal, with head protruding from one end and flippers on the sides.

When the totemic patterns were applied to flat surfaces, such as painted house screens, the designs had to be adjusted to fit. Once the principle was established of letting each totem be represented by stylized body parts, however, the problem was solved. The body parts were simply rearranged as necessary to fill up the given space in a pleasing manner. Sometimes the animal was simply "split" down the backbone and spread open to create a symmetrical design in one plane. The head appeared at the center of the design with one side of the body shown to the left and the other side to the right. Many silver bracelets are carved this way.

Sometimes the totem was just shown in a single profile, or as a double profile. Sometimes all of the necessary features were there, but out of order. This rearrangement of body parts can approach pure abstraction, as in the case of Chilkat blanket designs, which only experts can interpret. Always, though, the key design elements are there if you know where to look.

Killer Whale is portrayed with a double profile on a painted housefront in Angoon.

DESIGN COMPONENTS

Regardless of their media or subject matter, Southeast totemic artists adhered to certain conventional motifs. The components of this art form have undergone scholarly analysis in recent years, and certain names and definitions have come to be accepted as standard. The basic shape in Southeast Alaska totemic art is called the ovoid—the slightly rounded rectangle that is repeated over and over within a single design. Eyes are usually contained within an ovoid; sometimes the whole face or head is an ovoid shape as well. The ovoid illustrates the design principles of Native art: cor-

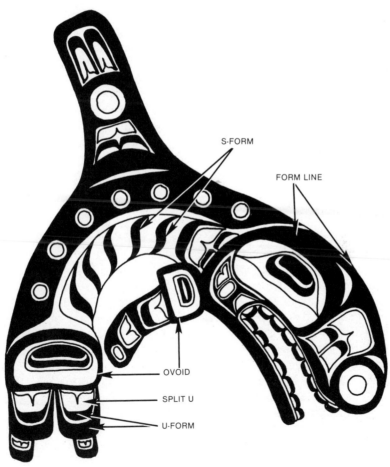

Jumping Killer Whale patterned after the design on a Tlingit hide shirt in the Berne Historical Museum.

ners are rounded, lines are curved, and everything is gently smoothed to make a flowing, pleasing shape.

The U-form is frequently an upside-down U, usually with a flattened top. This shape forms the ears of many crest animals and is used in details of tails and wings. Sometimes the U-form is divided in half to form a split U, a favorite device for feathers. U-forms can vary greatly in size and proportion. Some are tall and narrow, as for feathers, and others short and wide at the base.

The S-form is primarily used to fill up space or act as a bridge from one line to another. It, too, can vary in shape. Sometimes a series of S-forms represents ribs or a backbone.

All of these various components that make up a totemic design are contained within a continuous form line that defines the structure by outlining the major body parts. In a painted design the form line is usually black, while the secondary features are red or blue. In carved designs, the form line is seen on the surface of the wood while secondary motifs are recessed. Like all parts of the design, the form line is always curving, to create a continuous, controlled, flowing form.

In both carved and painted designs, a small face is frequently placed where two body parts join. This device is often seen in the figure of Beaver, where his tail joins with his body. The face also appears as the blowhole in Killer Whale. A face appearing within wings, however, indicates the power of flight. Within an eye, a face represents the life-force.

INTO THE CORPORATE ERA

After the first contact with the Russians when Chirikof's party went ashore, presumably near Sitka, in 1741, the Indians of Southeast Alaska saw ships from many nations. They traded furs for articles they did not have such as cloth, iron tools, kettles, and pots. These manufactured goods, and the practice of trading with the outsiders changed the pattern of their lives. They began to fit canvas sails onto their seagoing canoes; they adopted white men's garments in place of their own sewed skins and cedar bark shirts. Even when the Russian-American Company settled into Sitka, however, forcing the local Tlingit to abandon their homeland and camp in the shadow of the Russian community, the life-style of the majority of the Tlingit and Haida Indians living on the coast was not severely disrupted.

The first real devastation to come about as the result of contact with other cultures was smallpox, the scourge of aboriginal peoples. The English sea captain Nathaniel Portlock believed he saw many pockmarked faces when he visited near Sitka in 1787. He concluded the Spanish had brought the disease with them a dozen years before during the Pérez explorations. In 1836, smallpox broke out among the Tlingit in the southern

A small face within an eye usually represents the life-force. This is one of the Tired Wolf houseposts at Saxman.

range of the territory, perhaps spread northward from the British territories in Canada. This time the disease ran rampant through the Southeast coast and island chain. An estimated 50 to 60 percent of the Indian population—thousands of people—died. The smallpox spread from settlement to settlement along the coast to the north, eventually reaching the peoples of Bristol Bay, the Kuskokwim River, the Yukon River, and Norton Sound.

The U.S. purchase of Alaska from Russia had little immediate effect upon the Tlingit and Haida. The trading posts were more of an interruption to their life-style, as was the coming of missionaries. The discovery of gold and the birth of the commercial fishing industry in the late 1800s brought a substantial increase in the white population of Southeast Alaska and the development of new permanent communities. The Indians moved from their ancient villages to camp near the bustling mining towns or canneries where they could barter for goods or earn wages.

In the first years of U.S. possession, there were few laws to protect the white population and even fewer for Natives. In 1902, the Tlingit petitioned to attend white schools in Juneau and Ketchikan but were refused entrance. In 1912, they organized the Alaska Native Brotherhood with the aim of winning citizenship. This right was finally recognized in 1924. The same year, Tlingit attorney William Paul, Sr. won a seat in the territorial legislature.

Native peoples from all over Alaska gradually gained political sophistication and power. In 1971 their long efforts were rewarded by passage of the Alaska Native Claims Settlement Act, which awarded a cash and land settlement to reimburse the various Native groups for aboriginal lands that had been usurped by the U.S. government. Village, urban, and regional corporations were formed to manage the new resources. In Southeast Alaska, the final land selections for Native corporations will total 550,000 to 600,000 acres. Much of the acreage has been selected from prime timberland and many Native corporations have already entered the logging industry on a large-scale basis.

Common Plants of the Inside Passage

The plant communities are very similar all along the Inside Passage from Prince Rupert to Skagway. They are the result of the topography of the region, which consists of deep saltwater passages adjacent to mature coastal forests and high mountains, all occurring within a few thousand feet. This wide range of habitats existing in close proximity is one of the principal characteristics of Southeast Alaska.

HABITATS

From shipboard, Southeast Alaska appears to be all evergreens and salt water, but there are actually five distinct communities of vegetation. Lying close to the saltwater shore and along estuaries and riverbanks are marshlands or tidal flats made up of grasses, sedges, and other herby vegetation. Small willows and alder also grow at this low elevation and, in some locales, tall black cottonwoods.

The evergreen forest extends from sea level to timberline at two thousand or three thousand feet. The coastal forest of Southeast Alaska is the natural extension of the forest that stretches all along the Pacific coast from northern California to Cook Inlet. The southern forests are composed primarily of Douglas fir, but in Alaska, the dominant species are western hemlock and Sitka spruce. There is also a scattering of red cedar, Alaska cedar, and mountain hemlock. Southeast forests are generally old (usually

Forest openings reveal wet muskegs with low-growing shrubs and stunted trees. (U.S. Forest Service)

more than 150 years) and undisturbed by humans. Some of the mature trees are more than two hundred feet tall. Shrubs, ferns, and young trees grow beneath the tall cover, and the forest floor is littered with a thick layer of fallen logs and moss. These mature old-growth forests are called climax forests. They are in a natural cycle of growth and decay, which means that every stretch of woods contains many large, healthy trees; some small, young trees; and the remains of dead and dying trees that eventually will decompose to nourish the next generation.

In the forest openings are wet muskegs with pools of freestanding water. This community is characterized by natural bonsai—stunted, deformed trees that may be two hundred years old—as well as mosses, sedges, and low shrubs such as Labrador tea, high bush cranberry, blueberry, and crowberry. Primary among the trees are lodgepole pine (also called shore pine) and mountain hemlock.

Above the spruce and hemlock forest is a subalpine transition zone of scrubby trees such as mountain hemlock and a mat of low-spreading vegetation. Past tree line, above twenty-five hundred feet, begins the true alpine tundra community of tiny, low-growing plants such as heather, crowberry, nagoonberry, and alpine azalea that grow amongst the rocky outcrops.

Vegetation grows with astonishing rapidity in the early summer. This may seem surprising in an area with cool temperatures and little direct sunlight, but these factors are counterbalanced by long days. Even in Southeast Alaska, a summer day brings at least twenty hours of usable light. Within the space of a few weeks, barren, muddy hillsides are transformed into impenetrable salmonberry thickets that tower overhead. In the autumn, the process is reversed. The leaves linger on the berry bushes, turning yellow and mottled brown, until a late fall wind blows up. By morning, the trees and bushes are bare and winter has arrived.

As you travel throughout Southeast Alaska, you will begin to recognize the various trees, shrubs, and wild flowers that thrive in the wet coastal climate. Below are some of the most common plants of the region that you will see along the Inside Passage.

TREES

WESTERN HEMLOCK

Western hemlock is the most common tree in Southeast, forming more than 70 percent of the coastal spruce/ hemlock forest. These tall evergreens can grow to 190 feet with a 5-foot diameter trunk. The needles are dark green and shiny on top, and dull on the underside. Unlike spruce needles, they are short, soft, flexible, and rounded at the tip. They grow along two sides of the twig only, so the western hemlock twig is flat. The branches have a feathery

Western hemlock

appearance compared with the stiffer spruce; the tips are slender and curve down, especially when the five-eighth to one-inch cones have formed on the ends.

The better quality hemlock logs, those with straight grain, few knots, and a minimum of other defects, are used for general construction lumber.

Poor quality hemlock goes into pulp. Hemlock makes one of the best paper pulps and is also used for dissolving pulp, which is further processed into rayon, cellophane, and plastics.

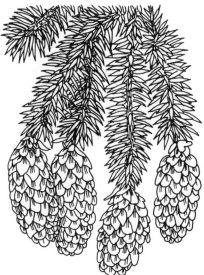

Sitka spruce

SITKA SPRUCE

The Sitka spruce is Alaska's official state tree and makes up 20 percent of the Southeast coastal forest. The tree can attain 225 feet in height and 8 feet in diameter, although 160 feet high and 3 to 5 feet in diameter is more typical. This tree is classic Christmas tree material. The needles are dark green on top, but silvery blue below. They are short, stiff, and sharp, and they grow all around the twig, exactly like a bottle-brush. If you put your hand around a spruce tip and squeeze, you will say "Ouch!" Not so with the hemlock. The 2 to 4-inch cones—considerably larger than the hemlock's—hang down from the branch tips.

Sitka spruce grows fast and is one of the most valuable trees in Alaska. Like hemlock, the better-quality spruce harvested in Southeast is cut into lumber. Spruce is an important wood for aircraft and glider construction, boats, ladders, and other items that require strength combined with light weight, and its excellent acoustical properties make it suitable for guitar faces and piano sounding boards. Sitka spruce also produces the highest quality wood pulp on the West Coast.

MOUNTAIN HEMLOCK

Mountain hemlock is the alpine counterpart to western hemlock. Although found at sea level, the mountain hemlock's range extends to thirty-five hundred feet, which is higher than the western hemlock or Sitka spruce cares to grow. The tree is smaller than the western hemlock, normally 50 to 100 feet high, but capable of stretching to 125 feet. In muskeg bogs and subalpine communities where soils are infertile, the tree takes on a severely twisted and stressed shape with very short branches, bonsai bends, and deeply weathered, gray bark. At times mountain hemlock hugs the ground, spreading horizontally as a low-lying shrub.

The needles of mountain hemlock are similar to those of western hemlock: shiny green, short, and soft. The difference is that they grow all the way around the twig for a fuller, bottlebrush effect. The cones resemble those of western hemlock but are longer. They are dark purple before they mature, deepening eventually to brown.

WESTERN RED CEDAR

Western red cedar grows in the southern part of the Panhandle, approximately from Petersburg south, mixed in with the rest of the spruce/hemlock forest. The tree is aromatic and the foliage is much different from that of either spruce or hemlock, the needles forming flat, fanlike sprays with one-half-inch elliptical cones appearing near the ends of the twigs. The wood from the red cedar resists rot and insects and is widely used for fence posts, shakes, shingles, and boat construction. The Tlingit and Haida Indians used this wood for their canoes, houses, and totem poles, and wove mats and baskets out of the rather stringy bark. The red cedar is a large evergreen, normally growing to 100 feet and sometimes as high as 130 feet.

ALASKA CEDAR

Alaska cedar, known also as Alaska cypress or yellow cedar, is the last of the five important conifers in Southeast. This cedar is found all along the coastal forest, but is not nearly as common as spruce or hemlock. Alaska cedar is smaller than the western red cedar, growing to a maximum height of one hundred feet. The leaf structure is the same flat, fanlike spray, but the tiny cones (less than one-half inch in diameter) are nearly round and more gray-colored than brown. The wood is durable, but soft and easy to work. The Tlingit and Haida Indians commonly used Alaska cedar for their carved canoe paddles, and it remains a favorite carving wood. Today Japan imports quantities of Alaska cedar and U.S. manufacturers use the lumber for windows, doors, and boats.

Alaska cedar

LODGEPOLE PINE

Lodgepole pine, or shore pine, is the only pine native to Alaska. Usually it is a twisted, scrubby specimen growing in the muskeg swamps of Southeast forest openings. In this mode the pine is only a few feet tall, often spreading horizontally rather than vertically. In better growing conditions, though, lodgepole pine can shoot straight up to forty feet. An inland variety found around Haines and Skagway grows even taller, to seventy-five feet. The tree is dark green with typical pine needles growing in pairs with a sheath at the base. The cones are up to two inches long and the wood very resinous. Lodgepole pines are prized by some southeasterners at Christmastime because they are a nice change from the usual spruce and hemlock and because they retain their needles longer than the other varieties of tree. They are too few to be harvested commercially.

ALDER

Red alder

Alder is the most common broadleaf, or deciduous, tree in Southeast Alaska. It appears from the size of a shrub to a small tree every place where the ground has been disturbed: along roads and ditches, on avalanche scars, by rivers and streams, on logging sites, and where glaciers have retreated. The smooth, gray-barked wood has long been used for smoking fish and game and is easily gathered for firewood. Alder is also preferred for some Native carving.

Three species of alder are present in Southeast. All have smooth, gray bark: shiny, dark green leaves with serrated edges (similar in shape to birch leaves); and small, dark, nutmeg-shaped nuts. The largest and most abundant species is red alder, which grows to forty feet. Sitka alder is slightly smaller, growing to thirty feet. This species grows along with red alder at lower elevations, but exists by itself at elevations above one thousand feet. The third variety, thinleaf alder, is found only in the northern part of the Panhandle, from Juneau to Skagway, where it grows mixed in with willows along streams.

Alder is known as a pioneer species, meaning that it follows disturbances to the ground such as avalanches or roadbuilding, quickly takes root, and improves soil conditions. When the evergreens appear and overtake them in size, the alders disappear because they are intolerant of shade.

WILLOW

Willows grow along with alders beside stream beds, beaches, and roads. Like alders, they grow fast and quickly take over sites that have been logged, burned, or otherwise cleared. They have light, gray-green leaves that are smooth and oblong in shape. In spring, they develop fuzzy caterpillar-shaped catkins that spread tuffs of white fluff everywhere. There are many varieties of willow in Southeast. The most common is the Scouler willow, followed by the Sitka willow and Barclay willow. In size the willows range from shrubs to small trees.

BLACK COTTONWOOD

The largest broadleaf tree in the area is the tall black cottonwood, which is common to the river valleys on the mainland of Southeast Alaska, including the Stikine, the Taku, and the Chilkat. The black cottonwood grows alongside the alder and willow trees but towers above both at eighty to one hundred feet. In 1965 a champion specimen was found near Haines (about five miles west of Klukwan on the Klehini River). The tree measured 101 feet in height with a circumference of 32 feet and 6 inches. A larger black cottonwood was found in Oregon in 1969.

At first glance the cottonwood might be taken for just another alder, since the two usually grow side by side. The cottonwood is much larger, though, and the leaves are pointed at the tip and smooth around the edges, in contrast with the toothed leaves of the alder. The black cottonwood is a handsome tree, and provides a touch of color in the fall when the leaves turn yellow-gold. The most famous cottonwood locale in Southeast is along the Chilkat River in the vicinity of Klukwan. Bald eagles gather in these cottonwoods by the thousands to feed on spawned-out salmon in late fall and winter.

MOUNTAIN ASH

The most colorful tree in Southeast is the European mountain ash. The tree has been introduced as an ornamental in many Southeast towns and grows to forty feet. Mountain ash is spectacular both in spring, when its clusters of tiny white flowers are among the first blooms to appear, and in fall, when its clumps of scarlet berries attract flocks of Bohemian waxwings and other migrating birds. One of the prettiest sights in Southeast is in late October or early November when the first snow has fallen on the mountain ash trees, which have lost most of their leaves but not

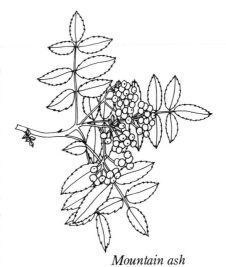

Mountain ash

their red berries. The foliage consists of delicate, fernlike sprays with many small, yellow-green leaves on a slim stem. The leaves turn bronze in fall. The bark is light gray and smooth. A native species of mountain ash grows as a tall shrub to about fifteen feet in forest openings, but is rare. It is smaller and less showy than the introduced tree.

A handful of other trees exist in Southeast Alaska but are less commonly seen or exist only in isolated spots. Among them are the dwarf Douglas maple (the only maple in Alaska), Pacific silver and subalpine firs, Pacific yew, quaking aspen, western paper birch, and Pacific serviceberry.

BERRIES AND OTHER FOREST PLANTS

Berrying is an important recreational activity in Southeast Alaska. Around late June, the berry fanatics start cruising the roads and trails, sniffing out the best patches for the summer's picking. When the jam and jelly jars have been hauled out for the ritual washing and the pails made ready, the expeditions can get underway. Berry-picking pails generally take two shapes: the two-pound coffee can and the yellow plastic container that Adams Old Fashioned peanut butter comes in. Holes are punched in the sides of the pail and the ends of a long scarf threaded through them and knotted. The scarf goes over the neck and the pail hangs in front of you, freeing both hands for picking. The berries—especially blueberries but also salmonberries, nagoonberries, and others—are an excuse to be with friends and enjoy the wild forest trails. Southeasterners like to store some of the summer fruit in the freezer to make blueberry muffins and sourdough salmonberry pancakes when the snow comes. The leftover goes into jam and jelly—Christmas presents for favored friends and relatives in the Lower 48.

Berry-picking is more than recreation for some older Alaska Natives whose culture was once heavily influenced by the cycle of food-gathering. For these people, collecting a certain quantity of berries every summer and preserving them for winter use is almost a ritualistic necessity, if no longer an economic one. One elderly Tlingit woman of my acquaintance has the use of only one eye and such severe arthritis that she can barely hobble with the help of a cane. When berrying time comes she is carried to the berry patch where she spends hour upon hour gathering in her winter's fruit.

SALMONBERRY

One of the first signs of spring in Southeast Alaska is the psychedelic pink blossom of the salmonberry. This star-shaped flower peeks through the bright green leaves in May, when nothing else is even close to blooming.

Salmonberries are a base plant of this region, running rampant over any available woodsy space. When the prickly canes reach their full summer height—easily ten feet—they form an impenetrable barrier. The fruit, appearing about July, appeals to bears. The berries are large and shaped like boysenberries or blackberries. Their color is quite remarkable: a true salmon-orange on some bushes and a dark red-orange on others. The flavor is mild but slightly tangy.

PACIFIC RED ELDER

When the salmonberries are already blossoming, the red elder, or elderberry, springs to life with clumps of lacy, white blossoms. This berry reaches the size of a small tree in Southeast. The elder, actually a member of the honeysuckle family, has brittle, woody branches and long, narrow leaves. Around August, grapelike clusters of tiny, shiny red

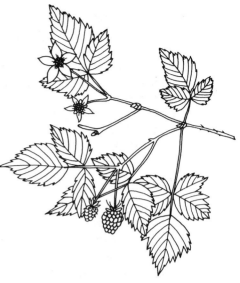

Salmonberry

berries form in place of the flowers—much to the delight of the crows. The fruit is bitter and affects some people adversely. (The elderberry that forms the basis for the excellent elderberry wines is a European species and not present in Southeast.)

Red elders are graceful shrubs that add color to many Southeast gardens. They are common in open areas of the forest or on the fringes of communities. A bank of elderberries makes a wonderful splash of scarlet against the dark green backdrop of spruce and hemlock.

BLUEBERRY

Blueberries are the preferred local berry in Southeast. There are several varieties, including some huckleberries. All of the varieties of blueberry are compact, but can reach six feet in height. The stems are woody; there are no thorns or prickles. The oval leaves are small and light green, and the spring blossoms, yellow-pink to bronze-pink, depending upon the variety, hang down in the shape of a bell. The berries vary, also, from blue to nearly black. One variety, the red huckleberry, is not blue at all but a bright, shiny red.

The most common variety is the early blueberry, the berries of which are covered with a light-colored powder or bloom. The Alaska blueberry is similar but the fruit is a shiny blue-black. Both varieties grow together. Many people insist that the latter variety is actually a huckleberry. The red huckleberry is rarer, to the dismay of local residents who enjoy them for their bright color and good jam-making qualities. All of these berries are delicious and most people simply mix them together since they grow side by side in the woods. On the muskeg at higher elevations are found two dwarf varieties: the dwarf blueberry and the bog blueberry. Both are low, spreading shrubs that never attain more than a couple of feet in height.

Some years the blueberries have a tendency toward worminess, alas. Nothing to be squeamish about—just dump your berries in a pail of water when you get back from the woods and soak them for a few hours. The worms (which are minute) become starved for oxygen and are forced to crawl out; then you rinse off the berries and proceed.

OTHER BERRIES

Blueberries and salmonberries are the most popular and common berries in the Panhandle, but by no means the only ones. For those who know where to find them, wild cranberries are a special treat in the fall. There are two creeping varieties that grow in bogs and alpine areas, and a bush variety that appears in the forest. The high bush cranberry is an extremely handsome plant that grows to twelve feet. The three-lobed leaves are sparse on tall branches and turn color with the seasons. The fruit, which is fairly large (three-eighths to one-half inch), elliptical, and translucent is a beautiful yellow-orange in summer and turns brighter with time. The high bush cranberries are flavorful and make wonderful jelly or syrup. Unfortunately, they are not common except along streams on the mainland.

The western thimbleberry is a common Southeast plant with large maple-shaped leaves. The flat, white blossom forms a compact pinky red berry shaped like a thimble. The shrub grows to five feet and is lush, but without spines. The fruit is edible but not profuse, and is not usually harvested today.

Southeast has several types of edible currants and gooseberries, as well as several ground berries. Of the latter, two that are unusual are the crowberry (sometimes called mossberry), a low, heatherlike plant with shiny, round, deep black berries that grows in bogs and upper tundra regions (including the rocky cliffs of the Juneau Ice Field at fifty-six hundred feet); and the rare nagoonberry that appears in low-lying meadows and bogs. The nagoonberry is a delicate little plant, growing two to ten inches off the ground, with three-lobed leaves and a red fruit shaped like a rounded, shiny raspberry. This berry has a superb flavor and is highly valued for jam, jelly, or wine—when you can find enough. Southeasterners have been known to share *anything* except the location of their secret nagoonberry patch. Small wild strawberries are also available in beach areas.

A berry to avoid is the poisonous baneberry, which has large, coarsely-toothed, lobed leaves and round red or white fruit, several to a stem. The bush grows in woods and thickets to three and one-half feet. As few as six berries have been known to cause dizziness, increased pulse, and stomach pain.

Devil's club is the ogre of the woods: a primitive-looking jungle plant with enormous leaves and treacherous spines. This plant reaches to ten feet and is a common inhabitant of the spruce/hemlock forest undergrowth. The elephantine leaves, up to a foot in diameter, are prickly on the underside. Even worse, the tall, snaking stalks are fitted with poisonous, sharp spines that fester and make a painful sore if they become imbedded in your skin. Devil's club can block your path through the forest, very unpleasantly, but, seen from a safe distance, the plant is quite attractive. In spring pale greenish white flowers develop on tall stalks, and turn into bright red berries in the fall (not edible).

Devil's club

The large leaves turn a pleasant yellow at the same time. As annoying as devil's club is on close encounter, it is one of the few hazardous plants in the woods. There is no poison ivy or poison oak in Southeast forests.

COW PARSNIP

Another common plant with elephantine leaves is the cow parsnip. This plant appears throughout Southeast Alaska along roadsides and in meadows, forest clearings, and many a domestic garden where it is not wanted. The plant has a hollow green stem that is striated like celery or rhubarb, hence the plant's two other names: wild celery and Indian rhubarb. On top are the gigantic many-lobed leaves and stalks that bear tight clusters of tiny white flowers in the spring. The flower clusters are so large and compact that they resemble a flat head of cauliflower.

Cow parsnip smells strongly "weedy," and the scent lingers on your skin and clothing for hours. Many people are allergic to the plant. The stems are edible and were routinely consumed by the Native peoples of Southeast in earlier times. To prepare cow parsnip you must first peel the stems; then the inside can be eaten raw or cooked like rhubarb in a little water. However, this is not advisable unless you are sure you are not allergic to the plant. With some susceptible people, even superficial contact will cause painful blisters on the skin. From a distance you might confuse cow parsnip with Devil's club because they both have large leaves, but the parsnip has the celerylike stalks with no spines. Also beware of confusing cow parsnip with deadly poison water hemlock which has a similar flower.

SKUNK CABBAGE

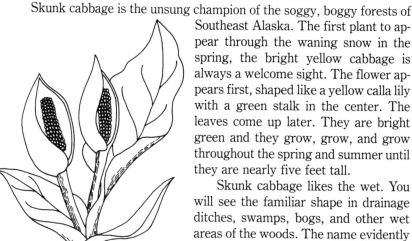

Skunk cabbage is the unsung champion of the soggy, boggy forests of Southeast Alaska. The first plant to appear through the waning snow in the spring, the bright yellow cabbage is always a welcome sight. The flower appears first, shaped like a yellow calla lily with a green stalk in the center. The leaves come up later. They are bright green and they grow, grow, and grow throughout the spring and summer until they are nearly five feet tall.

Skunk cabbage likes the wet. You will see the familiar shape in drainage ditches, swamps, bogs, and other wet areas of the woods. The name evidently comes from the strong odor of the plant (I have never noticed it, myself). The Tlingit used skunk cabbage for pit baking the way Easterners use seaweed in a clambake. The leaves contain large amounts of oxalic acid and should not be eaten.

Skunk cabbage

WILD FLOWERS

Despite its rainy disposition, Southeast Alaska has a full complement of wild flowers. A list of the commonly appearing varieties appears on pages 104–105. Below are a few of the better-known specimens that you may encounter during your rambles through the coastal forest.

The lovely blue-violet lupine grows to four feet tall along the coastal shore, along highways and roads, and in alpine areas. One of the most extravagant displays is along the highway just north of the Juneau airport, in the vicinity of Brotherhood Bridge. Fireweed is the showiest wild flower in the region. The tall variety grows to nine feet along roadsides, riverbanks, and in meadows. The plant has purple-pink flowers on a tall, leafy stem. Along forest trails, the small bunchberry forms a single greenish white flower with four petals in spring, and a red fruit in fall. Bunchberry is a dwarf form of dogwood and a common ground cover in the spruce and hemlock forest. The plant stands no taller than eight inches.

There are two types of violet: the yellow stream violet and the blue

Alaska violet. Both prefer damp locations. Southeast has many varieties of buttercup, a red-orange columbine, a purple-blue wild flag or iris, a wild rose, and the delicate blue forget-me-not, Alaska's state flower. Among the other species are two of special interest: a wild beach pea with red-violet flowers and tender pods that grows in beach sand; and a rare (outside of coastal Alaska) chocolate lily that grows in open grassy flatlands. This lily is colored deep purple brown and grows to twenty-four inches. The bulb is covered with ricelike pellets that are edible when cooked. The local Native peoples habitually included the pellets in their diet, accounting for the lily's other name: Indian rice. If you visit Southeast in early fall you might enjoy searching for clumps of Alaska cotton grass. Local residents are fond of using this tufted grass in dried floral arrangements.

Chocolate lily

COMMON WILD FLOWERS OF SOUTHEAST ALASKA

Cotton grass/Alaska cotton, *Eriophorum* species*
Skunk cabbage, *Lysichitum americanum*
False hellebore, *Veratrum eschscholtzii*
Indian rice/Chocolate lily, *Fritillaria camschatcensis**
Alp lily, *Lloydia serotina*
False lily-of-the-valley, *Maianthemum dilitatum*
Wild iris/Wild flag, *Iris setosa**
White bog orchid, *Habenaria dilitata*
Ladies' tresses, *Spiranthes romanzoffiana*
Heart-leaf twayblade, *Listera* species
Fairy slipper/Calypso, *Calypso bulbosa*
Coral root, *Corallorrhiza mertensiana*
Moss campion/Cushion pink, *Silene acaulis*
Dwarf water lily, *Nymphaea tetragona*
Yellow pond lily, *Nuphar polysepalum*
Mountain marigold, *Caltha leptosepala*
Marsh marigold, *Caltha palustris*
Western columbine, *Aquilegia formosa**
Monkshood, *Aconitum delphinifolium*
Yellow anemone, *Anemone richardsonii*
Narcissus-flowered anemone, *Anemone narcissiflora*
Cut leaf anemone, *Anemone multifida*
Cooley buttercup, *Ranunculus cooleyae*
Eschscholtz buttercup, *Ranunculus eschscholtzii*
Creeping buttercup, *Ranunculus repens**
Western buttercup, *Ranunculus occidentalis**
Sundew, *Drosera* species
Roseroot/King's crown, *Sedum rosea*
Grass of Parnassus, *Parnassia palustris*
Fringe cup, *Tellima grandiflora*
Alaska boykinia/Bear flower, *Boykinia richardsonii*
Laceflower, *Tiarella trifoliata*
Purple mountain saxifrage, *Saxifraga oppositifolia*
Luetkea/Alaska spirea, *Luetkea pectinata*
Goatsbeard, *Aruncus sylvester**
Marsh fivefinger/Cinquefoil, *Potentilla palustris*
Silverweed, *Potentilla egedii* var. *grandis*
Yellow dryas, *Dryas drummondii*
Eight-petaled dryas/Mountain avens, *Dryas octopetala*
Nootka lupine, *Lupinus nootkatensis**
Prickly wild rose/Nootka rose, *Rosa nutkana**

Beach pea, *Lathyrus maritimus*
Cranesbill/Northern geranium, *Geranium erianthum*
Touch-me-not, *Impatiens noli-tangere*
Stream violet/Yellow violet, *Viola glabella* *
Alaska violet, *Viola langsdorffii* *
Fireweed, *Epilobium angustifolium* *
Dwarf fireweed, *Epilobium latifolium* *
Western/Poison water hemlock, *Cicuta douglasii*
Cow parsnip, *Heracleum lanatum* *
Ground dogwood/Bunchberry, *Cornus canadensis* *
Pink pyrola/Wintergreen, *Pyrola asarifolia*
Single delight/Shy maiden/Wax flower, *Moneses uniflora*
Labrador tea, *Ledum groenlandicum*
Alpine azalea, *Loiseleuria procumbens*
Aleutian heather/Mountain heather, *Phyllodoce glanduliflora*
Alaska moss heather, *Cassiope* species
Bog rosemary, *Andromeda polifolia*
Pixie eyes/Wedge-leaved primrose, *Primula cuneifolia*
Rock jasmine, *Androsace septentrionalis*
Star flower, *Trientalis europaea*
Shooting star, *Dodecatheon* species
Broad-petaled gentian, *Gentiana platypetala*
Jacob's ladder, *Polemonium pulcherrimum*
Forget-me-not, *Myosotis sylvatica* *
Monkey flower/Wild snapdragon, *Mimulus guttatus*
Coastal paintbrush/Yellow paintbrush, *Castilleja unalaschcensis*
Mountain paintbrush, *Castilleja parviflora*
Lousewort, *Pedicularis* species
Poque/Broomrape, *Boschniakia rossica*
Butterwort/Bog violet, *Pinguicula vulgaris* var. *macroceras*
Twinflower, *Linnaea borealis*
Valerian/Mountain heliotrope, *Valeriana* species
Mountain harebell/Bluebell, *Campanula lasiocarpa*
Bluebells of Scotland, *Campanula rotundifolia*
Dandelion, *Taraxacum* species *
Goldenrod, *Solidago multiradiata*
Fleabane, *Erigeron* species
Arctic daisy, *Chrysanthemum arcticum*
Arnica, *Arnica* species
Seabeach senecio/Seabeach groundsel, *Senecio pseudo-arnica*
Yarrow, *Achillea borealis*

*   Very common

Wildlife of the Inside Passage

The coastal forests and waterways of Southeast Alaska nurture a huge variety of creatures. A few of them, such as the bald eagle and the humpback whale, are so rarely seen in most of the continental United States that their numbers in Alaska seem an embarrassment of riches and, for lovers of wildlife, probably worth a trip in themselves. For many of the other species, especially the larger land animals, just the opposite is true: although they exist in abundance, the chance of actually spotting a bear or a moose during the average cruise ship or ferry passage is slight. This is not to say that you won't see any wildlife on your trip, especially if you have time to linger in the more remote spots of Southeast. Here are the wildlife forms that are *common* to Southeast Alaska.

LAND ANIMALS

BLACK BEAR

The black bear, the smallest and most common species of bear in America, exists in the forests of much of Alaska. In Southeast, the black bear is at home on all of the mainland and most of the islands. Exceptions are the northernmost islands, including Admiralty, Baranof, Chichagof, and Kruzof. One of the highest concentrations is on Prince of Wales Island, across Clarence Strait from Ketchikan. You might easily glimpse one of these animals, as I have, ambling across one of the logging roads that bisect the island.

An adult black bear measures approximately twenty-six inches at the shoulder and can weigh up to two hundred pounds in summer when feed is plentiful. Although called *black* bears, the animals range in color from deep black to brown and even cinnamon, a fact that frequently causes them to be confused with their larger brown grizzly cousins. A very rare glacier variety with smokey blue fur appears sometimes in the northernmost part of the Panhandle around Yakutat. You can see a specimen, somewhat faded, of a glacier bear in the Sheldon Museum at Haines.

Black bears spend most of their time in summer browsing through open forested areas where they can find the salmonberries, blueberries, and other shrubs they like to eat. You are not likely to see one unless you happen to be in the forest, too. In late summer and fall, they turn to fishing for spawning salmon along shallow rivers and streams. In winter, when food is scarce, they enter a state of semihibernation characterized by a drop in metabolic rate. They are easily awakened, however, and may even leave their dens for short periods.

Spring may be the best time to spot black bears as they feed on tender new growth along beaches and in open meadows and hillsides. Look for clearings on the mountainsides (such as slide or avalanche scars) where the new vegetation has grown. The dark-colored animals are visible against the bright green cover or as they cross lingering patches of snow.

If you are in a semirural area and bent upon seeing a black bear no matter how degrading the circumstances, you might try the local garbage dump. It is a sad fact that bears that have been exposed to humans quickly become garbage addicts and would rather rummage through the garbage dump then forage through the woods. *Be cautious,* however, and do not approach the animals. Black bears give the impression of being less ferocious than other varieties because of their smaller size, but they can be just as lethal when protecting their interests—food, cubs, escape route, or private territory.

BROWN BEAR

The large brown bear, known also as the coastal brown bear and grizzly, is found throughout the Southeast mainland and on the northern islands, especially Admiralty, Baranof, and Chichagof.

Grizzly bear

Small populations occur on Wrangell and Etolin islands in the southern Panhandle. Brown bears and grizzlies used to be considered separate species, but studies have now shown them to be the same. However, bears living inland with primarily a vegetable diet (usually called grizzlies) are distinctly smaller than coastal bears that feed on high-protein salmon during the summer and fall.

Color is not a good test for distinguishing a brown bear from a black bear, since both species vary in color. Brown bears range from dark black-brown to blond. Size is a better indicator as the browns are considerably larger than black bears. Mature males weigh from five hundred to nine hundred pounds, and large coastal bears can reach fourteen hundred pounds. The brown bear also has a prominent hump over the shoulders (actually an extension of the powerful front leg muscles) and a roundish, massive head.

The brown bear is the most respected creature in the forest—truly the king. His powerful strength and substantial bulk leave him no enemies or predators... except man.

SITKA BLACK-TAILED DEER

The Sitka black-tailed deer is the most abundant game animal in Southeast Alaska, providing winter meat for many Southeast families. The name is aptly taken from the animal's small flag of a tail which is pure black on top and white underneath. The Sitka deer is a member of the coastal mule deer family which is native to the entire Pacific Coast from northern California through Southeast Alaska. The Sitka species is small, the average adult weighing from 100 to 150 pounds. The summer coat is reddish brown and turns dark gray in winter.

Home for these animals varies with the season. After the fawns are born in May and June, the deer begin moving out of the forest and up to the alpine meadows where they feed during the summer months (exactly the opposite of the bears, which come down from the mountains in the summer to feed off berries and salmon). When fall frosts limit the available food, the black-tails return to the forest and remain there throughout the winter and early spring, foraging among leaves and shrubs. If the snow is deep, they may be forced down onto the beach to search for dried grass or, in extreme conditions, seaweed. In spring and early summer, they move to the beach to nibble new grass and other succulent plants. You may see them there with their new spotted fawns, especially in the early morning, as you glide by in your ship.

MOOSE

Moose are found in only a few areas of Southeast Alaska, primarily in the mainland river valleys. The largest herd is located at the northern end of the Panhandle around Yakutat. Smaller herds roam near Haines, Berners Bay (on the mainland between Haines and Juneau), and along the Taku, Stikine, and Unuk rivers. You stand a good chance of encountering the large animals if you explore these rivers by small boat. Otherwise, you can only hope to see them grazing on the flats at the river mouths as you pass by on your ship. Moose are sometimes sighted on the large sandy flats at the entrance to the Katzehin River in Chilkoot Inlet, on the way to Haines and Skagway.

Moose are large animals, in the range of one thousand to sixteen hundred pounds for adult males. They spend much of their time knee-deep in swamps or shallow ponds, munching on willow twigs, weeds, and grass. Although slightly ludicrous in appearance with a mule-shaped body, small ears, and an improbably long nose, moose are greatly respected by local residents for their strength and ferocity, especially in defense of their young, and for their excellent meat. Many a southeasterner sets off resolutely every fall to "get his moose" to fill the freezer. The logistics of bagging a moose deserve considerable forethought, for a one-thousand-pound-plus animal yields a lot of meat to haul out of the woods. And there is nothing like butchering a moose in the middle of a swamp to dampen further enthusiasm for the hunt.

MOUNTAIN GOAT

If you have sharp eyes, you may be able to pick out a group of mountain goats in the high rocky outcrops that border the Inside Passage. Old-timers in the area have an irritating habit of peering out in the general direction of the sky and crying "Mountain goat!" as they cruise along the Southeastern fjords. The goats are there, all right, but they are mighty small to the naked eye. You have to look for small white dots that appear about half an inch high against the gray rock. You may be lucky and see them closer up, especially in Glacier Bay. Many pilots are cooperative about pointing out goats on the mountaintops as you fly overhead (over Misty Fiords, for example). You will have to look quickly, though, because you don't want to circle

Mountain goat

back and buzz the animals. Don't bother to get out your camera.

Mountain goats make their home in the most rugged and inaccessible parts of the Coast Mountains. Their hooves are fitted with cushioned pads that allow them to clamber up and down the sheer rock walls. Their coats are all white and shaggy, and they have long whiskers under the chin. The horns are black and short—not light-colored and curved like those of Dall sheep with which they are often confused (Dall sheep are not native to Southeast anyway). The goats spend the summer in high meadows where they feed off grasses and alpine shrubs. In winter they forage along the wind-blown ridges that are free from snow. Some may climb down to tree line and nibble at the hemlock trees.

RED SQUIRREL

The red squirrel is undoubtedly the most visible inhabitant of the coastal forest. You are likely to catch sight of one whisking along the spruce branches above your picnic table. You will hear this creature scolding you for some imagined transgression, because the red squirrel is a forest busybody. The red squirrel is not large—only eleven to thirteen inches long to the tip of its bottlebrush tail. The belly is white and the back and tail brown to rust. A white ring around each eye enhances an already bright countenance.

True to their reputation, red squirrels spend the summer months putting food by, collecting spruce cones and piling them in heaps for winter use. They make their nests in the trunks of trees and sometimes in dense foliage, but once the young are raised the squirrels live a solitary existence, each within a prescribed territory.

The red squirrel is Alaska's most common squirrel. The only other species in the state are the Arctic ground squirrel that inhabits the tundra and the northern flying squirrel. The latter is a resident of the spruce/hemlock forests throughout Alaska. It is nocturnal, however, and you are unlikely to see one.

GRAY WOLF

The wolf has gained a romantic image in Alaska in the past several years and the population is thriving. The most dense accumulations occur in Southeast where in some places there is one wolf per twenty-five square miles. Traditionally, the wolf has been hunted in Alaska for several different reasons. The thick fur is in great demand for parka ruffs (the part that surrounds the face when the hood is pulled over the head). A good quality wolf pelt is worth up to two hundred dollars to the hunter. Until the early 1970s, the wolf earned a fifty dollar bounty from the state of Alaska as well. The wolf also has been considered a threat to game animals such as moose, deer, and caribou that Alaskans use for food; indeed, the wolf-versus-moose controversy continues to rage in some parts of the state. Since statehood, the wolf has been accorded big game status, which means that, like other game animals, it can be hunted only under prescribed conditions.

The gray wolf occurs throughout mainland Alaska and on major islands in Southeast except for Admiralty, Baranof, and Chichagof. The color range extends from black to near white, with those in Southeast usually somewhat darker than those in the north. The wolf is a good deal larger than the average dog or coyote, the adult male weighing 85 to 118 pounds (the coyote weighs 25 to 40 pounds). In the north, wolves feed off moose and caribou, which has given them their bad reputation. In Southeast Alaska, their diet consists of deer and goats as well as small animals such as squirrels and the occasional bird or fish.

Unless you reach the remote areas of Southeast you are not likely to see a wolf, but it is not uncommon for independent boaters to spot the occasional animal prowling the shoreline in search of a meal, or to hear its captivating howl in the night.

Coyote

The coyote is a relative newcomer to Alaska, having migrated out of Canada's Interior. First noted shortly after the turn of the twentieth century, their numbers now range as far north as the Brooks Range. In Southeast Alaska they seem to exist on the mainland only and are not especially common. The coyote is about one-third the size of a wolf, averaging thirty pounds, with a coat varying from tan to gray.

The coyote's appetite for sheep and chickens has made the animal fair game in the Lower 48. In Alaska, where there are few sheep or chickens to prey upon, the coyote is forced to eat rabbits, birds, squirrels, and the like. There was a twenty-five dollar bounty in the state until 1969 that resulted in some hunting. Today coyotes are only occasionally trapped for their pelts and otherwise not much bothered. They are seldom visible. We once saw one in Gustavus, walking forlornly along in the snow and looking as if it would gladly chuck it all for a dog's life in front of the drawing room fire.

Other Animals

A raft of other animals inhabit the coastal forests. The porcupine is much in evidence in Southeast, as owners of dogs will testify. (I have ended more than one walk in the woods by pulling "porky" quills from the dog's nose and mouth.) The porky is nocturnal, but can sometimes be glimpsed plodding about the forest or along the road. The forest provides both shelter and sustenance, spruce bark (the inner layer) being a principal food. The porcupine's passage through the woods is highly visible: look for vertical bare patches on the tree trunks where a porky has dined off the bark. (There are some excellent examples along the Nature Trail at the Eaglecrest Ski Area in Juneau.) In summer, the porcupines switch from bark to a diet of leaves, tender branches, and buds.

Another Southeast resident is the beaver. Beaver pelts have been prized since the days of the Russian occupation and were used as a trade medium for many years. So many beaver were taken after the U.S. purchase of Alaska that they were protected in 1910. Beaver are still trapped, but under state regulation. In Southeast, beaver are most abundant near Yakutat and Juneau, but they live on other river drainages on the mainland, too, where they spend their time damming streams to satisfy their requirements for two to three feet of water year-round.

River otter

Of the other fur-bearing animals, the versatile land or river otter is at home on land as well as in both salt and freshwater. You can distinguish the river otter from the rare sea otter by the muscular tail, which makes up one-third of the animal's total body length of forty to sixty inches. The fur is dark brown, with some gray on the chin and throat. River otters are wonderful swimmers and can dive to at least sixty feet. In winter, they seem equally suited for snow and ice, where they run and slide and slip and tunnel just like children. They eat fish, supplementing their diet with shellfish and occasional birds. They might show up anywhere. In Wrangell, I once watched a pair from my hotel window. They were frolicking among the boats in the harbor as if they had nothing better to do in the world.

Other fur-bearing animals include the wolverine, much desired for its durable glossy brown fur used for parka trim; the marten or "American sable," Alaska's most widely trapped animal with one of the most beautiful of all furs; the pricey chocolate brown mink; and the classy ermine, which dresses in brown for summer but switches to white in winter. The charming sea otter, whose luxurious fur brought Russian traders to Alaska in the first place, is just now reappearing in Alaska waters after years of protection. These creatures once occupied the entire Pacific Coast from northern Japan through the Aleutian Islands and along North America to Baja California. At present they exist in good numbers in only a few locations, but they have been reintroduced in Southeast Alaska. With luck, perhaps the sea otter will be a familiar sight again one day. Your best chance of seeing them is probably around the northwest Chichagof and Yakobi islands area, near Elfin Cove.

Mammals not found in Southeast Alaska include the caribou and the Arctic fox, which frequent the Arctic tundra in the northern part of the state; the polar bear, which lives near the edge of the Arctic ice; and the big-horned Dall sheep, whose territory is the high mountains of Alaska's Interior and northern British Columbia. These animals will have to wait until your next trip to Alaska.

MARINE MAMMALS

Many species of whale inhabit the waters off the Alaska coast. Some are year-round residents, while others arrive for the summer months, preferring to winter in the more temperate waters off Hawaii or Baja California. Some whales are toothed, meaning they have large teeth that they use to catch—but not to chew—sizable prey that they then swallow whole. The others are baleen whales, which feed primarily on tiny shrimp-like organisms called krill. The krill is strained from the water by strips of bonelike material hanging from the whale's upper jaw. It was this baleen, or whalebone, that was so essential for ladies' undergarments and, along with whale oil, caused the creatures to be pursued by whalers in the nineteenth century. Oddly enough, the baleen whales, feeding on krill and microorganisms, are the giants of the deep; while the smaller whales, porpoises, and dolphins feed on meaty sea mammals and fish.

Since they are mammals, all whales must surface frequently to breathe air, which is when you have the opportunity to see them. They exhale through blowholes on their backs. Accompanied by a great deal of water vapor, the exhalations look like small geysers and are commonly known as spouting or blowing, hence the old lookout's cry, "Thar she blows." Often you will see the spout first which will be your clue to look for the whale. The usual sequence is spouting, then surfacing, then diving back to the deep. Sometimes the whale, especially the more acrobatic humpback, will leap clear out of the water on the dive. This is called breaching.

HUMPBACK WHALE

The humpback is a baleen whale and probably the most intensely watched whale in Southeast. This large whale, easily reaching forty-five to fifty feet, is active, frequently breaching and splashing about to the delight (and sometimes consternation) of nearby boaters. Some scientists think breaching may be warning behavior, or a territorial display, but its significance is not yet fully understood.

Humpback whale

Like many other species, humpbacks are migrating whales. They spend the winter in southern waters off Mexico or Hawaii where they breed and bear their young, but cruise as far north as the Bering Sea spring through fall. Unlike most other whales, humpbacks prefer to come in close to shore, feeding in the bays and fjords that outline the coast. Hence they are a familiar sight in many Southeast communities. You are virtually certain to see some of these elegant creatures on your summer cruise up the Inside Passage, if not up close then at least spouting in the distance. One group of about forty whales is known to feed around Frederick Sound, which is the large east-west channel at the south end of Admiralty Island and north of Petersburg. Look for them around the Five Fingers lighthouse. This area is rich is krill from late July through early August. A second area of concentration is Glacier Bay, where twenty or so whales habitually congregate. Large numbers of humpbacks also follow the herring runs in Auke Bay and Lynn Canal to the north of Juneau, and in Seymour Canal on the east side of Admiralty Island.

The humpback is dark in color except for the grooved belly. Three characteristics distinguish this whale: long pectoral fins, or flippers, which can measure up to fourteen feet; the huge tail that comes completely out of the water on the dive; and the distinctive hump that lies just in front of the small dorsal fin. The hump shows up in profile when the whales arch their backs to dive and gives the "humpies" their common name.

The humpbacks are the focus of considerable attention and study. They demonstrate a sophisticated feeding technique known as bubblenet feeding, which is used when the prey requires some herding. The whale, or sometimes a pair of whales, dives beneath the targeted food, such as a school of herring, and swims around the prey in an upward spiral, simultaneously exhaling through its blowhole. This creates a net of bubbles in the water that contains the confused fish. The whale then surfaces through the center of the bubble ring, jaws at the ready, and harvests the meal.

GRAY WHALE

Whale-watchers associate the gray whale, a baleen, with the California coast. Great numbers of gray whales are observed every winter as they migrate southward along the coast to their winter breeding grounds in the lagoons of Baja California. In spring they reverse the journey and spend June through October off northern Alaska where they feed on small shrimplike crustaceans that live near the ocean floor. That makes a round-trip journey of twelve thousand miles. Gray whales do not stay around Southeast Alaska like the humpbacks do, but they are frequently spotted as they pass through inside waters in early summer and late fall.

The most distinguishing feature of the gray whale is the pointed head that is usually covered with barnacles. There is no dorsal fin, and the flippers are much smaller than the humpback's. In color, this whale is mottled gray rather than black. In size, the gray is equal to the humpback, reaching a maximum length of fifty feet.

MINKE WHALE

The only other baleen whale common to Southeast is the minke or piked whale. The minke is the smallest baleen whale in the Northern Hemisphere, occasionally reaching thirty-three feet in length. These whales are grayish black on the top side, with a white stomach. Their most distinctive feature is a large sickle-shaped dorsal fin placed far back on the body.

Minkes are migrating whales and are found in many oceans from southern California to the Bering and Chukchi seas, where they spend their summers. When they are in southern waters they feed on krill, but their northern diet shifts to mackerel, cod, and herring. Look for them in Frederick Sound.

KILLER WHALE

The killer whale, also called orca from the Latin notation, is unmistakable in Southeast waters. In the first place, this whale has fantastic black and white markings, including a sparkling white chin, white flanks, and a white patch on either side of the head. Then, the male has an enormous triangular-shaped dorsal fin that stands out of the water like a shark's. In the adult male, the dorsal measures up to six feet. Whereas other whales may be traveling solo, killer whales are almost always seen in groups, or pods. The pods commonly contain as many as 25 or 30 whales, and herds of 150 have been spotted.

Killer whale

The killer whale is a toothed species, feeding on almost anything that moves in the ocean. Little is safe from this swiftest of whales that can swim at twenty-five knots and more. These "wolves of the sea" habitually go after seals, porpoises, squid, and many varieties of fish. Like land-based wolves, they are also capable of organizing their numbers to hunt down whales larger than themselves. The orcas themselves have no natural predators.

Killer whales average twenty-three feet in length and weigh eight to nine tons. They range all over the world and are frequently seen in the inside waters of Southeast Alaska. Chatham Strait and Stephens Passage are likely places to spot them. They have been known to attack boats, but whether or not their "killing" instincts extend to man is an unanswered question. This whale is an intelligent creature, a quick learner, and is often used in aquatic shows.

DALL PORPOISE

Another black and white sea creature commonly seen in Southeast is the Dall porpoise, which seems to delight in cavorting in the bow waves of fishing boats and pleasure craft. This porpoise ranges throughout the North Pacific from Baja California to the Bering Sea and feeds on squid and various small fish.

The Dall porpoise has a black body with white underside markings that extend halfway up the sides and sometimes tip the end of the tail and dorsal fin. There are many similarities between the Dall porpoise and the killer whale. Besides the obvious likeness in markings, both are extremely swift swimmers and fond of group travel. How can you tell them apart? First, the killer whale at twenty-plus feet is three times as large as the Dall porpoise, which reaches a maximum length of seven feet. And, the porpoise's dorsal fin is insignificant compared to the large upright triangle of the killer whale's. Finally, the porpoise delights in swimming close to the bow of your boat, but you are more apt to spot the killer whale off in the distance, chasing after something to eat.

HARBOR PORPOISE

The harbor porpoise frequents coastal bays and river mouths from the Arctic coast of Alaska to southern California. It is the smallest of the whale, dolphin, and porpoise family, reaching no more than five or six feet in length. In color the harbor porpoise is dark brown to gray, with a triangular dorsal fin toward the center of the back.

The harbor porpoise feeds on small fish and squid. This porpoise is most often seen alone, in pairs, or in small groups, but sometimes travels in larger company. You may see them swimming near the surface of the water, but not near your ship. The harbor porpoise is a reserved creature and does not go in for joyriding on the bow wave like the larger Dall porpoise.

My husband and I recently saw a pair of harbor porpoises as we were walking along the shore of Kootznahoo Inlet near Angoon on Admiralty Island. When we first spotted them, the tiny porpoises were slowly swimming and diving in the clear, shallow water just below the road. As we looked down upon their gray-black shapes with prominent dorsal fins, we decided we were watching a couple of large king salmon. When we got a look at their tails, which were whalelike and horizontal instead of salmon-like and vertical, we realized our mistake.

HARBOR SEAL

The resident species of seal in Southeast is the harbor or spotted seal, which is at home in both the North Atlantic and Pacific oceans. The harbor is a hair seal, as opposed to either a fur seal or sea lion, and is the only such seal in Southeast. Like all hair seals, the harbor seals are true seals: they have no ears and cannot rotate their hind flippers forward, making them clumsy on land. They are thus primarily water creatures, touching down on land to rest and bear their young. The harbor seal averages five to six feet in length, and varies in color from yellowish gray to blue gray with dark spots. The coat of stiff hair is used for parkas, moccasins, purses, and the like, which are available in the curio shops of every town.

Harbor seals are fish and shellfish eaters, consuming everything from herring to crab. They anger commercial fishermen because they are clever about stealing salmon from nets or off the trolling gear. A two-dollar bounty was in effect from 1927 and raised to three dollars in 1939, but was removed south of Bristol Bay in 1967. The Federal Marine Mammal Protection Act of 1972 limited seal hunting (and that of all marine mammals) to Alaskan Indians and Eskimos.

Harbor seals are the most common of all marine mammals in Southeast. You might spot them anywhere—in the open water, in a protected harbor, on rocky offshore outcrops, or on sandy beaches.

STELLER'S SEA LION

Last on the list of the common sea mammals to inhabit the Inside Passage waters is the Steller's sea lion. The brownish black sea lion is the largest of the eared seals, bulls reaching thirteen feet in length and weighing up to twenty-four hundred pounds. They have tiny, visible ears and, unlike the true seals, they are able to rotate their back flippers forward, making them more mobile on land.

The sea lion's province is the coastal waters from the southern end of the Panhandle to the Bering Sea. They favor remote areas with shallow, rocky bottoms where they can find the herring, rockfish, octopus, and shellfish that make up their diet. Like the smaller harbor seals, Steller's sea lions are fond of salmon and are a nuisance to the commercial fishing industry. They steal from gill nets and, even more irritating to fishermen, take large bites out of salmon that are trailing on the troll lines. Like seals, sea lions have been protected from indiscriminate hunting since 1972 and can be harvested only by Indians and Eskimos.

In winter, colonies of sea lions frequently gambol about the Juneau harbor in front of Merchants' Wharf. There is a sea lion rookery on Benjamin Island, at the entrance to Lynn Canal north of Juneau, that is especially busy in late May when the breeding season begins. The Alaska state ferries pass right by on the way to Haines and Skagway.

FISH AND SHELLFISH

SALMON

The best known fish in Alaska is surely the salmon. All five species of salmon exist in Southeast waters: the king salmon, known also as the Chinook (called spring salmon in British Columbia); the coho, or silver; the sockeye, or red; the chum, or dog; and the pink, humpback, or "humpie." The species differ from one another in several respects, including size, color, shape, anatomical details, spawning season, and life cycle. As far as the lay person is concerned, however, a salmon is a salmon on the plate: pink-fleshed (except in the case of white kings) and full of flavor.

The life cycle of the salmon is one of the most dramatic in nature. All species of salmon are anadromous, meaning that they spend part of their lives in freshwater and part in the sea. After hatching in the gravel stream beds, the salmon pass the next segment of their lives feeding and growing in the freshwater stream. The amount of time varies according to the species, from almost none in the case of pink and chum salmon to up to three years in the case of cohos. They then migrate downstream to salt water where they spend, again according to the species, from two to three years or more roaming the North Pacific. When they reach maturity, they migrate back to the stream in which they were hatched to spawn. Before reaching freshwater they eat voraciously because they will eat little once they start their upstream dash. It is at this point, while they are moving toward the stream mouth, that they become the targets of commercial and sport fishermen. The fisherman quickly learns this about salmon: when they are running you cannot keep them from biting, but when they're not there, they're not there.

The salmon spend as much as a few weeks at the entrance to the stream while their bodies readjust to freshwater. Then they begin the exhausting uphill battle to the spawning grounds. When their infallible instincts tell them that they have reached the place, the once beautiful salmon—now battered, torn, mortally weary and metamorphosed beyond recognition—carry out the spawning ritual. The females scrape a series of shallow nests, called redds, in the gravel with their broad tails and deposit several thousand eggs. The males spill their milt over the eggs, and the females brush gravel over the top. That is the end. Both males and females will die, usually within two weeks.

The fertilized eggs remain in their gravel incubators developing into embryo called alevins and then baby salmon called fry. When the fry are mature enough to swim downstream they are known as smolt. The smolt head out for the few good years in the great Pacific; then the cycle begins again.

The king salmon, Alaska's official state fish, is considerably larger than the other four species, commonly exceeding 30 pounds and frequently exceeding 50 pounds. The world-record king salmon taken in a fish trap off Prince of Wales Island in 1939, weighed approximately 126.5 pounds. (The salmon was not weighed until after it had been cleaned, so the weight is only an estimate.) This giant salmon—not very long, but chunky—is on display at the Clausen Museum in Petersburg. A record sport-caught king (93 pounds) was caught at Kelp Bay on the northeast coast of Baranof Island in 1977.

In Southeast, the king salmon runs extend from May through July. The major spawning runs are up the Stikine River near Wrangell, the Taku south of Juneau, and the Alsek south of Yakutat. Kings are capable of extremely long freshwater migrations. The northern kings that spawn in the headwaters of the Yukon River travel more than two thousand miles to reach their spawning grounds.

King salmon are commercial favorites because of their large size and good flavor, and they fetch up to eight dollars per pound at the retail market. Their flesh may be either red or white—why, no one knows. Although there is little difference in flavor, the white kings have always been undervalued because the flesh is not "salmonlike" in appearance. Local residents fish for kings year-round. A winter-caught king is considered a prime delicacy because of the flavorful fat that builds up over the winter months.

Next in size to the king is the coho, which reaches thirty-five pounds. Much loved by sport fishermen for its aggressive response to the hook, the coho is also valuable on the commercial market. The cohos enter the spawning systems from August through November, and sport fishing is good from July through September.

Sockeye salmon are the "money fish" of the Bristol Bay fisheries, where enormous quantities are netted and canned. The nickname "red salmon" comes from the spectacular coloration that the sockeye acquires while spawning: a brilliant red body and an olive green head. The sockeye is small compared with the king or coho, weighing only four to eight pounds in maturity. The fish also differs in eating habits, preferring a diet of marine plankton, chiefly small crustaceans. This makes the sockeye an elusive target for sport fishermen, who rarely hook the fish in salt water and never on bait. The fly fisherman sometimes succeeds and comes away with a good prize because the sockeye is desirable for eating fresh, for home canning, and especially for smoking.

The chum or dog salmon is the widest-ranging of any Pacific salmon. This species is found from the Sacramento River in California to the Mackenzie River in Canada, in the USSR, and in Japan. The fish takes its other name from the large doglike teeth that develop during the spawning season. Chums weigh up to eighteen pounds in maturity (some grow to thirty pounds), but are not sport-fishing favorites because they seldom strike a lure. Most commercially caught chum are netted. Unlike kings, cohos, or sockeyes, the young chum salmon do not spend a long time in freshwater, but feed in the estuary for a few months and then go out to sea.

Pink salmon are the smallest of the Pacific salmon, averaging only three and one-half to four pounds. They are also the shortest-lived, maturing at two years and setting off for the spawning grounds from late June to mid-October. Most pinks spawn within a few miles of the coast; some even spawn within the intertidal zone of the stream mouth. Like chums, the pinks spend no time in freshwater after they emerge from their gravel incubators. The fry swim up out of the gravel and head immediately downstream to salt water.

Despite such spunk, the pinks were not well regarded by either sport or commercial fisheries until recently, when the generally poor fishing tempted some fishermen to concentrate on the relatively plentiful pinks. They are netted, for the most part, and thus canned, and their flesh has a tendency toward mushiness. The nickname "humpy" comes from the spawning males which develop a pronounced hump on their backs after they enter freshwater.

PACIFIC HALIBUT

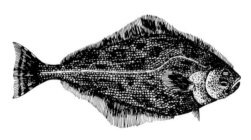

Halibut

Like the salmon, the halibut has traditionally been an important fish in Southeast Alaska. The Tlingit and Haida Indians elevated halibut fishing into a fine art. Their beautiful, carved wooden halibut hooks were proportioned to catch only halibut of the desired size, and their fishing skills were the envy of the early European explorers. Like everything in Alaska, halibut come in exaggerated proportions. Halibut weighing more than 300 pounds are brought in by sport fishermen every year. The largest on record is a 495-pounder caught near Petersburg.

The halibut is a flounder, or bottomfish, which accounts for its flat and generally goofy appearance. The fish starts life looking perfectly normal, but after about six months the left eye migrates across to join the right, and the halibut spends the rest of its days with both eyes on one side of its head. Then the fish turns over so the two eyes are uppermost, and what seems to be the top (the dark side) is actually the right side . . . very fishy indeed.

Left to their own devices, halibut live a long time. One old lady specimen was estimated to be forty-two years old. The juvenile halibut drive commercial fishermen crazy by latching onto the bait so that all the gear has to be pulled in. These small halibut are commonly called "chicken halibut," but a more apt description, which I happened upon in *Pacific Troller*, a wonderful book about commercial fishing (Alaska Northwest Publishing Company), is "ping-pong paddles."

Halibut is a good eating fish. The flesh is firm, beautifully white, mild tasting, and—if you can threaten the cook with something to keep him from overcooking it—moist and delicious. If you are lucky enough to catch a halibut for your table, here are two typically Alaskan things to do with it. Get some Krusteaz buttermilk pancake mix and add enough beer to make a batter that will not slide off your chunks of halibut. Fry in hot oil and eat. Or, cut your fresh, filleted halibut into small serving pieces and cover with white wine for up to two hours. Drain and roll in dry bread crumbs (preferably from homemade bread). Place in one layer in a buttered baking dish. Mix together two parts sour cream to one part mayonnaise and one part finely chopped onion and spread over the top, reaching clear out to the edges. Sprinkle with paprika and bake at five hundred degrees for fifteen to twenty minutes or until light brown on top and bubbling. This dish, called "Halibut Caddy Ganty," is prepared in the unparalleled kitchen of the Gustavus Inn (near Glacier Bay). I pass it on with the kind permission of the chefs. (This recipe and others from the inn appear in a small cookbook entitled *A Collection of Recipes from Gustavus Inn*, available in local book shops.)

TROUT

There are two important kinds of trout in the Southeast region. The cutthroat, which takes its name from two red stripes below the mouth, is found from Southeast Alaska north to Prince William Sound in sizes up to seventeen pounds. In freshwater the trout, like others of the family, frequently follow the salmon runs and feed on the new eggs. The cutthroats also are found in salt water.

Rainbow trout live in the river drainages as well as in freshwater lakes where they have been introduced. Some rainbows are seagoing, in which case they are known as steelheads. There is no difference between the two except that one lives in salt water and the other in fresh. The rainbow or steelhead is closely related to the Atlantic salmon and weighs up to twenty pounds. The world-record steelhead, however, was caught near Ketchikan in 1970 and weighed forty-two pounds, two ounces.

DOLLY VARDEN

Dolly Varden are welcome additions to the larder in Southeast. Many are sea-run, and they seem, on the plate at least, like a perfect combination of a salmon and a trout. Dollies are actually members of the char family. Many fishermen contend that they are in fact Arctic char, but the scientific community says not: while they are closely related, they differ anatomically in certain respects. (The true Arctic char does not exist in Southeast. Its realm is to the north in the coastal regions of the Alaska Peninsula, Bering Strait, and the Arctic.)

The dolly is salmon-shaped and silvery green in color. When fresh out of the water, the fish has distinctive red spots on the sides, like a rash. The spots fade with time but help the layman distinguish a sea-run dolly from a small salmon.

Dollies have an unusual life cycle. Like salmon, they spawn in freshwater and migrate downstream to salt water in their third or fourth year. Once at sea, however, they return every winter to a freshwater lake. Those that were spawned in a lake system return there. Those that were not have to find themselves a suitable lake. When mature, at five to six years, all the dollies return to their original streams to spawn. Many survive the spawn, however—perhaps as many as 50 percent—and return to sea. The fishing community condemns the Dolly Varden for eating salmon eggs and harming the salmon runs. The dolly does eat salmon eggs, but so do all trout.

Fully grown Dolly Varden reach up to twenty-two inches and weigh three pounds. They are easy to catch and well worth taking home. Their flesh is a delicate pink in color, like salmon, but troutlike in texture; the flavor falls nicely in between.

ARCTIC GRAYLING

The fantastic-looking Arctic grayling is a true Alaskan, dependent upon clear, cold streams and lakes that exist only in the north. The greatest concentrations are found in rivers on the north side of the Brooks Range, which is to say in the Arctic. Other populations exist in the Cook Inlet region and parts of the Interior. In Southeast Alaska, the grayling has been introduced successfully in some lakes, among them Antler Lake in the Juneau area; Big Goat, Tyee, and Manzoni lakes in the Ketchikan vicinity; and several on Prince of Wales Island.

The grayling grows slowly, reaching only twelve inches in six or seven years. Fully mature grayling might reach twenty inches, and some larger ones have been reported. Their diet consists of insects and the like which makes them a fly-fisherman's delight. If all of these things did not make the grayling a special fish, appearance would. The troutlike body is colored dark purple on the back with silvery green sides. On top is an enormous fanlike dorsal fin with reddish purple spots on a green background.

PACIFIC HERRING

The herring has never attracted much attention from sport fishermen except as bait for salmon, but this productive little fish has been an important contributor to the Southeast economy. The original Indian inhabitats of Southeast harvested both herring and herring roe for food. Herring roe are sticky and the female herring deposits them—in May, usually—on grass, kelp, or other surfaces in the intertidal area. The Tlingit learned to place spruce boughs in the water at the spawning grounds, and the herring obligingly covered the branches with their sticky eggs. The laden boughs were then removed from the water and hung out to dry. Exactly the same process takes place currently in the Cook Inlet and the Prince William Sound areas in the spring. There the herring deposit their eggs on strands of kelp. Divers are sent down to cut the kelp, which is salted or frozen with roe still attached and shipped to Japanese specialty markets.

The commercial herring fishery was launched on a grand scale in 1882 when the first herring reduction plant was built at Killisnoo on Admiralty Island. The products were fish meal, which was used as a fertilizer and food additive for livestock, and oil, which was used as as an industrial lubricant and detergent. In 1937, the greatest year of the herring industry, seventeen plants processed more than 251 million pounds of herring in Alaska. Salted and pickled herring was also produced in Southeast, especially during World War I. Both industries gradually declined, the last reduction plant closing in 1966. Today herring are harvested for bait and frozen whole.

The Pacific herring are blue-green fish averaging nine to ten inches in length. They run in schools of up to a million fish, which are in turn pursued by schools of salmon and other predators. One stretch of coastline north of Juneau has been dubbed the "milk run" by local fishermen who drag the area for the salmon that habitually chase after the herring that habitually frequent that stretch of water in the spring of every year.

There are many other species of fish in the fresh- and saltwater systems of Southeast Alaska, from the tiny, oily eulachon of the smelt family that was an important source of oil for Southeast Natives, to rockfish, sculpin, cod, and other bottomfish. The U.S. Forest Service publishes a small pamphlet, *Common Fresh and Saltwater Fishes of Southeastern Alaska*, that is a handy reference guide to the many local species.

CRAB

Southeast Alaska is blessed with a richness of crab. If you have a boat and a crab pot, all that remains is to find just the right place to set it down. Toss in a few fish heads, set the pot on the way to your favorite fishing grounds, pick it up at the end of the day, and there you are. Dinner that night might include any of the three varieties of crab that inhabit the Southeast coast: king, Dungeness, and tanner.

The famous Alaska king crab is not a true crab at all. The difference is that the spiny, spiderlike legs are jointed to fold backward and behind the body instead of forward and in front, like the Dungeness. True crab or no, the king crab is a fine specimen. By far the largest of the crabs, kings can grow to twenty-four pounds, although seven or eight pounds is the average commercial size. At that, they measure three feet from leg tip to leg tip. The meat of the king crab is sweet and firm, similar to lobster meat. Besides having excellent flavor, king crab is easy to eat. There is no cracking, picking, and sucking involved. Just snip the shell open with a pair of kitchen shears and the meat slides out in one piece. The body of the king crab is small compared with the legs, and is usually ignored.

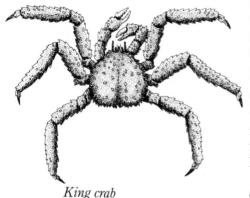

King crab

Dungeness crab is the familiar Cancer shape, a true crab, with eight forward-folding legs and two short claws. Compared with the king, the Dungeness has a large body, but full of good meat. Controversy continues over which of the crabs is better eating, and while I cannot settle the issue I can certainly put in my vote for the rich, succulent, gently flaking Dungeness.

The third candidate is the tanner crab, which usually is marketed under the name of snow crab. Also a true crab, the tanner looks something like a cross between the king and the Dungeness, with long, spindly legs. You frequently see the bulbous claws sold separately in the frozen food section of the supermarket. The leg meat is delicious but flakes into small bits as you remove it from the shell. Eating tanner crab is a somewhat wearing experience unless it is out of a can.

ABALONE

You rarely get the chance to taste Alaskan abalones because it takes a hardy diver to brave the frigid waters and bring them up. Abalones are abundant, though, the length of the Alexander Archipelago. Occasionally they can be plucked from the bottom at very low tides. The species of abalone that inhabits Southeast rarely grows larger than five and one-half inches. The meat is sweet and tender.

BIVALVES AND PARALYTIC SHELLFISH POISONING

In addition to crab and abalone, the Inside Passage yields several varieties of shrimp (including the tiny Petersburg species), cockles, scallops, octopus, sea cucumbers, sea urchins, mussels, and at least four varieties of clam. A word of warning here, however: *No bivalves (clams, mussels, cockles, scallops) in Southeast Alaska can be considered safe from the deadly paralytic shellfish poisoning, at any time of year.* This is a sad fact, but true. Paralytic shellfish poisoning (PSP) is caused by a toxin produced by a tiny organism known as a dinoflagellate (a similar dinoflagellate causes the sea condition known as the red tide). This organism is ingested by the shellfish, which absorb and store the PSP toxin in their bodies. The toxin is poisonous to humans, but does not harm the shellfish. Some shellfish retain the toxin longer than others; clams and mussels are the worst.

Symptoms of PSP show up only *after* the shellfish has entered the digestive tract, so do not try to "see if the clams are poisonous" by holding one to your mouth and waiting for your lip to go numb. Usually the symptoms occur within thirty minutes of eating the infected shellfish. They can include: a tingling or burning sensation on lips, gums, tongue, or face that gradually spreads to other parts of the body; dryness of mouth, nausea, vomiting; in later stages, shortness of breath, choking sensation, slurred speech, lack of coordination. If death occurs, which is seldom the case but does happen, the direct cause will be respiratory paralysis. There is *no antidote* to paralytic shellfish poisoning. If you experience any of the symptoms after eating shellfish, induce vomiting immediately and call a doctor.

Many residents of Southeast Alaska eat clams every year from beaches that they consider safe. I do not. I used to, occasionally, but I found that worrying about PSP took all the pleasure out of eating the clams anyway. Now I save clam and mussel-eating for places where I know they are safe, and, in Southeast Alaska, I console myself with crab, shrimp, halibut, trout, and five kinds of salmon.

BIRDS

Some 278 species of bird are found in Southeast Alaska. Many are year-round residents, while others stop off on their way to or from nesting grounds and winter homes that may be ten thousand miles apart. If you are interested in identifying some of the Southeast birds, Robert Armstrong's *Guide to the Birds of Alaska* (Alaska Northwest Publishing Company) is a useful source. The notes about each species are not as detailed as those of an Audubon guide, but the color photographs let you see what the birds look like up close. Another good reference guide is *Birds of Southeast Alaska, A Checklist*, a pamphlet prepared by the U.S. Forest Service in conjunction with the Alaska Department of Fish and Game and the Juneau Audubon Society. A complete list of birds commonly appearing in Southeast Alaska during at least two seasons of the year appears on pages 131–133. Here are some of the most noticeable birds that you may encounter during your trip through the Inside Passage.

BALD EAGLE

No matter how many times you hear about the bald eagle population in Southeast Alaska, you will not believe the number of eagles you will see until you actually get there and start counting. Bald eagles are everywhere: in the treetops, on the beach, soaring close over the water, wheeling high in the sky. Southeast Alaska has almost an embarrassment of eagles—some fifteen thousand by official guess.

The bald eagle was selected as the national emblem by Congress in 1782. Adult males and females look identical, with pure white head and tail, yellow hooked beak, deep brown body, and a wingspan of up to eight feet. The young birds are a mottled brown and white with a dark beak to match. They look rather like the golden eagle but the latter is rare in Southeast and you should not have a problem confusing the two. Bald eagles acquire their adult plumage in their third or fourth year.

There is no other bird that you could mistake for the adult bald eagle. You will soon learn to pick out their white heads glistening in the tops of the spruce and hemlock trees that line the shore of the Inside Passage. The narrow passageway from Sergius Narrows through Neva Strait on the approach to Sitka is one of the best places to view eagles. The U.S. Forest Service interpreters on board the Alaska ferries are apt to initiate an eagle count to see how many eagles can be spotted along this thirty-mile stretch. The highest number to date is ninety-four.

You will probably see eagles launch themselves into the sky and glide above the surface of the water, using their keen eyes to spot an easy meal. Bald eagles feed on herring, smelt, and spawned-out salmon, and turn to birds and small mammals when they cannot find fish. Basically, they are scavengers, and as such are commonly seen feeding at garbage dumps.

One of their favorite meals is spawned-out salmon that clog the upper reaches of many Southeast rivers, among them the Chilkat River, near Haines. Natural warm springs keep this river flowing long into the winter when other waters are frozen. The eagles—some thirty-five hundred of them—congregate in the tall cottonwoods along the Chilkat River flats below the village of Klukwan to gorge on the dead and dying salmon from October through January. This incredible sight is the largest gathering of bald eagles anywhere in the world. The best viewing is from mile 18 to mile 22 on the Haines Highway (west out of Haines toward the Alaska Highway). The state of Alaska has recently established the forty-nine-thousand-acre Chilkat Bald Eagle Preserve to protect this gathering of eagles and their habitat. Other concentrations of eagles occur along the shoreline of Admiralty Island, where there is an average of two nests per mile around the 678-mile shore, and on the Stikine River, especially in the spring.

Bald eagles build their nests in the tops of large, old, spruce or hemlock trees that grow close to salt water or mainland rivers. Eagle nesting trees average three and one-half feet in diameter and four hundred years in age. The nests are constructed of branches, small sticks, and moss. Since the birds add to the nests every year rather than build anew, the structures have been known to reach eight feet in diameter and seven feet deep. Do not miss the superb "eagle tree" on the ground floor of the Alaska State Museum in Juneau. This exhibit includes a bald eagle nest, eagle eggs, and mounted specimens of juvenile and adult birds.

Eagles are protected by law in Alaska as elsewhere. In places where logging threatens to interfere with their nesting habitat, the U.S. Forest Service and U.S. Fish and Wildlife Service have identified known nesting trees so that logging crews can give them a wide berth. Of course, eagles have not always been treated so well in Alaska. The territorial legislature placed a fifty-cent bounty (later raised to two dollars) on the big birds in 1917 because they were considered a threat to spawning salmon and to the young foxes that were being raised on fox farms. The bounty was lifted in 1953, but not before an estimated 128,000 birds had been killed.

The cry of the bald eagle is the only incongruous thing about this bird. From its size and stature you would expect a mighty scream, but the eagle communicates in a series of dainty cheeps that build to a high-pitched *kleek-keek-eek-eek-eek-eek*.

COMMON RAVEN

The second important bird in the Southeast aviary is the raven. The ink black raven has been winging through the dripping spruce forests for as long as human memory can recall. The ancestors of today's Tlingit and Haida Indians gave the bird a central role in their ancient mythology and legends and celebrated its character in songs, dances, and artistic designs.

Until you see one up close, you might confuse the raven with the Northwestern crow, which also lives in Southeast year-round. Both are black all over. The raven, though, is surprisingly large, measuring more than two feet in length, against the crow's seventeen inches. The raven also has a much larger bill than the crow's and a pronounced brow. And the raven produces a unique sound: a throaty, melodious *klok* or *kla-wock* that is entirely different from the raucous *caw-caw* of the crow.

STELLER'S JAY

The Steller's jay is one of the handsomest birds of the coastal forest. Upright and bold, with an electric blue and black plaid coat and a black head crest, this jay is immediately recognizable. A year-round resident in Southeast, the jay, like the red squirrel, is a notorious busybody. I have

Steller's jay

often watched two or three Steller's jays taunting a bald eagle. While the eagle rests stoically on a spruce limb, the jays flap about from branch to branch, chattering imperiously. Eventually the eagle gives up in disgust and flies away. For all of their bickering and bullying, the jays are some of the most entertaining figures in the forest and great favorites of mine.

The Steller's jay takes its name from the Bering expedition of 1741. When Vitus Bering set out to explore the uncharted sea to the east of Russia, he took with him the naturalist Georg Wilhelm Steller. With the ship anchored off of Kayak Island near Yakutat in order to replenish the water supply, Steller went ashore to collect specimens of plants and birds not found in Asia or Europe. Among his finds was a brilliant blue, high-crested jay that he recognized as native to North America. The Steller's jay was proof that Bering had found a land that was separate from Russia.

BLUE GROUSE

Another year-round resident of the forest is the blue grouse, sometimes called the spruce hen. The bird is in fact chicken-shaped with a brown-to-gray and white speckled body, a black tail with a band of pale gray at the top, and the feathered legs common to the grouse and ptarmigan family. These game birds live in mature forest stands and among the dwarf trees that dot the muskeg in the alpine areas. The females build their nests on the ground and it is not unusual to come upon a hen with her batch of chicks as you are walking through the woods or grassy openings in early summer. In winter, the grouse are up in the trees. During the mating season, the woods echo with the muffled *huh-huh-huh* of the courtship call. The peculiar sound is produced by air sacs on each side of the male's neck and is responsible for the grouse's nickname, "the hooter."

Of the four species of grouse found in Alaska, the blue grouse is the most common in Southeast (others include the spruce grouse and ruffed grouse). It is the largest of the grouse and a popular game bird, with the males often reaching three and one-half pounds.

ROCK PTARMIGAN

Ptarmigan are closely related to grouse and similar in appearance, but they are smaller (two-thirds to one and one-half pounds) and have feathered feet—a great bonus in this climate. Of the three species of ptarmigan in Alaska, only the rock ptarmigan lives in Southeast. (The willow ptarmigan, which is the state bird, inhabits most of the rest of the state.) In summer, the ptarmigan is a mottled brown with white wings, but winter brings out an all white coat except for a bit of black on the tail and (in the male) a band of black through the eye. Ptarmigan are nomadic in winter, wandering from slope to slope in search of a meal of birch buds or willow.

CANADA GOOSE

The Vancouver Canada goose is the largest of the several subspecies that frequent Alaska, weighing as much as sixteen pounds in the fall. Many are year-round residents of the Southeast tide-flats. One of the largest congregations frequents the tidelands around Juneau where they can be viewed from the Egan Expressway. The Canada goose is

Canada goose

unmistakable: a large bird with brownish gray back and wings, a long, black neck and a black head with white cheeks. When they are feeding on the grasslands they look oddly like miniature dinosaurs with their long necks curved down to the ground.

Canada geese mate for life. The Vancouver variety nests in shore grass, under conifers, or in muskegs. They are rare among geese in that they actually have been known to land in trees.

DUCK

Several varieties of duck brave the Southeast winters. Among the year-round residents are the ubiquitous mallard, the fancy-dress harlequin, the common merganser and red-breasted merganser, and two species of scoter. The white-winged scoter and surf scoter are perhaps the most familiar ducks in Southeast. They raft upon the salt water in large groups. The expression "ducks in a line" is very appropriate to scoters. You often see them diving down beneath the surface to look for fish and popping back up again, one by one.

RUFOUS HUMMINGBIRD

Among the first birds to arrive in spring, sometimes before the snow is even gone, are the rufous hummingbirds. The male is a cheery sight in the drab dog days of winter's end with his orange coat and irridescent red throat. The female is more green in color and lacks the brilliant red throat. They haunt Southeast gardens, impatiently awaiting the bright blossoms of spring. The hummingbird, fewer than three and one-half inches long, flies a good many miles to summer in Alaska. In late fall the rufous heads south again to spend a warm winter in Mexico.

PESTS

Unfortunately, the winged creatures of Southeast Alaska are not limited to the bird family. Most of the stories you have heard about insects in Alaska are not true—at least about Southeast Alaska. The swarms of gigantic mosquitoes that hang from your eyelids are creatures of the northern tundra with its inviting pools of freestanding water. Southeastern insects are more apt to be too small to swat.

Usually there is enough breeze to keep insects at bay. If the air is still and the bugs are pesty, your best bet is to roll down your sleeves, button your collar, put on a hat, smear yourself with whatever brand of repellant is popular this year, and try to relax. Nothing seems to draw biting or stinging insects more quickly than an overheated, sweaty, enraged human being.

Basically, the pests fall into three categories. Mosquitoes really are not that troublesome in Southeast Alaska. Those that are around seem to be slow-moving and somewhat dim. In your hotel room at night, for instance, they are easy to hunt down and kill. Campers get the worst of them and a mosquito flap on your tent is certainly in order. White-sox are vicious, tiny, black, biting flies that swarm about your body and try to crawl under your clothes. Failing that they are happy to bite *through* your clothes. White-sox (the name comes from their silvery white legs) are capable of a nasty bite; on some people, the raised red spots can itch for days. You do not necessarily feel the bite at the time though. The bite you *do* feel at the time—a prolonged prick—comes from the no-see-um. Your skin swells up immediately and the itch comes and goes for days. These gnatlike insects like the damp—a nice sweaty forehead, for example. If they are nearby, they will light on any exposed piece of skin—ears are an especially favorite meal. No-see-ums seem tuned to your state of mind. If you can stay calm and go about your business, they likely will not be a bother; but start getting anxious about them, perspiring and breathing heavily, and they will fulfill your worst fantasies.

Scientists now think that some of these biting beasts may be attracted to the carbon dioxide that humans expel. Hold your breath!

COMMON BIRDS OF SOUTHEAST ALASKA
(PRESENT DURING AT LEAST TWO SEASONS)

Common loon, *Gavia immer**
Arctic loon, *Gavia arctica*
Red-throated loon, *Gavia stellata*
Red-necked grebe, *Podiceps grisegena*
Horned grebe, *Podiceps auritus*
Black-footed albatross, *Diomedea nigripes*†
Sooty shearwater, *Puffinus griseus*†
Fork-tailed storm-petrel, *Oceanodroma furcata*†
Leach's storm-petrel, *Oceanodroma leucorhoa*†
Pelagic cormorant, *Phalacrocorax pelagicus*
Great blue heron, *Ardea herodias*
Whistling swan, *Olor columbianus*
Canada goose, Vancouver, *Branta canadensis fulva**
White-fronted goose, *Anser albifrons*
Snow goose, *Chen caerulescens caerulescens*
Mallard, *Anas platyrhynchos**
Pintail, *Anas acuta*
American green-winged teal, *Anas crecca carolinensis*
American widgeon, *Anas americana*
Greater scaup, *Aythya marila*
Lesser scaup, *Aythya affinis*
Common goldeneye, *Bucephala clangula*
Barrow's goldeneye, *Bucephala islandica*
Bufflehead, *Bucephala albeola*
Oldsquaw, *Clangula hyemalis*
Harlequin duck, *Histrionicus histrionicus**
Common eider, *Somateria mollissima*
White-winged scoter, *Melanitta fusca deglandi**
Surf scoter, *Melanitta perspicillata**
Black scoter, *Melanitta nigra*
Common merganser, *Mergus merganser**
Red-breasted merganser, *Mergus serrator**
Sharp-shinned hawk, *Accipiter striatus*
Bald eagle, *Haliaeetus leucocephalus**
Marsh hawk, *Circus cyaneus*
American kestrel, *Falco sparverius*
Blue grouse, *Dendragapus obscurus**
Rock ptarmigan, *Lagopus mutus**
Sandhill crane, *Grus canadensis*
Black oystercatcher, *Haematopus bachmani*

Semipalmated plover, *Charadrius semipalmatus*
Black-bellied plover, *Pluvialis squatarola*
Greater yellowlegs, *Tringa melanoleuca*
Lesser yellowlegs, *Tringa flavipes*
Spotted sandpiper, *Actitis macularia*
Black turnstone, *Arenaria melanocephala*
Northern phalarope, *Phalaropus lobatus*
Common snipe, *Capella gallinago*
Short-billed dowitcher, *Limnodromus griseus*
Western sandpiper, *Calidris mauri*
Least sandpiper, *Calidris minutilla*
Pectoral sandpiper, *Calidris melanotos*
Rock sandpiper, *Calidris ptilocnemis*
Dunlin, *Calidris alpina*
Glaucous-winged gull, *Larus glaucescens* *
Herring gull, *Larus argentatus* *
Thayer's gull, *Larus thayeri*
Mew gull, *Larus canus* *
Bonaparte's gull, *Larus philadelphia*
Arctic tern, *Sterna paradisaea*
Common murre, *Uria aalge* *
Pigeon guillemot, *Cepphus columba* *
Marbled murrelet, *Brachyramphus marmoratus* *
Rock dove, *Columba livia* *
Great horned owl, *Bubo virginianus* *
Short-eared owl, *Asio flammeus*
Rufous hummingbird, *Selasphorus rufus*
Belted kingfisher, *Megaceryle alcyon* *
Western flycatcher, *Empidonax difficilis*
Violet-green swallow, *Tachycineta thalassina*
Tree swallow, *Iridoprocne bicolor*
Barn swallow, *Hirundo rustica*
Steller's jay, *Cyanocitta stelleri* *
Black-billed magpie, *Pica pica*
Common raven, *Corvus corax* *
Northwestern crow, *Corvus caurinus* *
Chestnut-backed chickadee, *Parus rufescens* *
Brown creeper, *Certhia familiaris* *
Dipper, *Cinclus mexicanus* *
Winter wren, *Troglodytes troglodytes* *
American robin, *Turdus migratorius*
Varied thrush, *Ixoreus naevius*
Hermit thrush, *Catharus guttatus*
Swainson's thrush, *Catharus ustulatus*

Golden-crowned kinglet, *Regulus satrapa*
Ruby-crowned kinglet, *Regulus calendula*
Water pipit, *Anthus spinoletta*
Bohemian waxwing, *Bombycilla garrulus*
Starling, *Sturnus vulgaris* *
Orange-crowned warbler, *Vermivora celata*
Yellow warbler, *Dendroica petechia*
Yellow-rumped warbler, *Dendroica coronata*
Wilson's warbler, *Wilsonia pusilla*
Pine grosbeak, *Pinicola enucleator*
Common redpoll, *Carduelis flammea*
Pine siskin, *Carduelis pinus* *
Red crossbill, *Loxia curvirostra* *
White-winged crossbill, *Loxia leucoptera* *
Savannah sparrow, *Passerculus sandwichensis*
Dark-eyed junco, *Junco hyemalis* *
Tree sparrow, *Spizella arborea*
Golden-crowned sparrow, *Zonotrichia atricapilla*
Fox sparrow, *Passerella iliaca*
Lincoln's sparrow, *Melospiza lincolnii*
Song sparrow, *Melospiza melodia* *
Lapland longspur, *Calcarius lapponicus*

*   Year-round resident
†   Outside waters

Sights Along the Waterway

As you travel through the Inside Passage, you will observe a variety of wildlife, from seabirds to breaching humpback whales; forested islands that seem suspended in space; tall mountain peaks; and ice blue glaciers flowing into the sea. But there is more to Southeast Alaska than breathtakingly beautiful scenery, and your shipboard vantage point will allow you to peer in at life as it is truly lived in this northern neck of the woods.

For people who inhabit the communities along these waterways, the Inside Passage is a transportation corridor, a lifeline to the outside world. There are no connecting roads along the shore. All day long, the narrow passageways hum with activity as vessels work their way north and south. Fishing boats are frequent sights in the summer and fall. You will see them with nets spread in the water and unloading the catch at the dock. Passenger cruise ships are another summertime phenomenon. Some twenty different vessels make scheduled visits to Southeast Alaska between May and October of every year. Alaska Marine Highway ferries and commercial tugs and barges are year-round denizens of the waterway.

You may notice that the water itself is not as empty as it first appears. Southeast Alaska is still relatively free of man-made debris, but nature has strewn the water with old logs and clumps of seaweed. In winter the occasional iceberg passes by on a one-way journey to oblivion. There are interesting navigational aids along the route, especially in the narrow channels, and floats to mark the location of private and commercial crab pots. On the shore are signs of clear-cutting where the timber industry has been at work. You will also pass staging areas where logs are rafted together for the trip to the mill. Always there are unexpected little scenes that are visible only from your special shipboard view: a homesteader's cabin tucked in the trees at water's edge; a sailboat riding at anchor in a quiet cove; an ancient cemetery with marble monuments poking above the grass; a cluster of abandoned cannery buildings; a glimpse of weathered totem poles guarding their secrets of the past; a derelict boat marooned on the tide; a secret beach, perfect moon of sand—can you ever find it again?

If you travel the Alaska Marine Highway System during the summer months, a U.S. Forest Service shipboard interpreter will be on board your state ferry to point out and explain sights along the route. The interpreter program is a cooperative arrangement between the state of Alaska and the U.S. Forest Service. The Forest Service provides the interpreters as well as maps, books, brochures, and films for their shipboard presentations. The Alaska Marine Highway System provides passage, accommodation, and meals. The Forest Service personnel present films and short, informal talks on such topics as the bald eagle, humpback whale, glaciers, and the Tongass National Forest; they also give historical introductions to each Inside Passage community. Through such exercises as "eagle counts" while passing through some of the especially narrow passages, they manage to involve you in the passing scene.

The interpreters are equipped to answer questions about virtually every facet of life in Southeast Alaska, from where to find a campground to what date the Russians settled in Sitka. They have extensive information files on board as well as a good library of books and pamphlets about Southeast Alaska that they will lend to you during the voyage.

Some of the cruise ships also have special resource personnel aboard such as someone from the Alaska Cruise Lectures organization of Ketchikan. One of their members may board your vessel at the point of departure and stay aboard for the entire cruise. The cruise lecturers are well prepared on every topic, but, as residents of Ketchikan, they can provide a personal perspective of contemporary life in Southeast Alaska.

TROLLERS, GILL-NETTERS, AND SEINERS

Late each spring, when the snow leaves the mountains, the collective thoughts of southeasterners turn to salmon. Sport fishermen dig favorite poles out from behind the piles of skis, while commercial fishermen begin sharpening their hooks and mending nets. Along about May, the floats come alive with a frenzy of hull scraping and painting.

Commercial salmon fishing is heavily regulated by the state of Alaska, payment for the years of overfishing that depleted the stocks almost beyond repair. Under the Limited Entry Program, the state licenses commercial fishermen according to the type of gear they use, and limits the number of licenses. Then, come fishing season, the Alaska Department of Fish and Game determines how long the commercial harvest will last in each location, according to the strength of the salmon runs. Depending on the type of gear, the allowable fishing periods, called "openings," can be as brief as a few hours. Gone are the days when a commercial fisherman could go out in the spring and fish until he couldn't stand it any longer.

Three different types of boat are used for salmon fishing in Southeast. Two of them use nets to trap the salmon, while the third employs hooks. You are likely to see all three as you travel around Southeast in the summer.

TROLLERS

Troll fishermen fish with baited hooks or lures that are trailed through the water from long poles extended from the side of the boat (sometimes from the front as well). Each pole has a large stainless steel line attached to it with several hooks, so that an average-sized troller might have up to sixty hooks in the water at one time. When fishing, the troller is recognizable by the long poles, or outriggers, extended horizontally over the water. When the boat is not actively fishing, the poles are pulled up to a vertical position alongside the center mast. Power-trollers are equipped with hydraulically powered winches that haul in the heavy gear. On hand-trollers, fishermen crank in the lines by hand. Troll-caught salmon, usually kings or cohos, are the highest quality fish on the market. They are removed from the line as soon as they strike and immediately killed, gutted, and iced in the hold where they stay until they are unloaded at a cold storage facility for further tidying up and freezing. These salmon end up as steaks in the fresh or fresh-frozen case in your supermarket or on your plate at Seafood Sam's down the street. Only a small percentage of salmon leaves Southeast Alaska in an unfrozen or uncanned state. Those that do come from the troll fishery. A trawler, incidentally, is something else entirely: a large fishing vessel that pulls a net bag through the water. There are no salmon trawlers in Alaska.

GILL-NETTERS

Gill-netters are the smaller of the two net-fishing salmon boats. The net is wound around a large spool-shaped reel on the stern. When the boat is in position, the net is let out in a line stretching across the current from the boat. The end of the net is marked with a buoy. The top of the net is supported by floats and the bottom, fixed with weights, hangs straight down in the water like a curtain. The salmon, heading for their spawning stream, swim into the net headfirst. The size of the mesh prevents them from swimming forward, and when they try to back out they are caught by

A troller cruises slowly along, outriggers extended over the water. (Alaska Department of Fish and Game)

the gills, hence the name gill net. After a time the net is hauled in over the reel and the salmon are plucked off (this is called "picking salmon").

Gill nets catch fish of only a certain size and shape. Smaller fish swim through the mesh, while larger specimens simply knock up against it and swim away undamaged. Gillnetted salmon usually sustain some damage and are more suitable for canning than fresh-freezing. As done on trollers, the salmon are killed, cleaned, and iced on board.

On some gill-netters, the reel is mounted on the bow of the boat instead of the stern. These are known as bow-pickers. Whether bow-mounted or stern-mounted, the reel is what to look for to identify a gill-netter. The newer boats are made of fiberglass and have a long, low profile (no mast), something like a large riverboat with a cabin. Some boats are outfitted for both trolling and gillnetting, so they have both poles and drum.

The gill-net fishery is tightly controlled. Openings are few and very specific as to allowable hours and location. As a result, so many gill-netters may be crowded in one spot that your ship will have to weave through an obstacle course of nets. Not long ago, while traveling to Skagway aboard the ferry *Matanuska*, our progress up Lynn Canal was blocked by gill-netters whose nets were stretched across the inlet to take advantage of a

The spool-shaped reel on the stern labels this boat a gill-netter. (Alaska Department of Fish and Game)

twenty-four-hour opening. Even with field glasses it was impossible to tell which net belonged to which boat until we were upon them, and we ran over one of the nets. Miraculously, the net slid under our keel and popped up again unharmed.

PURSE SEINERS

Purse seiners are the largest boats in the fleet. They run to fifty-eight feet in length and function as vacuum cleaners, cleaning up everything in their path. Using a nineteen-foot power skiff, the seine crew sets the large seine net out in a circle from the mother boat. Then they tighten the bottom of the net with a drawstring—called "closing the purse"—and haul the works aboard. Inside will be a little of everything: seaweed, sea urchins, halibut, sharks, junk-fish, and—with luck—a substantial quantity of salmon. All this is sifted through, the salmon kept and the rest thrown back. Whereas a troller or gill-netter can be operated by a one- or two-man crew, the seiner requires a crew of six.

Purse seining is at once the most efficient and least discriminating method of catching salmon. The fish reach the dock in the worst shape of any commercially caught salmon. They are iced and off-loaded directly to cannery tenders (large vessels that run supplies of ice out to the fishing grounds and bring back the fish) or cannery docks where they are cleaned and processed. All purse-seined salmon are canned.

Seiners are amazingly homogeneous in appearance. All have a boom with a circular power winch at the top to hoist the heavy net onto the large afterdeck. When the boat is underway, the net with its floats is coiled on this afterdeck like a mass of intestines, and the power skiff rides upside down on the stern. The most interesting view of purse seiners is from the air. Should you be sight-seeing by plane around Southeast about July, you might be able to look down and see the seine nets scribing perfect circles on the water.

LONG-LINERS

Southeast enjoys good halibut fishing, too. Petersburg is the halibut capital of the region, but you will see the big halibut boats (up to sixty feet) in many Southeast harbors. Commercial halibut fishermen fish with long-lines. A longline is made up of a series of eighteen-hundred-foot (approximate) line lengths, called skates, to which leaders with baited hooks are at-

Seiners are the largest boats in the fleet. Look for the circular power winch.
(Alaska Department of Fish and Game)

tached. The skates are tied together to form one line several miles long. Large halibut boats might have fifteen miles of gear in the water.

The line is laid down on the bottom of the ocean (halibut are bottom feeders) and the ends marked with floats. When the halibut have had a chance to get on the hooks, the line is reeled in over a drum at the stern, similar to the gill-netter's drum, and the halibut are lifted off. The fish are iced in the hold and taken to a cold storage plant where they are processed and frozen for shipment to the Lower 48.

PROMISE OF PROFITS

Commercial fishing has become big business in Alaska, requiring enormous capital investment with only the promise of substantial profits in a good year. The problem for many fishermen is that the combination of low fish runs and heavy regulation has meant few good years of late. Today a new fishing vessel equipped with modern electronic navigation and fish-finding equipment costs between one hundred thousand dollars and five hundred thousand dollars, depending on the type of vessel. To those monthly bank payments must be added the cost of fuel, insurance, and supplies. On the return side of the equation, the price paid for salmon at the dock might range from some three dollars per pound for troll-caught red kings to a few cents per pound for seine-caught pinks sold in the round (not cleaned). A very good seine fisherman (a "highliner") might gross one hundred thousand dollars a season; a very good troll or gill-net fisherman might gross forty to fifty thousand dollars; but the average fisherman seldom does much more than meet expenses.

Even while fishermen are going bankrupt, commercial fishing enjoys a certain aura of romanticism. The old-man-and-the-sea image lingers even in the face of short seasons and high interest rates. For the few weeks of the year (days in some cases) that the commercial fisherman is allowed to fish, he is still master of his vessel and takes orders from no man.

Despite the specter of five-hundred-thousand-dollar boats and batteries of expensive electronic equipment, there is still room in the fisheries for the small-scale fisherman who goes out in his twenty-foot skiff with a couple of handlines and brings in a few fish every week. This fisherman will not make a living this way, but if those fish happen to be kings, they could bring in one hundred dollars apiece—enough to pay expenses and buy a few cases of beer.

CLEAR-CUTTING

As you cruise along the larger islands such as Chichagof and Prince of Wales, you will notice bright green squared-off patches on the hillsides amid the surrounding forest. These are areas that have been clear-cut: evidence of the timber industry at work. The bright green color is from the new growth that is taking form where the old trees were cut.

Most of the forested land of Southeast Alaska is Tongass National Forest (some seventeen million acres). Like all national forest lands, the Tongass is open to many different activities, from recreational hunting and fishing to commercial mining and logging. The U.S. Forest Service tries to manage the land so that all of these activities can be carried out simultaneously without damage to timber, water, wildlife habitat, or recreational value.

The Alaska National Interest Lands Conservation Act passed by Congress in 1980 specified that four and one-half billion board feet of timber could be harvested from the Tongass over the following decade. About two million acres of forest will be harvested over the next one hundred years. The timber harvest is carried out by commercial logging companies that buy the timber from the Forest Service at auction. The highest bidder wins the right to harvest the timber within a specified area.

Clear-cutting is the method most commonly used for harvesting spruce and hemlock stands in the Tongass. Clear-cutting means cutting down every tree within a specified area, as opposed to selecting and removing only the best specimens and leaving the rest alone. Logging companies favor clear-cutting in the difficult terrain of Southeast Alaska because of its obvious efficiency: they can concentrate all of the road building, cutting, and hauling in one small area. Selective cutting requires some fancy techniques such as helicopter logging, which are dangerous, expensive, and inefficient.

Clear-cutting also increases the productivity of the forest by replacing uneven old-growth stands of mixed value with easy-to-harvest high-value trees of uniform size and spacing. And, the new stands have a higher percentage of spruce than old-growth forest because clear-cutting makes way for the full sunlight that the more desirable spruce requires. By the time a clear-cut patch has regenerated and matured, the tree mix will be 50 percent hemlock and 50 percent spruce, versus 70 percent hemlock and 30 percent spruce in the old stands. In 90 to 125 years, the patch will be ready to harvest again.

Clear-cutting remains a controversial practice. Conservationists consider the technique both unsightly and damaging to the environment and to wildlife. Most of the damage is from erosion, blockage of salmon-spawning streams with debris, or destruction of protective habitat or forage areas for wildlife. The industry maintains that these adverse effects can be avoided with proper safeguards and management. One management change that has lessened these effects has been a reduction in the maximum allowable size of a clear-cut from more than two thousand acres to just one hundred. The average-sized clear-cut in the Tongass National Forest today is seventy acres.

You may see other signs of the logging industry during your trip through

A-frame hoists lower bundles of logs into the water for the trip to the mill.

Southeast. A-frame hoists at the water's edge are used to lower bundles of logs into the water, where they are formed into log rafts for the trip to the mill. The logs are corralled by a perimeter of boom logs chained together in the shape of a rectangle. The log rafts are towed to the mill by powerful tugboats called "bullboats" because they "bull" the logs around.

Most hemlock logs cut from the Tongass, and some spruce, wind up at pulp mills at Sitka and Ketchikan where they are turned into high-grade dissolving pulp used in industrial processes such as the manufacture of rayon or plastic. High quality spruce logs are taken to sawmills and processed, usually for export to Japan.

NAVIGATIONAL MARKERS

You will notice several types of navigational marker along the Inside Passage route. Some are red, some green, some blinking, others not. All of these markers are navigational aids that the Coast Guard has positioned to mark safe passageways through difficult channels or harbor entrances. Most of them are buoys that are anchored to the ocean floor. Their color, shape, and number are all clues to how the passage should be navigated.

The color of the buoy indicates to which side the boat should pass. Red buoys are kept on the right, or starboard, side of the vessel when returning from sea (in other words, inbound, heading upstream, or entering the harbor), as in the mariner's expression, "red right returning." Black buoys are kept to the left, or port, side. When outbound, or heading out to sea, the situation is reversed. Buoys painted with black and white vertical stripes mark the center of the channel and can be passed on either side. Port and starboard buoys are also numbered consecutively from the beginning of the passage to the end. Red buoys are always even-numbered; black buoys always odd-numbered. Midchannel markers are not numbered. In very shallow or narrow channels, such as Wrangell Narrows between Wrangell and Petersburg, mariners must thread their way from buoy to buoy very carefully to avoid running aground.

Coast Guard crew members hoist a lighted buoy aboard a tender for routine maintenance. (U.S. Coast Guard)

The color of a buoy is backed up by its shape. Regular red buoys, called nuns, are pointed or cone-shaped on top. Black buoys, called cans, are can-shaped or cylindrical. Lighted buoys are topped with battery-powered red, green, or white lights that flash intermittently at night to give mariners their position. They are also identified with reflective markers called daymarks—square-shaped and odd-numbered in black, white, or green for port; triangular, red, and even-numbered for starboard.

Groups of small, round floats that you see bobbing on the surface of the water, usually red, are not navigational aids, but buoys marking the location of commercial crab pots. Lest you find yourself tempted to pull one up, you should know that a full-sized commercial crab pot can measure six to seven feet across, weighing more than five hundred pounds. Pulling someone else's pot is considered a tacky piece of business anyway.

LIGHTHOUSES

Among the most picturesque sights along the Inside Passage are lighthouses, and there are several on the route from Prince Rupert to Skagway. Congress provided for the building and maintenance of lighthouses in U.S. waters as early as 1789, but none was constructed in Alaska until 1900. Before then the only navigational warning light on the entire

The Cape Decision lighthouse is one of twelve that stood sentry over the Inside Passage. (U.S. Coast Guard)

Alaska coast was the seal oil lantern burning in the cupola atop the governor's residence on Castle Hill in Sitka (replaced by a simple post light after the mansion burned in 1894). Eventually, twelve manned lighthouses stood watch over the Inside Passage.

Those that are still operational differ in appearance except for their tall white towers and red roofs. The octagonal Eldred Rock lighthouse—still the original structure—is the most unusual. From south to north, the lighthouses you will pass along the Inside Passage include: Tree Point, Dixon Entrance (lighted 30 April 1904); Mary Island, Revillagigedo Channel (lighted 15 July 1903); Cape Decision, Sumner Strait (lighted 15 March 1932); Five Fingers, Stephens Passage (lighted 1 March 1902); Point Retreat, Lynn Canal (lighted 15 September 1904); Sentinel Island, Lynn Canal (lighted 1 March 1902); Eldred Rock, Lynn Canal (lighted 1 June 1906); Cape Spencer, Cross Sound (lighted 11 December 1925). You will also pass the Canadian Green Island and Lucy Island lighthouses just out of Prince Rupert.

Originally all of the lighthouses were manned by a lighthouse keeper (sometimes a family) who lived in splendid isolation from the usual cares of the world. Today the lights are automated. The last manned light station in Alaska was Five Fingers, which was fully automated in the summer of 1984.

The original lenses from three of these lighthouses are displayed in museums around Southeast. Check in the Tongass Historical Society Museum in Ketchikan, the Alaska State Museum in Juneau, and the Sheldon Museum in Haines.

THE NARROWS

The Inside Passage contains two stretches of water that are extraordinarily narrow. Wrangell Narrows and the connecting passages of Peril Strait offer unparalleled closeup views of the Southeast landscape and its most popular inhabitant, the bald eagle. As your ship negotiates the narrow twists and turns, you will also get a firsthand look at the navigational aids that mark your passage. Not every ship is able to negotiate these tight channels. Alaska ferries, however, pass through them on their scheduled runs between Wrangell and Petersburg, and to Sitka. If you have a choice, schedule your trip so that you make the passage in daylight. If you must make the trip at night, it is worth getting out of bed to watch as your ship glides between the red, green, and white blinking lights that mark the route.

WRANGELL NARROWS

Wrangell Narrows is the most famous waterway in Southeast Alaska. Winding like a narrow ribbon for twenty-one miles between Mitkof and

Kupreanof islands, the narrows terminates at Petersburg to empty into Frederick Sound. At one point along the way, this chute of rushing water closes to one hundred yards. More than seventy navigational markers guide the helmsman through the passage. Passing through Wrangell Narrows brings you so close to shore that you can almost reach out and grasp an evergreen. At night the waterway is a maze of winking colored lights. (Alaskans have nicknamed it "Christmas Tree Lane.") Your ship glides silently between them as dark cliffs loom overhead.

The passage is so squeezed—an average half-mile wide at high tide—that the current rips through the narrows at up to eight miles an hour with every tidal change. The tide enters and exits from both ends. The channel was dredged to an average low-tide depth of twenty-six feet in the 1940s, but has since silted in another four feet. The shallowest point is currently nineteen feet. Large ships, such as the Alaska Ferries, do not attempt Wrangell Narrows unless the water measures at least two feet above average low tide.

Wrangell Narrows is the preferred route between Wrangell and Petersburg for all types of vessel—fishing boats, tugboats with log rafts, state ferries, and private cruisers. There is ample room for small craft to pass, but large ships remain in radio contact with each other and pass at prearranged wide spots in the road. Fog is the helmsman's worst enemy in Wrangell Narrows. Even with radar, ship captains delay passage until the next tide, if possible, rather than grope their way through the maze of markers. If thick fog descends en route, the best choice is to anchor well off to the side and wait for it to lift.

PERIL STRAIT

Peril Strait is a diagonal cut between Baranof and Chichagof islands. that forms a shortcut to Sitka. The waterway takes its name not from hidden rocks in the water, but from an incident that occurred during the time of the Russian occupation in 1799. That year, a party of Aleut hunters on their way from Sitka to Russian headquarters at Kodiak stopped to camp on a beach where they found quantities of mussels. More than one hundred Aleuts died from the debilitating illness that we know as paralytic shellfish poisoning. The Russians named the waterway Pogibshe, meaning deadly, which has come down to us in English as Peril Strait. The passage narrows at Poison Cove, where the fateful mussels were collected, and Deadman Reach, where the hunters ate their last meal.

From there Peril Strait closes to almost a ditch in a series of zigzagging passages leading to Sitka. The first is Sergius Narrows. From buoys to shore is a distance of three hundred feet and the tide rushes through at speeds close to nine and one-half miles an hour. Large ships can pass only when the tide is slack. Now you pass through Kakul Narrows and emerge into Salisbury Sound, which is open to the Pacific. Beyond some jewel-like islands in the distance you can see the ocean, and you probably can feel the Pacific swell. The passage narrows again into Neva Strait and constricts still further to Whitestone Narrows before opening again to Olga Strait and Sitka Sound.

The thirty-mile stretch encompassing Sergius Narrows and Whitestone Narrows is one of the best places to view eagles in Southeast Alaska. As you glide between the forested islands, the bald eagles virtually line up in the treetops to greet you. The Forest Service interpreters on board the state ferries are fond of initiating eagle counts along this route. (Our group counted sixty-two.) You also have a good chance of seeing deer at the water's edge, and sharing the tight passage with tugboats and log rafts on their way to the pulp mill at Sitka.

Bald eagles are especially prevalent along Sergius and Whitestone narrows approaching Sitka. (John Schoen)

AN INTERNATIONAL BOUNDARY

The boundary between the United States and Canada is not exactly a "sight" because it is invisible, but you will pass over the line on your way from Prince Rupert to Ketchikan. The boundary line extends from the southern point of Prince of Wales Island to the mainland at the entrance to the Portland Canal. The border follows the Portland Canal inland to the Coast Mountains and continues along the range from peak to peak to the vicinity of Skagway. From Skagway the line turns abruptly westward and stretches almost to the sea again but stops at Mount Fairweather, parallels the Saint Elias Mountains to Mount St. Elias, and then jumps onto the 141st meridian for a straight run northward to the Arctic Ocean.

The boundary was fixed in a treaty between Britain and Russia in 1825. The southern line was established at lat. 54°40′ N., but Britain's Hudson's Bay Company retained the right to use navigable rivers in Russian Alaska to reach their inland posts in Canada. When the United States purchased Alaska from Russia in 1867, the old boundaries were retained with only minor adjustments.

Towns and Villages of the Inside Passage

The towns and villages that border the Inside Passage are as ruggedly individualistic as Alaskans themselves. Some, like Juneau and Skagway, were born out of the gold rush while others, Sitka and Wrangell for example, date from earlier periods in Alaska's history. Petersburg has retained the atmosphere of a busy fishing depot, while Ketchikan is unabashedly a mill town. Despite substantial differences in character, all Southeast communities have one thing in common: a working waterfront. No matter where you visit, you will find busy commercial docks and at least one boat harbor, where a lot of the life of the town is lived. A visit to the commercial fishing harbor in summer will reward you with a view of fishermen mending their nets and getting the rest of their gear in order. In the early morning or evening especially, when the light is flat, it is pleasant to spend an hour walking among the brightly colored boats, reading the names, and tasting the salt on the air.

OF SPECIAL INTEREST

Southeast communities also share a deep appreciation for their roots, even though the roots may extend back fewer than one hundred years. All of the larger towns have excellent *local history exhibits*. History buffs will discover relics from the gold rush, the steamship era, or the heyday of the salmon canneries. Local museums also contain fine displays of Tlingit and

Ketchikan's busy harbor is crowded with fishing boats, pleasure craft, and exotic cruise ships.

Haida artifacts.

A few communities offer outdoor *salmon bakes*. There are first-rate operations in Juneau and Haines, and smaller outfits start up in other communities from time to time. The salmon is grilled over an open alder fire, usually in a spectacular setting such as alongside a gold-bearing stream. Don't be put off by the thought of eating out-of-doors. All of the salmon bakes provide covered dining areas to shelter you from the rain.

Something else you should not pass up is a *Tlingit or Haida dance per-*

Juneau's Gold Creek salmon bake is one of several in Southeast. The salmon is grilled over a traditional alder fire.

formance. The only groups presently performing on a regular basis are the Cape Fox Dancers of Saxman (Ketchikan) and the Chilkat Dancers of Haines. Most of the other Southeast towns also have Native dance groups, and occasionally one of them will muster a public performance. The Sitka Ga Jaa Heen Dancers have scheduled performances for visitors some years. A dance exhibition is probably your only chance to hear Native language and music. The dance also brings to life the colorful blankets, fantastic masks, and elaborate head-dresses that are otherwise seen only in museum displays.

At several stops you can take "flightseeing" trips over some of Southeast's spectacular scenery. Taking to the air in a bush plane or helicopter is a truly Alaskan experience. You will gain a new perspective on this silent, peaceful land as your tiny craft maneuvers between glacier-capped peaks or skims along the water's edge. Popular excursions include tours over the ice fields straddling the Coast Mountains, trips to nearby glaciers (helicopter glacier tours land you right on the ice), and flights across Misty Fiords and Glacier Bay national monuments. From Juneau, you can combine an ice field flight and salmon bake with an excursion to Taku Glacier

Lodge (see *The Remote Inns*).

If *hiking* (or strolling) suits your frame of mind, you will find developed trail systems in every town. When you arrive consult the local visitors' center and U.S. Forest Service office for brochures and other information about nearby trails. Advance reading for serious trekkers might include Margaret Piggott's *Discover Southeast Alaska with Pack and Paddle* (The Mountaineers), which outlines trails in all of the major towns (including the historic Chilkoot Trail from Dyea to Lake Bennett). Anyone contemplating a hike in Southeast, whether a morning's berry-picking excursion or a week's ridge walk, should be prepared to encounter mosquitoes and the infamous Southeast rain.

SHOPPING FOR LOCAL ART

If the heart of Southeast is down at the docks, the soul can be found in the many galleries displaying the work of local artists. One of the singular aspects of Southeast Alaska is the high caliber of local art work, which includes traditional Native crafts such as wood and silver carving as well as graphic arts, painting, sculpture, pottery, and weaving. You will find Southeast artwork on sale in galleries, book shops, and private studios in all of the larger communities and featured aboard Alaska state ferries.

A piece of local art can make a satisfying remembrance of your trip to Alaska, and meandering through the galleries is a good way to get out of the weather and meet local residents. Before you shop, though, you should be aware of some facts about prints. Original or hand-pulled prints—whether silk-screened or printed from wood block, linoleum block, lithographic stone, or etched metal plate—are valued by collectors because they are made in small editions, usually of two hundred or fewer, from a master image created directly by the artist. Each print is signed and numbered by the artist. Because they are produced by hand, the prints differ slightly one from the next, which adds to their uniqueness. Commercial reproductions are less valuable because they are the products of a photographic process. While they are produced in signed and numbered limited editions, the edition usually numbers from five hundred to one thousand prints. An artist can also produce an unlimited edition of a work, in which case the print has no value whatever to the serious collector. If you are concerned about the value of a print as a collector's item, look for low-numbered editions. Of course the primary value in acquiring local art is personal satisfaction: buying a print or a painting out of admiration for the artist's work and for the memories it brings back of your trip. You will find a lot of high-quality art in Southeast Alaska that is not expensive (ten dollars to one hundred dollars), and it will give you pleasure for years to come. What follows is a miniguide to contemporary artists who live and work in Southeast Alaska.

Art items for sale in a Sitka shop are contemporary versions of Southeast Native themes.

The two leading artists in Southeast today are *Rie Muñoz* and *Nancy Taylor Stonington*. You can find their works for sale in most larger communities in Southeast Alaska. Muñoz, a longtime Juneau resident, is known throughout Alaska for her colorful watercolors, commercial reproductions, and original silk-screen prints depicting people and scenes from daily Alaska life. Her special interest is the Native cultures of Alaska, and she has made a concentrated effort to record some of their cultural traditions before they vanish completely. Her folksy renditions of Southeast community scenes are equally popular. A recent Muñoz innovation has been the translation of some of her works into wall tapestries at the world-renowned weaving capital of Aubusson, France. One of these tapestries is on permanent display in the lobby of the Bank of the North in Juneau.

Nancy Taylor Stonington spends part of each year in Idaho, but devotes so much time to painting the Southeast Alaska landscape that she qualifies as a local resident. Her medium is watercolors; original paintings are available as well as commercial color reproductions. Stonington is extremely prolific. She enjoys immense popularity in Southeast, where the misty gray-green panorama is a match for her soft watercolor palette.

Florals are another Stonington specialty.

Other well-known artists produce consistently but not necessarily in great volume. You will find some of their work for sale at one or another of the galleries or shops in Southeast. *Dale De Armond* of Juneau produces very small editions of hand-printed wood-block prints and fine wood engravings of a variety of local subjects, including animals, birds, and figures from Southeast Native legend and mythology. Her work is much admired for its bold design and fine execution. *Jo Ann George* of Angoon, a Tlingit village on the west coast of Admiralty Island, creates distinctive pencil portraits of Angoon and other Tlingit-inspired subjects. *Cha Cordova* of Wrangell carves fossil ivory. Her ivory jewelry takes unusual shapes, frequently small faces or floral designs, and her larger decorative sculptures approach the abstract.

The list of producing artists is virtually endless, but here are some other local artists to look for. Ask for their work in galleries, shops, and art fairs, especially within their own communities.

JUNEAU

Kitty Bauer, silk-screened prints, stone lithographs, and watercolors of Alaska landscapes; *Judy Cooper*, naive-style renditions of Juneau scenes in linoleum-block, wood-block, or silk-screened prints and commercial reproductions; *John Fehringer*, soft and intricate airbrushed paintings and reproductions showing Alaska scenes, from Juneau cityscapes and Mount McKinley to sailboats and floatplanes; *Sharon Lobaugh*, oil paintings and watercolors of Southeast landscapes in bold composition; *Bill Ray, Jr.*, stone lithographs, pen-and-ink and fine charcoal drawings depicting Alaska figures, wildlife, and Native and abstract imagery; *Donna Standerwick*, oils, watercolors, and color lithographs of Southeast waterfront locales; *Skip Wallen*, limited-edition stone lithograph portraits of people and wildlife, superbly crafted and greatly admired (look for his note cards in bookstores and galleries, too).

GUSTAVUS

Carole Baker, watercolors of still lifes and local scenes; *Kate Boesser*, large-scale wood-block prints of hidden figures in heavy grain pattern.

HAINES

Pete Andriesen, limited edition silk-screened prints and note cards from pen-and-ink drawings of Alaska scenes and wildlife; *Teri Bastable*, hand silk-screened cards and prints with a wild flower motif; *Sue Folletti*, carved silver jewelry with Northwest Coast Indian motif; *Tresham Gregg*, wood and metal sculpture and graphics with Tlingit- and Haida-inspired designs; *Fred Shields,* silver and gold jewelry; *Madeleine Shields,* silk-screened notes and prints; *Gil Smith,* oil and acrylic paintings, primarily scenics; *Jenny Lyn Smith,* carved silver jewelry and silk-screened prints with traditional totemic designs; *John Svenson,* watercolors and silk-screened prints of mountain scenes and mountaineering. In addition, the artists at *Alaska Indian Arts* produce traditional Northwest coast wood and silver carving.

KETCHIKAN

George Estrella, carved silver and gold jewelry, often with a fish motif; *Doug Hudson,* sculptured wood murals; *Dick Miller, Elizabeth Rose,* and *Mark Wheeler,* watercolor renditions of local scenes.

METLAKATLA

David Boxley, silk-screened prints and carved and painted bentwood boxes, paddles, and masks, using traditional totemic design motifs but with a flair.

SITKA

Johnny Avatock and *Rick Booth,* carved silver bracelets and other jewelry; *Norman Campbell,* quiet Southeast scenes of treed islands, rocks, and water in fine pencil drawings with watercolor blush; *Mary Croxton,* watercolor paintings and limited edition reproductions of local scenery and wildlife; *Keith Greba,* scrimshaw jewelry and decorative pieces with wood and brass presentations; *Dale Hanson,* carved ivory and cast pewter sculptures of wildlife; *Cheryl Les,* watercolor images of wildlife, flowers, fishing boats, and other local scenes; *Phillip Slattery,* handsome, heavy necklaces of trade and other rare beads and polished ivory.

SKAGWAY

Barbara Kalen, oil paintings and note cards of local landscapes and scenes of the historic White Pass and Yukon railroad; *Ann Miletich-Warder,* impressionistic watercolor and colored pencil images of glaciers, forest, and other Southeast landscapes; *David Present,* ivory scrimshaw and sculpture in distinctive modern designs.

WRANGELL

Lavon White, acrylics and watercolors of local landscapes.

Not included here are the dozens of potters, weavers, basket makers, photographers, and other fine craftspeople of Southeast Alaska.

PRINCE RUPERT
Population 16,500

Prince Rupert, terminus for both the Alaska and Canadian ferries and just ninety miles south of Ketchikan, is the true start of the trip up Alaska's Inside Passage. A fishing town at heart, Rupert is home to the same types of fishing vessel that you will see the length of the Southeast Alaska Panhandle. Totem poles spring into view—heritage of the Haida Indians whose ancestral home was the Queen Charlotte Islands and the Tsimshian who lived on the mainland—and the gift and curio shop windows display jewelry and decorative art with totemic designs. The flavor is definitely Alaskan. Rupert is thoroughly Canadian, however, and there are sights to remind you of the town's English heritage, too, like the coat of arms above the Provincial Court House. If you have an extra day before catching your ship, plan to explore some of the sights of Prince Rupert. The town is good for walking, with most of the intriguing features within a few blocks of major hotels. You may see Soviet freighters and other exotic foreign ships docked at the impressive port facilities.

BACKGROUND

Prince Rupert was born out of the wilderness as the western terminus of the second Canadian transcontinental railroad in the early 1900s. (The first went to Vancouver.) The new town, located on Kaien Island at the mouth of the Skeena River, was named in a competition sponsored by the Grand Trunk Pacific Railway, with a $250 prize going to the person who could come up with a name that was "purely Canadian" and not more than three syllables. The winning entry (submitted by a Miss Eleanor M. MacDonald of Winnipeg) honored Prince Rupert, a cousin of King Charles II of England and first governor of the Hudson's Bay Company that was chartered in 1670. The prince died in 1682, but he is remembered in this city as one of the earliest entrepreneurs in Canada.

The town has remained a transportation center, linking the Canadian Pacific Coast to the rest of Canada by rail, highway, air, and water. From the port of Prince Rupert, you can travel north to Alaska by Alaska state ferry, or south to the Queen Charlottes and Vancouver Island on the British Columbia ferry system. Fishing, especially for halibut, has been a mainstay of the Prince Rupert economy since World War I. The community supports large salmon and halibut fishing fleets and four fish-processing plants. There is also a sizable wood products industry, including a Skeena

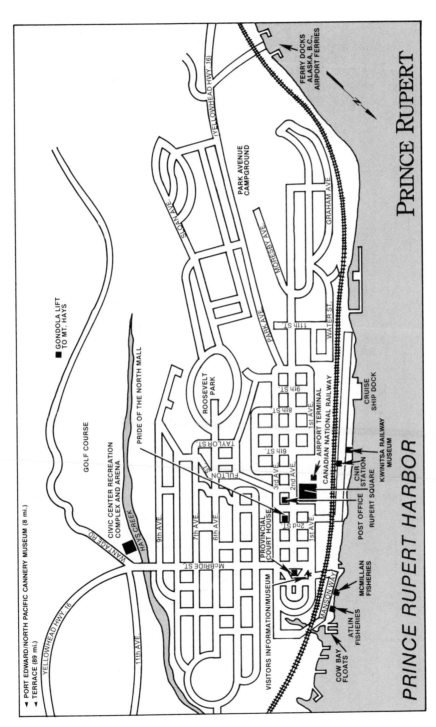

PRINCE RUPERT

PRINCE RUPERT HARBOR

FERRY DOCKS
ALASKA, B.C.,
AIRPORT FERRIES

(YELLOWHEAD HWY. 16)

PARK AVENUE
CAMPGROUND

SLOAN AVE.

MORESBY AVE.

PARK AVE.

GRAHAM AVE.

WATER ST.

11th ST.

GONDOLA LIFT
TO MT. HAYS

PRIDE OF THE NORTH MALL

ROOSEVELT
PARK

GOLF COURSE

CIVIC CENTER RECREATION
COMPLEX AND ARENA

HAYS CREEK

WANTAGE RD.

9th ST.

8th ST.

6th ST.

1st AVE.

TAYLOR ST.

FULTON

3rd AVE.

2nd AVE.

AIRPORT TERMINAL

CANADIAN NATIONAL RAILWAY

CNR
STATION

CRUISE
SHIP DOCK

KWINITSA RAILWAY
MUSEUM

POST OFFICE

RUPERT SQUARE

1st AVE.

2nd AVE.

9th AVE.

7th AVE.

6th AVE.

PROVINCIAL
COURT HOUSE

McBRIDE ST.

VISITORS INFORMATION/MUSEUM

McMILLAN
FISHERIES

ATLIN
FISHERIES

COW BAY
FLOATS

MANSON WAY

11th AVE.

▸ PORT EDWARD/NORTH PACIFIC CANNERY MUSEUM (8 mi.)
▸ TERRACE (89 mi.)
   YELLOWHEAD HWY. 16

The coat of arms over the entrance to Prince Rupert's Provincial Court House is reminiscent of an English heritage.

Cellulose pulp operation eight miles from town, and extensive deepwater port facilities.

GETTING THERE

You can reach Prince Rupert by car, train, plane, or ship. Prince Rupert is the western terminus of Yellowhead Highway 16 from Prince George (450 miles), Jasper, Edmonton, and other points in the Canadian Interior. At Prince George, the Yellowhead meets north-south arteries leading to the Alaska Highway and Vancouver. The Canadian National Railway (VIA Rail Canada) reaches Prince Rupert from Prince George; the terminal is conveniently located at the downtown waterfront.

Both Canadian and Alaska car ferries call at Prince Rupert. The Alaska ferry runs north from Rupert and back, stopping at Inside Passage ports, but not between Prince Rupert and Seattle. British Columbia ferries travel between Prince Rupert and the Queen Charlotte Islands and south to Vancouver Island. There is daily air service from Vancouver and several nearby towns. The airport is on Digby Island, a short ferry ride from Prince Rupert.

TO SEE AND DO

Prince Rupert is compact enough that, once established downtown, you can easily take in the major sights on foot. The *Prince Rupert Visitor Information Centre* is located right in the city center at the corner of First

Nineteenth-century cannery buildings on the Skeena River near Prince Rupert have been preserved as part of the North Pacific Cannery Museum.

Avenue and McBride. The Canadians have done a clever thing here, combining a small museum, art gallery, and visitors' center in one pleasant building (although ground has been broken for a new museum building across the street). Just inside the entrance you will find a natural history exhibit with a display of local birds. Here is your chance to get acquainted with the raven and the bald eagle, the two most important birds of the Northwest cultures and prominent representatives of the wildlife you will see along the Inside Passage.

The *Museum of Northern British Columbia* encompasses the themes of Prince Rupert's history: the railroad, canneries, timber, and mining. Exhibits include a representative sampling of Northwest Coast Indian artifacts. Here you can see your first Chilkat blanket (faded but still beautiful), button blanket, carved wooden masks, and trade beads. There are good displays of cedar bark and skin clothing, baskets, and lidded bentwood boxes. Be sure to notice the large copper shields. These shields, called tinneh, were used as a form of currency (along with blankets and other items) by the early coast peoples. Some, such as those in the museum, were painted with the owner's crest. Also, do not miss the collection of carved argillite. Argillite, a soft shale stone, comes from Skidegate Inlet in the Queen Charlotte Islands. Haida craftsmen began applying their traditional totemic designs to argillite in the early nineteenth century and found themselves with a valued trade item.

The *Art Gallery* displays the work of local artists and hosts traveling shows from other parts of Canada. There is an excellent gallery shop with books on Northwest Coast art and prints by leading Haida artists such as Bill Reid, Freda Diesing, and Robert Davidson. Carved silver jewelry, masks, and other art objects are for sale as well.

Prince Rupert is a good place to just ramble about town and see where you end up. The *sunken gardens* behind the Provincial Court House are a monument to creative problem solving. After ground had been excavated to erect the court house, the building site was relocated several yards uphill to take advantage of the view. The terraced flower beds were created to fill the gaping hole that was left. You will also come upon several *totem poles*— you may even see a pole being carved at the *carving shed* near the museum. If you like Chinese food, you will love Prince Rupert for its numerous *Chinese restaurants. Seafood,* of course, is another Rupert specialty.

My favorite walk in Prince Rupert is down to the *waterfront* where the highly aromatic scents from the canneries waft along the salt air. As you exit from the visitors' bureau, turn right and right again on First Avenue. Go down the hill and bear left on Manson Way. The road crosses the railroad tracks and you will find yourself at the cannery docks where the fishing boats off-load their cargoes of halibut and salmon. On the street side, your progress may be interrupted by workmen wheeling cartfuls of fish to and from the cold storage plant.

Now continue along the waterfront, keeping the water on your left, until you reach *Smile's Seafood Restaurant* overlooking the Cow Bay floats. There is an outer room with booths and an inner dining room overlooking the waterfront. View aside, the two best things about Smile's are the atmosphere—you will be convinced you are the first tourist to ever walk into the place—and the menu. Where else can you order (in addition to the expected offerings of salmon and halibut), a sardine sandwich, smelts, smoked Alaska black cod, halibut cheeks (fishermen consider them the best part), an oyster burger, or an abalone burger? Smile's is terrific. My husband and I first went there in 1969 and the place has changed little since. Next door to Smile's, the spiffy new *Breaker's Pub* makes a more genteel alternative for waterfront dining.

On the waterfront behind the VIA rail station, you will discover the small *Kwinitsa Railway Museum.* Installed in the historic Kwinitsa Station, restored and relocated from its original site on the Skeena River, the museum exhibits station artifacts and items pertaining to the 1914 arrival of the Grand Trunk Pacific Railway from Winnipeg—the first train to cross the Canadian prairies to the West Coast.

Prince Rupert's *gondola lift* operates to the 1,850-foot level of Mount Hays. In winter (if snowfall has been sufficient), the Mount Hays Sky Ride lifts you to alpine skiing with lodge, cafeteria, restaurant, and ski rental shops. In summer, the ride affords a stroll through alpine meadows plus a view of the Queen Charlotte Islands and, to the north, Alaska. The gondola terminus is on Wantage Road, which skirts the municipal golf course.

Head for Smile's when you are in the mood for abalone burgers, smoked black cod, and other seafood treats.

(Take a cab.) Ask at the Visitor Information Centre about tours of the state-of-the-art *grain elevator* and *coal terminal,* and *flightseeing* by float-plane or helicopter.

Eight miles from Prince Rupert, the village of Port Edward is the site of the delightful *North Pacific Cannery Museum.* The complex of white clapboard buildings was one of the nineteen salmon canneries built at the mouth of the Skeena River in the late 1800s. The main cannery building has been converted into an informal but dynamic museum of maritime history. Arranged comfortably throughout the spacious room are all kinds of commercial fishing equipment, including mock-ups of a halibut long-liner and salmon troller that kids can climb in and explore, and exhibits on old-style can manufacturing (by hand), net making and mending, and different commercial fishing techniques. The walls and floors are festooned with old nets, glass and wood floats, mounted fish specimens, flags, and colorful salmon can labels.

Other buildings along the wooden boardwalk house an art gallery and cafe (originally the mess house). More enterprises (perhaps a bed and breakfast?) wait in the wings as additional structures are readied. Although North Pacific last canned fish in 1971, commercial fishermen still tie up to the wharf to make repairs or mend their nets. If you want to drop a line in the water, *Bob's Bait & Tackle* will rent you a rod.

Festivals in Prince Rupert include *Indian Cultural Days,* in June, when Native people from coastal villages and the interior gather to perform traditional dances and display crafts and Native foods. During the second weekend in June, *Seafest* celebrates the city's maritime heritage with contests, races, and a friendly "sea feast" competition among local restaurants.

KETCHIKAN
Population 14,300

Ketchikan has a habit of collecting epithets: "Alaska's First City," because it is the first stop on the way north through the Inside Passage; "Salmon Capital of the World," for the tremendous fishing industry that founded the town; and, more dubiously, the "Rain Capital." Technically, Ketchikan is not the rainiest place in Southeast (that distinction goes to the community of Little Port Walter on the southern tip of Baranof Island where there is measurable precipitation approximately 239 days of the year), but the average yearly rainfall of 162 inches has led local wags to comment: "If you can't see Deer Mountain, it's raining; and if you can see it, it's about to rain."

Another saying about Ketchikan, coined by my husband, is: "We're going to stay here in Ketchikan as long as it takes to get a good night's sleep!" This sentiment is equally apt, because Ketchikan is a robust, fun-

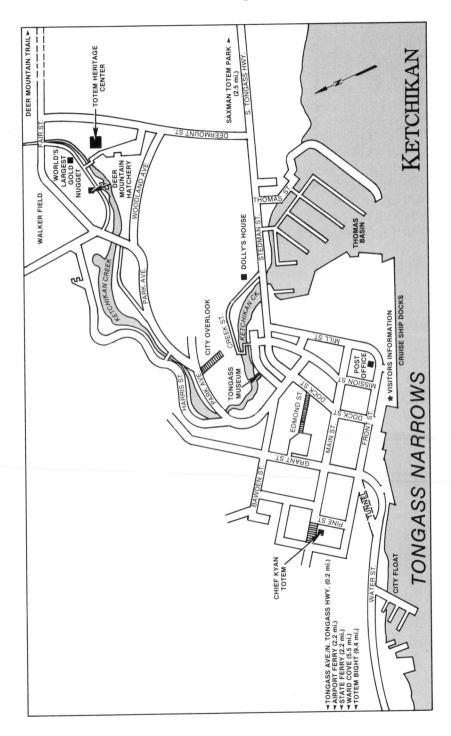

filled town where there's always something going on. On a given summer day, a cruise ship might be moored along the wharf, the seine fleet getting ready to put to sea, and the salmon milling about below the Ketchikan Creek Bridge. Restaurants and bars throb with loggers in from Prince of Wales Island, Natives in from booze-free Metlakatla, fishermen waiting for the next opening, and office workers plotting the weekend's excursion. Outside, the streets are choked with cars moving from one end of the road to the other. There is a sense of activity and purpose in the air.

In the past, Ketchikan has projected something of a rough-and-tumble mill town image. But a stroll through the city center today reveals a forest of hanging flower baskets and the jewellike Whale Park—indications that the rough edges are wearing away. Even the dismally antiquated downtown hotels are enjoying some renovation and face-lifting. You'll enjoy your stay in this lively waterfront city.

BACKGROUND

Ketchikan lies on the western coast of Revillagigedo Island, ninety miles north of Rupert via the Marine Highway. Like other Southeast communities, the town is squeezed into a narrow ribbon of land between the mountains and the sea. Revillagigedo is a real tongue twister; most people shy away from saying the word aloud. The name is Spanish, the island having been named in honor of the Count of Revilla Gigedo who was viceroy of Mexico in the late 1700s. The correct Spanish pronunciation is

"Alaska's First City" on the Inside Passage is renowned for salmon, rainfall, and commercial activity.

Rheh-bee-ya-hee-'hay-tho. The best bet is to emulate local residents and shorten the name to Revilla, which, Anglicized, or "Alaskacized," then becomes Ruh-'vil-la.

The name Ketchikan is derived from a Tlingit word that is commonly translated to mean "the salmon creek that flows through town" or the "thundering wings of an eagle." Both translations are technically correct, but there is more to the story than that. According to Ketchikan's premier historian Mary Balcom, a Tlingit Indian established a summer fishing camp near Ketchikan Creek long before the present community was founded. Because he was called Kitschk, the camp was known at Kitschk-hin or Kitschk's stream, the Tlingit word hin meaning water, river, or stream. The Americans and Europeans who began to frequent the area could not pronounce this or would not try, so they shortened the word to Kitskan, which has come down to us as Ketchikan. (Bear in mind that the Tlingit, like the Haida and Tsimshian, had no written language, so Tlingit words written with the English language alphabet have been spelled phonetically, with differing results.) The name Kitschk can be literally translated to mean "the thundering wings of an eagle," or the sound of the eagle's wings in flight.

The Tlingit fishing camp was well established by 1883 when a small salmon saltery was built at the mouth of Ketchikan Creek. Two years later, there were canneries at the nearby communities of Quadra on the mainland and Loring on Revillagigedo Island. In 1887, the Quadra cannery was moved to Ketchikan and the settlement we know today was born. The Tongass Packing Company packed fifty-five hundred cases of salmon that first year, the beginning of an industry that grew to more than a dozen canneries producing more than two million cases of salmon a year, earning Ketchikan the title of Salmon Capital of the World.

Mining contributed to the growth of the settlement when gold was discovered in the area in 1897. Good copper deposits were located on Prince of Wales Island the same year, and the community was launched on another tack. Lumber production started at about the same time. The Ketchikan Spruce Mill was moved from its first location on Prince of Wales Island to Ketchikan in 1903 to provide lumber to manufacture packing boxes for the canneries. The mill remained the focal point of downtown Ketchikan, in recent years producing cants (sawed logs) for export to Japan. The local economy was dealt a blow when the mill—now owned by Louisiana-Pacific—was relocated to Annette Island. Louisiana-Pacific's pulp mill, built at Ward Cove in 1954, produces a dissolving pulp used to manufacture plastics and other synthetics. The Cape Fox Native Corporation is logging corporate lands around Ketchikan as well.

The salmon fisheries declined in the 1940s and nearly collapsed in the 1970s, mostly from overfishing, but the industry is gradually recovering. While only two canneries operate currently in Ketchikan, the fresh fish market is growing rapidly—3.5 million pounds of fresh seafood were air-freighted out of Ketchikan in 1986. *Silver Lining,* a leading seafood processor and smokery, produces a product that closely resembles the home-smoked salmon Alaskans prepare for themselves. Buy a packet while you are in Ketchikan or other Southeast communities and enjoy this traditional Southeast delicacy on a cracker in your hotel or stateroom at night.

Mining is still a viable industry: not gold or copper anymore, but molybdenum, a silver-white metal used in the production of stainless steel. The U.S. Borax and Chemical Corporation is in the process of developing what may be the world's largest molybdenum deposit at Quartz Hill, which is located, rather awkwardly, in the middle of the new Misty Fiords National Monument forty miles southeast of Ketchikan. Once under way, production is expected to continue for a seventy-year period. Like all Southeast towns, Ketchikan relies on both tourism and government to flesh out the economy.

GETTING THERE

You can reach Ketchikan by air or by water. There is daily jet service from Seattle and Juneau. The airport is located on Gravina Island, across Tongass Narrows from the city of Ketchikan. A small ferry shuttles passengers and automobiles between the airport and the airport ferry terminal, a little more than two miles north of the Ketchikan city center, near the Alaska state ferry terminal. Ketchikan is a port of call for both mainline ferries traveling north and south along the Inside Passage and for smaller vessels serving Metlakatla, Prince of Wales Island, and Hyder. Most cruise ships tie up at the city dock on the downtown waterfront.

TO SEE AND DO

Ketchikan has a number of attractions near the city center that can be seen on foot and others that require a bus or automobile trip out the road. The central sights can all be viewed on the *walking tour* that has been outlined by the Ketchikan Visitors' Bureau. This two-mile amble requires two to three hours and takes in the major attractions of Creek Street, the Totem Heritage Center, Deer Mountain Hatchery, and the Tongass Museum: all relatively flat terrain. Along the way you will get a look at some of Ketchikan's famous staircases leading to residential neighborhoods high in the clouds. If you can muster the strength to climb the stairs to the *City Overlook* off of Park Avenue (Upland Way on the Walking Tour map), you will be glad you made the effort when you reach the top and look down over Creek Street, the floats at Thomas Basin, and the cruise ships passing along Tongass Narrows. First stop, then, in the city should be the *Ketchikan Visitors' Bureau,* dockside on Front Street, to obtain a copy of

Climb to the City Overlook and view Creek Street and boat-filled Thomas Basin. Tongass Narrows is beyond.

the Walking Tour map and other brochures.

Front Street, where the cruise ships dock, is lined with hotels, eating establishments, and gift and souvenir shops. The nicely redecorated *Gilmore Garden* in the Gilmore Hotel lobby is inviting for cocktails, meals, or a special concoction from the espresso bar. *Charley's Restaurant* near Mission Street is popular for lunch, dinner, and cocktails. Toward the spruce mill end of Front Street is the *Pioneer Pantry.* You should lean your elbows on the counter for at least one meal at this venerable establishment. The menu runs to BLTs, grilled cheese sandwiches, chicken-fried steak, liver-and-onions, and meatloaf—no funny business like quiche at the Pioneer. The *Scanlon Gallery* on Mission is an excellent spot to buy Southeast art.

Ketchikan is truly a marine city, with interesting activities occurring the entire four-and-one-half-mile length of the waterfront. Much of the business district hangs over the water on pilings. If you have not arrived by boat, it is worthwhile getting out on the water to view the city from this angle. Consider taking one of the *waterfront cruises* offered by Outdoor Alaska (check with the visitors' bureau for details).

Creek Street is one of the most photogenic sights in all of Southeast Alaska. The wooden boardwalk—lined with homes, art galleries (try the *Morning Raven Gallery* at 20 Creek Street), and small shops—juts out over Ketchikan Creek. Creek Street was the red-light district of Ketchikan during the rowdier days of the twenties and thirties when loggers and fishermen came to town looking for entertainment. The twenty-odd houses were permanently closed in 1953. Yet another Ketchikan saying is that Creek Street was the spot where "both fish and fishermen went upstream to spawn," a concept that greatly influences the plot of Ketchikan's own rip-roaring, home-grown summer musical melodrama, *The Fish Pirate's Daughter* (highly recommended).

Number 24 on the right, painted peppermint green with a red door, is *Dolly's House.* Big Dolly Arthur arrived in Alaska in 1914 at the age of twenty-six and exercised her considerable charms until Creek Street was closed. Dolly continued to live in her house, however, until she moved into a nursing home at age seventy-three, and many of her personal furnishings are still there. Recently Dolly's House has been restored as a small museum that offers a glimpse into her life and times. A photo of Dolly in the front room shows a spirited "Big Blonde" type of generous proportions. At five-foot-eight she was not called Big Dolly for nothing, and her weight ballooned to 240 pounds in later years. The dining room table is set for company and the bottle of bootleg whiskey (the bottle, at least) stands at the ready in a tiny wet bar positioned strategically over the creek. A quick toss through the trapdoor took care of any incriminating evidence. Upstairs in the bedroom, Dolly's clothes hang in the wardrobe and her chunky pink and red costume jewelry sprawls on the dressing table. There is a small admission charge, which buys you a guided visit. Next door, at *Parnassus* (28 Creek Street), you will meet Ms. Lillian Ference, who presides over this delightful two-story bookstore (new and used), giftshop, and espresso bar.

The Totem Heritage Center at 601 Deermount Street is a repository for original, unrestored totem poles that have been retrieved from the deserted Tlingit communities of Tongass and Village islands and the Haida village of Old Kasaan. The collection, the largest in Alaska, totals more than thirty poles and fragments. Five are on display in the central gallery, and you will be struck by their size. Surrounding the gallery are glass cases displaying art and artifacts. Be sure to note the set of traditional wood-carving tools made by Tsimshian artist Jack Hudson. Each piece is beautifully decorated and shaped to fit the carver's hand.

The Totem Heritage Center is also used for workshops in Native crafts such as wood carving, beading, basketry, and silver engraving. As you explore the center you may see young artists sorting and stringing beads and working on dance blankets or other projects. In the beading room, notice the handsome copper and wood screen depicting Raven with the sun and moon.

Outside the Totem Heritage Center stands a new totem pole carved by Tlingit artist Nathan Jackson in 1979. This pole, called the *Raven–Fog Woman pole,* recalls the story of the mythical hero Raven and Fog Woman, his wife, who created the first salmon. According to this legend, Raven went fishing with his two slaves to gather the winter's food supply, but managed to catch nothing but bullheads. As they were returning to camp, a heavy fog engulfed their canoe and they lost their way. Suddenly, a woman appeared in the canoe. She asked Raven for his spruce root hat, which she took in her left hand. All of the fog disappeared into the hat and Raven was able to find the way home. Fog Woman became Raven's wife and produced sockeye salmon for him out of baskets of spring water like rabbits out of a hat. When she had produced enough salmon to fill many smokehouses, Raven forgot his former hunger and began to mistreat her. She left him to return to her father's house, and as she walked into the sea, all of the salmon followed, leaving Raven nothing to eat but the bullhead.

The pole depicts Raven at the top, easily recognized by his wings and straight beak. He is holding a bullhead on a line. Beneath him, his two slaves, Gitsanuk and Gitsanqeq, also hold bullheads. At the bottom of the pole is Fog Woman, with the spruce root hat in her left hand and a salmon in her right; and below her, two salmon. This is a beautiful pole. As in the original totem poles, most of the wood has been left natural, so you can see that the carving truly started life as a tree. The colors—earth red, black, and copperish green—are used for accent only.

Across Ketchikan Creek via a footbridge from the Totem Heritage Center and past the "world's largest gold nugget"—chained in place, of course—is the Alaska Department of Fish and Game's *Deer Mountain*

Hatchery. This facility releases 150,000 young coho and an equal number of king salmon each year into Ketchikan Creek, where they migrate downstream into Thomas Basin and salt water. After a hazardous life at sea, the surviving adults return to the hatchery to spawn. They are captured in holding pens, and the eggs and milt are taken to produce the next generation of salmon. The baby salmon or fry are reared at the hatchery for about two years. After they begin feeding they are called fingerlings. When they reach four to eight inches, they are known as smolts and released to the wild. Deer Mountain Hatchery also produces 10,000 steelhead trout yearly.

At any given time the hatchery population exceeds 600,000 fish in various stages of development. Hatchery workers were measuring the young salmon fry the day we visited. Depending upon the month, you may be able to see adult fish returning to the hatchery. The kings spawn from the end of July through August, and coho the end of November through December.

The *Tongass Historical Society Museum* at 629 Dock Street has one of the nicest sites of any museum anywhere. The building, which also houses the public library, practically straddles Ketchikan Creek. Inside, you can hear the sound of water rushing beneath your feet. The museum embraces all of the themes that thread through Ketchikan's history, including Native cultures, mining, and fishing. The collection is not large; you can walk through the exhibits in an hour.

A new exhibit, "This Is Our Life," focuses on the changing cultures of Southeast Native peoples. Showcases reveal a lifestyle rich with creativity.

Big Dolly Arthur exercised her charms at number 24 until Creek Street was closed in 1953.

You will see beautiful and functional spruce root and cedar bark baskets, bentwood boxes and elaborate feast dishes, a button blanket expensively ornamented with abalone buttons and dentalia shells, and a large Chilkat blanket (look closely at the fringe to see the dark strands of cedar bark spun into the mountain goat wool). A carved wooden crest hat in the shape of a salmon comes from the Dog Salmon clan on Prince of Wales Island. Elders of the Tlingit, Haida, and Tsimshian peoples guided the preparation of the display and explained how the artifacts were made and used. Their stories add a special dimension.

The museum also has the original lens from the Tree Point light station at Dixon Entrance. The lens, originally illuminated by a kerosene vapor lamp, was donated to the museum when the light was replaced by a rotating beacon in 1963.

The totem pole outside the museum, *Raven Stealing the Sun*, was commissioned by the City of Ketchikan to honor the Tongass Tlingit who originally inhabited the area. The figures recall the story of Raven, who brought light to the world by stealing the box of daylight from a chief on the Nass River (see page 69). The pole was designed and carved by Tlingit artist Dempsey Bob and raised in 1983.

As you are enjoying your walk around Ketchikan, make your way to the corner of Main and Pine streets where you will find one of Ketchikan's typical high wooden staircases, a 1904-vintage turreted house, and the *Chief Kyan totem*. This pole is a copy of an earlier totem that stood in a different location in town. The top figure is Crane. Thunderbird is below, with

Ketchikan carver Nathan Jackson (right) works on a new totem pole with Steve Brown (left foreground) and Ernest Smeltzer.

According to legend, anyone touching the Chief Kyan totem will have money within twenty-four hours.

outstretched wings, and Bear on the bottom. Legend has it that anyone touching the pole will have money in their hands within twenty-four hours.

Three miles south of Ketchikan on the South Tongass Highway, the world's largest collection of totem poles has been gathered at *Saxman Totem Park.* The village of Saxman was formed in the late 1800s by Tlingit from Cape Fox and Point Tongass villages. It is named for Samuel Saxman, a schoolteacher who was lost with two other men in the winter of

The spectacular Sun and Raven, at the entrance to Saxman Totem Park, recalls several Raven adventures.

1886 while they were hunting for a new village site. The twenty-four totems were brought to the site from abandoned villages on Tongass, Cat, Pennock, and Village islands and from the old Cape Fox Village at Kirk Point under a U.S. Forest Service and Civilian Conservation Corps project in the 1930s. Some were repaired and restored and others completely replicated—a process that continues today.

The park is located on the uphill, or left, side of the highway as you proceed south. At the entrance stands what is probably the most photo-graphed totem in the park: *Sun and Raven.* This spectacular pole, originally carved in 1902 as a memorial column, recalls several Raven myths. Raven is at the top, with his characteristic straight beak. The corona around his head represents the Sun, who entertained Raven during the Deluge. The eye-shaped designs on his wings, with small faces inside, symbolize the power of flight and Raven's ability to change form.

The three small figures between Raven's wings are the Children of the Sun. Below them is the face of Fog Woman, Raven's wife, who produced salmon out of springwater. Next is Raven again, diving after Frog to the bottom of the ocean to visit the creatures of the sea.

Slightly uphill from Sun and Raven are the *Tired Wolf houseposts.* The posts were carved in approximately 1827 for members of the Wolf phratry who had once crossed paths with a particular wolf. According to their story, the men of Forest Island House were out fishing one day in their canoe when they came upon a wolf swimming for shore. He was so ex-hausted that his tongue lolled out of his mouth. They rescued the wolf and took him to live with them, and the animal became a faithful companion and helped them to hunt. In the carvings, the wolves' tongues are hanging out of their mouths. The long tail up the back of each post distinguishes Wolf from Bear. Notice the small face that forms the pupil of the eye in one of the wolves. This was a carver's device to symbolize the life-force.

The body of the totem pole collection is arranged in a wide grassy area at the top of the street. In front of them are two more sets of houseposts: Ravens on the left and Bears on the right. Look to the right to see the *Lincoln pole.* This is a replica. You can see the original pole in the Alaska State Museum in Juneau. The precise history of this famous totem has been lost to the past, but the carving was erected on Tongass Island in 1883 to com-memorate the clan's first sighting of a white man many years previously. The carver evidently used a picture of President Lincoln as a model for the figure wearing a stovepipe hat at the top of the column. At the base of the pole was Raven, the clan crest, and the pole was known as the Proud Raven pole.

The plain shaft with the single lonely figure at the top wearing a potlatch hat is the *Seward pole,* which was carved about 1885 to com-memorate Secretary of State William Seward's tour of Tongass Island in 1869. During his visit, Seward was entertained by the clan chief. He was given a ceremonial spruce root hat, furs, and a carved and painted chest. On the pole the secretary is shown seated on the chest and wearing the potlatch hat. Some say the Seward pole is actually a ridicule pole that was erected because Seward did not reciprocate the hospitality shown him by the people of Tongass Village.

Be sure to notice all of the Frog totems in the park. Besides the Frog figure on the Sun and Raven pole, there is a mortuary column showing

Some say the Seward pole, carved about 1885 to commemorate Secretary of State William Seward's visit, is actually a ridicule pole.

Raven poised for flight on top and Frog midway down the shaft, and the *Frog Tree*, with two Frog totems atop a crosspiece on an upright support. The latter pole was erected in memory of a woman whose name was Two Frogs on a Drifting Log. The legend tells of a young Tlingit woman, the daughter of a chief, who went to live with a tribe of frogs in a lake near their village. The father was eventually able to rescue her and bring her home, but she was unable to eat human food and soon died.

Another pole you will enjoy examining is the *Loon Tree*. The top figure is Loon, the crest figure of a particular Tlingit clan. Below Loon are three bear cubs making their way headfirst to the base of the pole. The cubs represent the story of Kats, who married a she-bear that appeared to him in human form and was ultimately killed by their cub-children. Kats's bear-wife is at the bottom of the pole, holding the human figure of Kats between her front paws. The Kats legend is a favorite topic for totem poles. You will see many other carvings representing Kats, his wife, and their cub-children in Southeast totem parks.

If you want to learn more about the poles in Saxman and other totem collections, the standard reference book is *The Wolf and the Raven* (University of Washington Press) by Dr. Viola Garfield of the University of Washington Department of Anthropology, and Linn Forrest, who was the U.S. Forest Service architect in charge of the Civilian Conservation Corps totem restoration project. The authors were actively involved in the restoration project and have tried to document the history of each totem. The book is available in paperback in most Southeast bookstores. (*The Wolf and the Raven* also documents the poles in Totem Bight and Klawock totem park.)

Saxman Native Village includes a visitor information center with interpretive exhibits, a gift shop, carving shed, and newly completed *Beaver Tribal House.* In summer, the community hosts scheduled performances of the *Cape Fox Dancers,* Saxman's traditional Tlingit dance group, and the *Naa Kahidi Indian Theater,* presenting a dramatization of an ancient Tlingit myth.

Beyond Saxman, the South Tongass Highway leads to a small sawmill at *Herring Cove.* You will probably see rafts of logs in the water awaiting the planer. The *George Inlet Lodge* (mile 12) serves waterfront dinners on Fridays and Saturdays. The road ends at a powerhouse at mile 12.9. If you are looking for a place to put a line in the water on the way back, stop at mile 4.5 (Mountain Point) where you can see the red marker number 18 on a point in Tongass Narrows. There is good fishing here for pink salmon in July and August.

Northward out of Ketchikan, the North Tongass Highway extends for 18.4 miles. Midway along is the Louisiana-Pacific pulp mill at Ward Cove, which produces a high-grade dissolving pulp for industrial use. Roads lead inland to the *Ward Lake Recreation Area* with several attractive national forest campgrounds and picnic shelters. A gravel road continues through Cape Fox Corporation lands to Lake Harriet Hunt, where the Ketchikan Ski Club operates a small ski tow in winter. Much of the land on both sides of the road has been recently clear-cut. If you have never had the chance to observe the effects of clear-cutting, this is a good place to look, but remember that the land is privately owned. On the left of the Tongass Highway at mile 9.4 is *Mud Bight,* a much-photographed community of float houses that is left high and dry on the mud at low tide.

At mile 10, on a point overlooking Tongass Narrows, is *Totem Bight State Historic Park,* the site of another fourteen restored or replicated totems and a community house. A bight, incidentally, is a small cove or bay along the coastline, in this case in Tongass Narrows. A short trail leads through the forest to the park. The site, with its gentle beach and salmon stream, was formerly used by the Tlingit as a summer campsite. The en-

The community house at Totem Bight overlooks Tongass Narrows. The spot was formerly a Tlingit campsite.

trance to the trail is guarded by two Haida mortuary carvings, an Eagle with a Chilkat blanket design on the front and a Thunderbird. Both are copies and neither is considered a good example of Haida art. The Chilkat blanket pattern is especially out of character with traditional carving conventions.

The community house was constructed by the Civilian Conservation Corps to replicate an early nineteenth-century clan house with painted housefront, carved corner posts, and a tall totem pole at the entrance. An oval hole in the bottom of the pole frames the doorway into the house. The interior is fashioned in typical style. There is a central fire pit for cooking and heating and a wooden platform around the perimeter where the inhabitants sat, slept, and stowed their belongings. The interior houseposts are also carved, as they were in early times.

The entrance pole celebrates several Raven stories. Raven is at the top with outstretched wings and the box of daylight at his feet. Of special interest is the Killer Whale, easily identified by the tall dorsal fin and small face representing the blowhole. The freestanding pole on the point in front of the community house symbolizes several different stories. The bottom figures are most recognizable. They include, in descending order: Frog, Cormorant (with outstretched wings), Raven, Halibut, and Grizzly Bear. Halibut appears less frequently than some of the other crest figures. In this instance his broad tail is folded down over his back.

The other totems in the park are arranged along a pleasant path overlooking the water. Some are Haida in origin; others are Tlingit. The Alaska Division of Parks has prepared an informative brochure identifying each pole. Pick up a copy from the visitors' center in Ketchikan. I particularly like the Totem Bight version of the Kats story. Kats's bear-wife is crouched at the top of the column and her bear tracks lead up the simple cedar shaft. Another unique pole features Halibut positioned crosswise atop a square post.

Totem Bight is a lovely spot to linger among the totems and watch the ship traffic pass on Tongass Narrows. It should be noted, though, that this is a historical park with no fires, food, or camping allowed. You can enjoy your picnic at the U.S. Forest Service campground at *Settlers' Cove*. Continue past Totem Bight and take the road to the left at the end of the highway. You will find a boat launch, camp sites, and picnic tables. A path leads along the beach to the right. You duck into the mossy forest, following the trail and the sound of rushing water, and come to a bridge that forges the stream.

If your timing is right on the way back to town, consider dropping into the *Clover Pass Resort* (approximately mile 14; follow the signs) for cocktails or dinner. (Dinner reservations are recommended.) This casual waterfront complex of rental cabins, dining room, lounge, float, and rental boats is popular with local residents and out-of-town visitors alike. Fishing is the watchword, from one of the rental boats or available fishing charters. Whether you arrive by boat or car, the food is excellent (try the prawns) and there is always something happening out at the dock.

In addition to the usual parade, Ketchikan puts on a ripsnorting *Logging Carnival* on the Fourth of July with such events as ax throwing, choker setting, powersaw bucking, ax chopping, and pole climbing. The contests are held in town (on Walker Field off Park Avenue) and they are superb entertainment for everyone. A lot of the fun for visitors is listening to the good advice shouted by the knowledgeable spectators. The combination of the parade, Logging Carnival, and evening fireworks display over Tongass Narrows recommends Ketchikan as a destination over the Fourth. Other annual Ketchikan celebrations include the *Festival of the North,* a winter arts and music gala; the *Great Alaska Sportfishing Championship,* a one-day fish-off between disc jockeys from radio stations across America (June); and the *Blueberry Festival* and street fair in August. Ketchikan's *King Salmon Derby* takes place over Memorial Day weekend and the two following weekends in June.

Ketchikan is the nearest departure point for plane or boat excursions

The ripsnorting Ketchikan Logging Carnival draws an enthusiastic Fourth of July crowd.

into *Misty Fiords National Monument*. "Misty," as the locals call it, lies roughly thirty miles east of Ketchikan: a 2.2 million-acre wilderness encompassing the east side of Revillagigedo Island and a portion of the mainland between Behm and Portland canals. The area was set aside for protection in 1978. Within the monument the deep fjords of Walker Cove and Rudyerd Bay penetrate the wilderness with sheer rock walls rising to three thousand feet. The untouched wilderness of Misty Fiords is accessible only by floatplane or boat. Wildlife is prevalent and the bays and coves offer good fishing, camping, photography, and wilderness exploration. The U.S. Forest Service maintains fourteen cabins within the monument that can be rented for fifteen dollars a night. Those on salt water have mooring buoys nearby. (For reservations and information write *Ketchikan Ranger Station, U.S. Forest Service, 3031 Tongass Avenue, Ketchikan, Alaska, 99901;* telephone *(907) 225-2148.*)

For many visitors, Misty Fiords is most conveniently viewed from the air. All of the air taxi services in Ketchikan offer flyover trips. The flight takes approximately an hour and a half. The pilot takes you down Tongass

The 2.2 million-acre Misty Fiords National Monument is a brief floatplane ride from Ketchikan. (U.S. Forest Service)

Narrows and up over Behm Canal. You may see purse seiners, eagles' nests, or mountain goats along the way. Once inside the monument, the pilot usually sets down in the upper reaches of one of the bays and shuts off the engine so that you can spend a few minutes appreciating the solitude of the mountain wilderness. Looking out at the alpinelike setting, you are likely to forget that you are still on salt water and ask the pilot how far above sea level you are. You will not be the first to be disoriented. At least one Ketchikan operator, Outdoor Alaska, offers combination cruise and flight tours into Misty Fiords. If you have a little more time at your disposal, going at least one way by boat will give you a more relaxed view of this spectacular corner of Southeast Alaska.

For those traveling the Inside Passage in private boats, the U.S. Forest Service has taken special care to provide safe moorage within the monument. There is a government dock and a buoy at Mantzanita Bay, and a number of anchor buoys have been placed within the monument. Contact the *Ketchikan Ranger Station, U.S. Forest Service, 3031 Tongass Avenue, Ketchikan, Alaksa, 99901,* for the latest information on boating and camping in Misty Fiords. Kayaking in Misty Fiords is increasingly popular—contact *Southeast Exposure, P.O. Box 9143, Ketchikan, Alaska, 99901*; telephone *(907) 225-8829*, for guided kayak trips into the monument. As always in wilderness Alaska, be extremely wary of bear, especially around salmon streams. There are brown bear in the area.

A last word of caution: you may not get blue skies for your trip to Misty Fiords. Misty earns its name and reputation by soaking up more than 150 inches of rain and snow a year.

WRANGELL
Population 2,400

Wrangell is a solid frontier town taking its time about entering the twentieth century. If it were not for the busy waterfront, the town could just as easily be a gold-mining camp in the mother lode country of California or a hamlet in Kansas or Missouri. You sense a strong spirit of independence in Wrangell. The false-fronted buildings along Front Street all have different shapes and designs. Each stands alone, aloof from the next. The streets are broad and paved. There are wide sidewalks—room to pass without jostling your neighbor and room to grow. Some of the spaciousness is due to the two devastating fires that have rampaged through the downtown business center. The more recent, in 1952, destroyed all of the waterfront side of Main Street, which at the time was built on pilings over the water. The burned-over area was subsequently closed with fill, but the devastation left a permanent gap along the waterfront.

Tugboats in Wrangell Harbor await the next assignment.

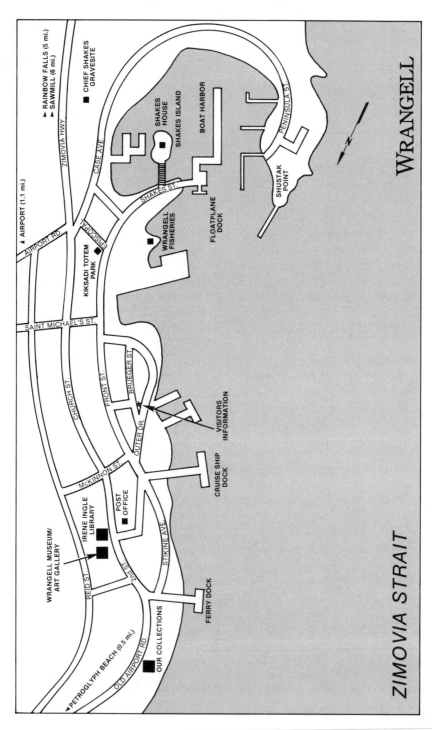

The false-fronted buildings along Front Street in Wrangell reflect a spirit of independence.

BACKGROUND

Wrangell's multinational history has been the direct result of the town's proximity to the swift-flowing Stikine River that reaches 330 miles from the Southeast mainland into British Columbia. Located on the northern tip of Wrangell Island, just seven miles from the river delta, Wrangell has been a terminus for river activity since the Tlingit Indians first used the Stikine to trade with the Athapaskans in the Interior.

At the time of the Russian occupation of Alaska, the Stikine delta and neighboring islands were the home of a powerful group of Tlingit Indian clans that came to be known as the Stikines. The chief of the Stikines was Shakes, the fourth in a succession of chiefs of that name. (The seventh and last Chief Shakes died in 1944.) His village, known as Kots-lit-na, was situated on Wrangell Island, approximately twenty miles to the south of the present town of Wrangell. About 1811, the Russians began trading with the Tlingit for the valuable furs such as beaver and land otter that were obtained up the Stikine.

The story of the modern settlement of Wrangell begins not with the Russians, however, but the British. In the early 1800s when the Russians were busy relocating their headquarters from Kodiak to Sitka, the British Hudson's Bay Company controlled the fur trade in Canada. They moved their posts farther and farther west until they reached the Pacific, where they ran smack up against the Russian-American Company in their bid for the Native fur trade. In 1825, the two countries signed treaties fixing the boundaries between Russian-America and Canada. The agreements gave the Hudson's Bay Company the right to use navigable Southeast streams to reach their posts in Canada, providing no Russian settlement stood in the way. Increasingly desirous of reaching the fur supply on the mainland just beyond the Russian coast, the Hudson's Bay Company decided to establish a post on the Stikine, which would give them easy access to the Interior and an easy exit to move the furs to market.

Before the British could set this plan in motion, the Russian-American Company got wind of the scheme. The Russians sent their own expedition, commanded by Captain-Lieutenant Dionysius Zarembo, to cut off the British from the Stikine trade by establishing their own fort at the river mouth. In 1833 they began building Redoubt Saint Dionysius (redoubt meaning fort) on the shore of a sheltered bay (now Wrangell Harbor) on the northern tip of Wrangell Island. The fort, the second non-Native settlement in Southeast Alaska, was named for Zarembo's patron saint. When the British arrived—too late—to build their own fort, they were met with a show of force and made to back down. The Russian flag was raised over Redoubt Saint Dionysius on 26 August 1834.

Once the crisis had passed, the British managed to get what they wanted anyway. In 1839 the Russian-American Company agreed to lease to the Hudson's Bay Company all of the mainland coast from Portland Canal at the southern border of Russian territory to Cape Spencer west of Glacier Bay for a period of ten years. The price was two thousand land otter skins annually, plus a quantity of provisions such as wheat and salt beef that were always in short supply. Under this arrangement, Redoubt Saint Dionysius passed into British hands and assumed the name Fort Stikine.

Under the British flag, the Stikine settlement became a major trading center for the neighboring Tlingit Indians. Chief Shakes had already moved his community from Kots-lit-na to the small harbor area now known as Shakes Island. Other clans lived nearby on Wrangell Island and on the mainland. In exchange for valuable furs, the Indians were given manufactured items that they wanted such as cloth and the rich wool Hudson's Bay Point blankets.

Fort Stikine was abandoned in 1849. When Alaska was sold to the United States in 1867, the trading settlement was received by the U.S. Army. Once again the name was changed, this time to Fort Wrangell for Baron Ferdinand von Wrangell, who had been the chief manager for the Russian-American Company from 1830 to 1836 when Redoubt Saint Dionysius was founded. The Army built new quarters on a rise near the site of the old fort. Fort Wrangell closed in the 1870s with all of the other army posts in Alaska except Sitka. Some of the buildings were purchased by a retired army supply officer who opened a trading post.

Wrangell was the jumping-off point for three different gold rushes to the Interior. In 1861 the Stikine strike, the first gold strike to affect Alaska, took prospectors upriver to a spot called Buck's Bar. Captain William Moore transported the prospectors from Wrangell to Buck's Bar aboard his steamer the *Flying Dutchman*. By the time the second wave of prospectors arrived in 1873 on their way to the new strikes in the Canadian Cassiar district, the non-Native population of Wrangell had dwindled to three. Once again the quiet outpost was transformed into a boomtown as fortune seekers geared for the trip into the wilderness, then spent their hard-won diggings on the way back out again. Wrangell was suddenly the busiest spot in the territory. An estimated three thousand people went up the Stikine and packed into the Cassiar in 1874. Three years later, the first mission school in Alaska was opened at Wrangell. By 1880, steamers ran directly to Wrangell from Portland and Victoria, British Columbia.

When the Cassiar rush ended, Wrangell subsided into inactivity once more. Historian Hubert Howe Bancroft reported in 1886 that the fort was deserted and the town "nearly so, except by Indians. . . . The main street is choked with decaying logs and stumps, and is passable only by a narrow plank sidewalk."

The town rebounded with the rush to the Klondike in 1898, as prospectors scrambled to get to Dawson in the shortest possible time. Some of them elected to follow the Stikine to Telegraph Creek and hike 160 miles overland to the headwaters of the Yukon. But by the time this strike had run its course, Wrangell had gained an economic toehold with two canneries and a sawmill.

These industries continue to dominate the economy. The number one industry in Wrangell today is lumber. Wrangell Forest Products operates the largest sawmill in Alaska, six miles south of town. The downtown harbor houses a sizable fleet of trollers, gill-netters, and seiners, plus a large cannery and cold storage plant and several smaller seafood processors. Besides salmon, they package halibut, crab, and the prized local shrimp, from salad size to beefy prawns.

Wrangell is a scrappy town. The community has stuck it out for more than a century, through good times and bad. Consider the *Wrangell Sentinel*. The newspaper started publication on 2 November 1902, and contines today—the oldest continuously published newspaper in Southeast.

GETTING THERE

So far, Wrangell has not been a regular stop on most cruise ship itineraries. This is changing, though, with the introduction of smaller and more maneuverable vessels that frequent the smaller Southeast ports. The Alaska state ferries do call at Wrangell on their way between Ketchikan and Petersburg (both northbound and south), and the ferry terminal is right in the center of town. The airport, with daily jet service to cities along the Seattle to Juneau route, is one and one-half miles north of town.

If you are traveling by ferry, it is well worth arranging your itinerary to get off for a day at Wrangell. There are comfortable accommodations both in town and out the road. The harborside Stikine Inn is unmatched for convenience and a spectacular setting, but bring your earplugs to stop the beat of the rock band that plays in the lounge at night or ask for a room in the new addition. *Harding's Old Sourdough Lodge* and the *Roadhouse Lodge* (mile 4 Zimovia Highway) are good alternatives.

TO SEE AND DO

Wrangell is so small that you can walk to all of the major attractions. Since the state ferry docks downtown, you can stroll through the community even if you are in port for only an hour or two. Whether you arrive at the state ferry terminal or the city dock, angle off to your right to Outer Drive and Brueger Street, where you will find the *Visitors' Information Center* in a small A-frame hut. There you can get a visitors' guide, brochures, and other information you need. The area toward the water is what is known as the "downtown fill area." This is the part of town that was filled in after the 1952 fire destroyed the waterfront side of Front Street that had been built on wooden pilings.

Front Street continues southward toward the boat harbor. You will pass old false-fronted wooden buildings, each painted a different color and design. Some show the founding date: "Biehl's, 1898," for example. At the intersection with Episcopal Street, you come to Wrangell's latest addition, pocketlike *Kiksadi Totem Park.* Four new totem poles, exact replicas of historic Wrangell-area carvings, stand in the tiny park surrounded by plantings of shrubs and trees. The *One-Legged Fisherman pole,* at the upper left of the park, represents a Tlingit myth about a supernatural being of the Eagle clan known as the one-legged fisherman (in the pole, however, he is given two legs). The one-legged fisherman used a magic harpoon to catch salmon, which he strung up on ropes, as shown in the carving. The original version of the tall pole at the front, the *Kiksadi pole,* was carved in the 1890s to honor a chief of the Kiksadi clan, whose crest figure, the Frog, appears near the top.

When you reach the end of Front Street, Shakes Street leads out to the harbor and the seafood-processing plants. On the way you will pass the Marine Lounge, which is the site of the original Russian fort, Saint Dionysius. A footbridge takes you to *Shakes Island*, a grassy compound of cottonwood and mountain ash trees with a replica of the Shakes community house and several totem poles.

Shakes House, like the community house at Totem Bight in Ketchikan, was constructed as part of the Civilian Conservation Corps's totem restoration project in the 1930s. In this case, the building was meant to be a replica of the house where the various Chiefs Shakes lived after the clan moved from Kots-lit-na. All of the lumber and support poles were hand-adzed to give the house an authentic look and, like the original dwellings, no nails were used in the construction. The green and black Bear totem framing the entrance was painted and carved on the interior screen in the original Shakes House.

Unfortunately, the interior of the house is not usually open to view. It is arranged in the traditional style with a central fire pit for cooking surrounded by two tiers of wooden platforms for sitting, sleeping, and storage, and has a smoke hole in the roof. A carved and painted wooden screen separates the chief's private quarters from the common room. Instead of the original Bear design, the screen is decorated with the design from a Chilkat blanket that belonged to the Shakes family. The interior houseposts were originals brought from the old village in the 1800s. Now more than two hundred years old, they have been removed for restoration and eventual display elsewhere

Shakes House is a replicated Tlingit community house of hand-adzed lumber and no nails. (John Schoen)

in Wrangell. Replicas have been carved to replace the originals in Shakes House. The Shakes Island house was dedicated at a great potlatch in 1940 that was attended by Indian leaders and other dignitaries from Southeast Alaska. The next chief in the Shakes line, Kudanake, age seventy-six, took the occasion to assume formally the title of Shakes VII, which he had never taken. He was the last of the Chiefs Shakes.

Besides the community house, Shakes Island houses several totem poles from the Wrangell area. Some of the poles belonged to the Shakes clan, while others were copied from poles owned by neighboring clans. The two short poles directly in front of the house at the left are replicas of memorial poles. If you go around behind them you can see the carved niches where the ashes of the deceased would have been placed.

The *Bear-up-the-Mountain pole* with bear prints leading to the Bear figure at the top, is similar to the Kats pole at Totem Bight but recalls a different story. This pole commemorates the ancestors of the Shakes family who were led up the highest peak in the area by a grizzly bear to escape the great flood. The clan took Bear as their crest and the pole symbolizes their tracks up the mountain to safety. The original version of this pole was a memorial to the younger brother of Chief Shakes VI.

To the left of the Bear-up-the-Mountain pole stands the *Gonakadet pole*. The original version of this pole contained the ashes of Chief Shakes VI's father and mother. The carving recalls the story of a young man who slew a legendary lake monster called Gonakadet. The youth found that by putting on the monster's skin he could swim under the lake waters indefinitely and catch salmon and halibut for his family to eat. However, he had to return each morning before the ravens called. One morning he failed to come home and his wife found him dead on the beach, still inside the monster's skin. From that day on, the village people called the youth by the name of Gonakadet. One night Gonakadet's wife heard him calling out to her to climb onto his back and hold on tight! She did as he bid and he took her to his home beneath the water. Gonakadet and his wife are seen only occasionally, but the sighting is always considered good luck.

Visitors are usually delighted by the *Three Frogs totem* that overlooks the boat harbor to the right of Shakes House. This pole, a copy of a ridicule pole that once stood in Wrangell, features three green Frog totems on top of a plain shaft. The story involves three women from the Kiksadi clan of Tlingit who married three of Chief Shakes's slaves. Shakes demanded that the Kiksadis pay him for the upkeep of the women since they were living with the Wrangell clan. The Kiksadi chief refused even to acknowledge their existence since they had disgraced the clan by marrying slaves, so Shakes erected the Three Frogs totem—Frog being the Kiksadi crest—to shame him into paying. There is a difference of opinion about what happened next: some say the Kiksadis never paid, and some say they did.

Stories of some of the other poles on Shakes Island are contained in a

The original version of the Three Frogs ridicule pole was erected to shame a Tlingit chief into paying a debt.

pamphlet entitled *The Authentic History of Shakes Island and Clan*, by E. L. Keithahn (Wrangell Historical Society). You can obtain a copy at the Wrangell Museum.

 Chief Shakes' gravesite is across the boat harbor from Shakes Island on the uphill side of Case Avenue. The plot is enclosed within a Russian-style picket fence with two Killer Whale totems on top. This is the grave of

Shakes V, who was head of the clan when the British occupied Wrangell and at the time of the American purchase. There is no need to walk up to the site as there is nothing to see beyond the Killer Whales and the fence except a pleasant grove of trees.

Back in the center of town, *Church Street*, not surprisingly, contains the community churches. The First Presbyterian Church is remarkable for a large, red, neon cross that shines for miles out to sea at night. The cross, erected in 1939, is used as a navigational light by local mariners. The church is the oldest American protestant church in Alaska, dating from the time of the first mission school in Wrangell. The building was founded in 1879, but was severely damaged by fire on two occasions. The structure has been extensively renovated. The Saint Rose of Lima Catholic Church next door is the oldest Roman Catholic parish in Alaska.

A few more yards along Church Street is the *Irene Ingle Public Library*. There are two totem poles in front and a small collection of petroglyphs beside them in the grass. These strange rock carvings, of undetermined age, have been found throughout Southeast Alaska. Archeologists have been unable to agree upon their significance, but many think they were a type of boundary marker. Some of the etched designs are clearly shaped like animals; others appear to be faces. Some just seem to be abstract scribbles. The clearest image among the library petroglyphs is in the left-hand group. If you look on the larger stone at the rear, you can easily make out two heart-shaped faces with large, round eyes. (The most extensive collection of petroglyphs in Wrangell is at the Petroglyph Beach north of town. See below.)

Rock carvings have been found in many locations in Southeast Alaska. They may have been primitive boundary markers.

The *Wrangell Museum*, next door to the library, is housed in the city's first schoolhouse, which was erected in 1906. The building has proved versatile through the years, hosting at various times the library, the morgue, a doctor's office, and city hall. The museum is operated by the Wrangell Historical Society and the collection is devoted to local Wrangell history. Of the Native artifacts, one of the most interesting pieces is a ceremonial Tlingit dance blanket depicting a Bear design made by a Wrangell woman more than thirty years ago. The Bear totem is outlined in abalone shell buttons and thousands of tiny beads. There are 232 buttons in the border alone.

Other notable items in the Native exhibit include some excellent carved wooden halibut hooks, cedar bark and spruce root baskets, and a small Tlingit canoe from the local area. If you have visited Shakes Island, you will want to look at the photo display of the original Shakes House and the last Chief Shakes, Shakes VII, attending the 1940 potlatch in his ceremonial regalia.

Equipment buffs will enjoy the communications room containing the old Campbell press that printed the *Wrangell Sentinel* until more modern equipment was installed in 1965. There is also a late-1800s linotype, an old letter press, and other pieces of machinery.

The main exhibit room contains an assortment of items connected with Wrangell and the surrounding territory, among them some small, lidded copper kettles of a type that the Hudson's Bay Company first sent to Canada around 1782. There is a Russian iron float of a type used to suspend fishing nets, a collection of old cameras, and a fabulous still that was found on a nearby island. I think my favorite item might be—and you will have to ask one of the staff members to unearth it and show you how it works—a collapsible wooden crate that came from Chas. Benjamin's store in Wrangell. Now there was a good idea.

There is a selection of local history and art books on sale in the lobby, as well as note cards, Wrangell garnets, and some gift items. Before leaving the museum building, duck into the *Wrangell Art Gallery* to shop for local art.

If you walk up the road from the ferry terminal and turn left on Stikine Avenue, following the sign to the petroglyphs, you can have a lovely stroll amidst typical Southeast trees and wild flowers (lots of forget-me-nots). The salmonberries bordering the road ripen in July, enabling you to nibble as you amble along. After a few minutes you will come to a barnlike building on your left with a sign that reads *Our Collections*. Our Collections is a hodgepodge of miscellanea that has been lovingly gathered and protected over a lifetime in Wrangell by Bolly and Elva Bigelow. Whether or not you should visit the Bigelows' private museum is a matter of personal inclination. To some, the Bigelows' barn is distressingly reminiscent of a garage in need of a cleaning. Others—the types that like to root around at garage sales—will wax poetic over the treadle and hand-crank sewing machines, old trapping gear, lanterns and binnacles, waffle irons, and copper wash kettles. My husband, for instance, was quite overcome by the cooperage tools—where else, says he, can you find a complete set of instruments expressly created for making barrels? You may get a charge out of the old costume jewelry or the valve off the *Matanuska*. Our Collections is memo-rabilia, curiosities, old things—in no particular rhyme or order. Be sure to corner the Bigelows and hear their story about whatever item captures your imagination.

Perhaps another five minutes beyond the Bigelow house is the *Petroglyph Beach*, one of the most unusual sights in Southeast. Scattered along the shore are perhaps forty different petroglyphs (no one knows exactly how many) within the space of a few yards. To get to the beach, start looking for the sign pointing to the petroglyphs just after you have passed a mobile home park on your right. A wooden boardwalk will take you from the road to the beach. The wooden planks are slippery in the rain, so wear beachcombing shoes and be careful.

You need a tide below the twelve-foot level to find the petroglyphs. They are not signed, so locating them is something like an Easter egg hunt. Here are some hints: when you get to the end of the boardwalk, turn to your right and walk along the beach, keeping you eyes on the rocks between you and the water. You will see lots of strange images looking back at you. Continue on until you come to a large rock outcropping and a shingled house. Walk straight toward the water from the rock outcropping, and you will see a spiral on a nearby rock. Look away to your right and you will see a big face. There are many more.

Hunting for petroglyphs makes a pleasurable family expedition. The mysterious images appear and disappear according to the light and whether the rocks are wet or dry. You may want to take paper and crayons with you and try some petroglyph rubbings. (Mark the paper, not the petroglyphs; the museum staff will tell you how.) Rice paper works best. Charcoal is not recommended because it gets very messy in the damp conditions. Some local residents use fern to make rubbings. Strip off the leaves, crush them into a ball, and rub them lightly over the paper. *Norris Gifts* and *Wrangell Drug* on Front Street sell rubbing supplies. If you do not have time for the Petroglyph Beach, you can make rubbings on the several petroglyphs in the Wrangell Museum.

The Stikine River is the playground for Wrangell residents. Since 1980 the river has been protected as part of the 443,000-acre *Stikine–Le Conte Wilderness* that takes in much of the mainland between Wrangell and Petersburg. There is plenty of wildlife, including moose, and good fishing, hunting, boating, and camping. Charter services are available to view the river by boat, river raft, or plane. You might even enjoy a dip at the Chief Shakes Hot Springs Recreation Area twelve miles up the river. The facilities, built by the forest service, include an enclosed wooden bathhouse

Bolly and Elva Bigelow show some of the collectibles they have garnered through the years.

in a forest glade, and an outdoor tub that overlooks a meadow of lupine and distant mountain range. Not surprisingly, the hot springs receive heavy local use in summer. The mosquitoes can be fierce, but the setting is spectacular.

A garnet ledge on the river delta produces semiprecious stones. The ledge was deeded to the children of Wrangell and the Boy Scouts of America by one of Wrangell's civic leaders many years ago. Others wishing to dig for garnets must pay a small fee. (Permits are sold at the Wrangell Museum.) Digging your own garnets is not necessary, though, as they are sold in local shops. It is more fun to buy them from local children who greet you at the ferry or cruise ship dock with muffin tins full of purple stones. Starting at twenty-five cents apiece, they are inexpensive and unusual souvenirs of your trip to Wrangell. (You can examine a chunk of the garnet ledge in the Wrangell Museum.) You can also arrange sightseeing trips to LeConte Glacier, about twenty-five miles north of Wrangell, and Anan Creek, thirty miles south, a prime bear-observation site. Plenty of fishing charters are available, too.

Like other small towns, Wrangell puts on a rousing down-home *Fourth of July celebration* with fireworks, loggers' rodeo, and parade. Local residents contend that Wrangell's loggers' contests are better than those of other communities because *real* loggers compete instead of professional contestants drawn by the prize money offered elsewhere. The "Wrangellites" also put on the *Tent City Winter Festival* on the first weekend in February to celebrate the role that Wrangell played in three gold rushes

Locating petroglyphs is like an Easter egg hunt. Clint Sturdevant, former assistant director of the museum, points one out.

and give residents some relief from the winter wearies. There is a food and craft fair and lighthearted contests such as beard-growing and tall tales. The Wrangell *King Salmon Derby* takes place in May.

PETERSBURG
Population 3,300

Petersburg is set apart from other Southeast communities by a deeply felt Norwegian heritage. The townspeople celebrate their Scandinavian origins during the renowned Little Norway Festival that takes place annually on Norwegian Independence Day and in the attractive *rosemaling* (traditional Norwegian tole painting in floral design) that is patiently applied to shop fronts on Nordic Drive.

The other thing that distinguishes Petersburg from other Southeast communities is a predilection for business. This is a cannery town. With four seafood processing plants, and the largest home-based halibut fleet in Southeast, fish and fishing are the dominant themes.

Except for the Little Norway Festival, there is little activity planned around tourists in Petersburg. You will find a friendly but businesslike atmosphere with hardworking residents who are intent upon capitalizing on the present rather than falling back upon the past. Nevertheless, Petersburg can be disarmingly casual. It is the only place I have ever rented a car without filling out any paperwork.

BACKGROUND

Petersburg is situated on the extreme northern tip of Mitkof Island. It is the last stop on the Marine Highway line before reaching Juneau, northbound, and the prize that awaits mariners who have navigated the twenty-one-mile Wrangell Narrows.

The town was founded by Peter Buschmann, who migrated from Norway to Tacoma, Washington, with his wife and eight children in 1891. Six years later, he was homesteading a site along Wrangell Narrows that showed potential for a year-round fish-processing industry. Not only were both salmon and halibut in abundance, but there was a natural harbor, timber to build with, and a ready supply of ice from the Le Conte Glacier just twenty-five miles away.

Other Norwegians followed Buschmann to his spot on Wrangell Narrows and they set to work developing a neat, well-planned, Scandinavian-style community. By 1900 the Icy Straits Packing Company, with Buschmann as manager, had put in a sawmill, wharf, warehouses, bunkhouses, and a store, as well as packed 32,750 cases of salmon. The fishermen brought in salmon for the cannery in the summer and fall and went after

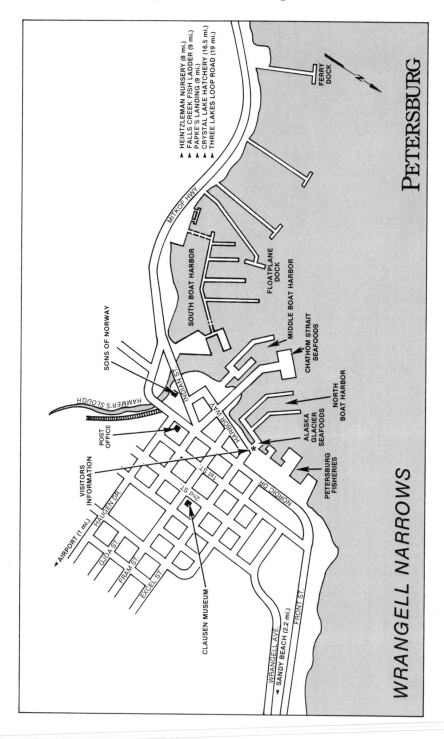

halibut in the winter. Peter Buschmann's new community, called Petersburg, grew into a stable, year-round enterprise, in contrast to the mining towns that were subject to cycles of boom-and-bust.

The salmon industry was successful, but it was halibut that put Petersburg on the map. The fine white fish was much in demand for East Coast markets. Fresh halibut could be packed in glacier ice, shipped by steamer to Seattle, and forwarded to the East without spoiling. (The criteria for spoilage were perhaps a little different in those days.) Petersburg emerged as the halibut capital of Alaska and retains the title today.

At the height of the cannery era, as many as eight seafood-processing plants operated simultaneously in Petersburg. While the volume has subsided somewhat, Petersburg is still the major fish-processing community in Southeast, with four processing plants and a reduction plant that produces fish meal from scraps. Petersburg Fisheries, Buschmann's old company, has operated continuously since its founding and is now a subsidiary of Icicle Seafoods. Besides salmon and halibut, the town processes crab, herring, and the tiny, delectable Petersburg shrimp that are fished within a twenty-five-mile radius of town. Petersburg ships 150,000 pounds of shrimp to market annually.

Timber is the second important industry. Twenty-five million board feet of spruce, hemlock, and cedar are harvested each year from nearby lands. Timber is also *grown* in Petersburg at a U.S. Forest Service nursery south of town.

GETTING THERE

As with all Inside Passage communities except Haines, Skagway, and Hyder, access is by water or air only. The trip between Wrangell and Petersburg via the twenty-one-mile Wrangell Narrows is among the most exciting legs of the Marine Highway. Alaska State Ferries make the trip regularly on the north to south run. The ferry terminal is about one mile south of town— too far to walk with anything but the merest wisp of a suitcase. Only some of the smaller "exploration class" cruise ships currently include Petersburg in the Southeast itinerary. They dock right downtown at one of the boat harbors. There is daily jet service between Petersburg and other Southeast communities with connections to the rest of Alaska and the Lower 48.

TO SEE AND DO

Petersburg is an artist's delight, whether the medium is oils, watercolors, or color film. So many images leap to the eye, from kerchiefed cannery workers in tall rubber boots to old wooden buildings reflected in Hammer's Slough. Just stroll about town and take in the boat harbors and

A boatload of Dungeness crab arrives at the Petersburg Fisheries dock. Petersburg is still a major fish-processing community.

halibut fleet, canneries, rosemalinged store- and housefronts, and the natural scenery of Wrangell Narrows. Even the sidewalks are decorated with inset brass designs. Stop in at the *Chamber of Commerce Information Center* at Harbor Way and Excel streets and pick up a town map. Petersburg streets have recently been renamed for famous old boats of the commercial fishing fleet.

At the north end of town are the fish-processing plants of Petersburg Fisheries (Buschmann's old company). No tours are available at any of the canneries, but there is plenty of activity outside. You should walk past Petersburg Fisheries and far enough around the bend to the north to see Wrangell Narrows opening up into Frederick Sound.

Toward the south end of town are the boat harbors, *Chatham Strait Seafoods*, and *Hammer's Slough*, a small saltwater inlet lined with stilt-houses along a narrow, wood-planked street. The *Sons of Norway Hall* at the entrance to the slough was begun by Peter Buschmann in 1897 and completed in 1912. The enormous barnlike structure, painted white with red rosemalinged shutters, stands on pilings above the slough and is one of the most photographed buildings in Petersburg. *Husfliden*, upstairs, sells Norwegian imports and local arts and crafts, including expert rosemaling by Naomi Welde, the manager. The local chapter of the International Sons

Weathered houses on stilts line the shore of Hammer's Slough, where the street is still planked with wood.

of Norway organization is still helping to preserve Petersburg's Norwegian heritage. *Helse,* a restaurant and natural foods store at Sing Lee Alley and Harbor Way, serves homemade soup and bread, huge cinnamon rolls, sandwiches, and the like to popular acclaim.

The *Clausen Memorial Museum* (Second and Fram streets) is most notable for its heritage of the sea room that is dedicated to fish and fishing. There hangs the world record king salmon (estimated weight 126.5 pounds) that was caught in a fish trap off Prince of Wales Island in 1939. The salmon was cleaned before weighing so the record weight can only be estimated. The record chum salmon is here, too, weighing in at 36 pounds.

The museum excels at illustrating the workings of commercial fishing gear. You will come away understanding the differences between long-lining, trolling, trawling, gillnetting, and seining. There is a model fish trap, a commercial crab pot, old cotton and linen fishing nets, canning equipment dating from the days when cans were soldered shut, a couple of early model outboard engines, and the original lens from the Cape Decision lighthouse. The lens was in place between 1932 and 1968 when it was replaced by a rotating beacon. Another exhibit contains tools used in fox farming, an important cottage industry in Southeast during the 1920s.

The outer room of the Clausen Museum is devoted to early

Petersburg, beginning with photos of Peter Buschmann and his wife Petra and some of their possessions. Those who enjoy cross-country skiing on to-day's lightweight equipment should take a look at the incredibly long and wide handmade skis dating from 1920. The rest of the collection consists of assorted paraphernalia that found its way into the community in earlier times. I enjoyed looking over the old-fashioned collars and collar buttons, ladies' high-top shoes, and a wooden hat stretcher—things that are not around today.

Even if you do not go into the museum, walk up to the building to see the *Fisk* (Norwegian for "fish"), an eleven-foot bronze fountain sculpture of halibut, salmon, and herring that has come to be regarded as the symbol of Petersburg. The sculpture was created by artist Carson Boysen for the 1967 Alaska Centennial as a celebration of all Southeast fish. A similar theme inspired the *wood and copper mural* on the outside wall of the museum, a community project organized by the Petersburg Arts and Crafts Guild in 1977. Do not be surprised if you see a strange-looking boat as you wander around town. It is the *Valhalla,* a Viking ship that puts to sea in May of each year for the Little Norway Festival (see below). The *Valhalla* was built in 1976 to welcome the Tall ships sailing into New York for the nation's Bicentennial celebration. The citizens of Petersburg later purchased the vessel for their community.

If you have a free afternoon in Petersburg, rent a car and drive out *Mitkof Highway.* The road extends to the south along Wrangell Narrows, past the seafood-processing plants and the Alaska state ferry terminal, to mile 34. At mile 9 is the *Frank Heintzleman Nursery,* a U.S. Forest Service tree farm that produces up to one million Sitka spruce seedlings a year for use in reforestation projects throughout Alaska. (B. Frank Heintzleman was a longtime regional forester for Alaska and governor of the territory from 1953 to 1957. Heintzleman Ridge near Juneau is also named for him.) The nursery has no official visitor program, but you are welcome to go out and look around. The facility engages in research related to reforestation in dif-ferent regions of Alaska and elsewhere in the world. Scotland, which lies on nearly the same latitude as Southeast Alaska, was one of the first users of Sitka spruce seedlings for reforestation because the species grows fast and is hardy. The Heintzleman Nursery progeny have a survival rate of more than 90 percent.

At approximately mile 10 on the right side of the highway is the *Falls Creek Fish Ladder.* Stairs lead from the parking area to a bridge from which you can watch migrating coho and pink salmon maneuver upstream in late summer and fall. Just past the sign to the fish ladder, look for another road on the right leading off to *Papke's Landing,* a favorite recreation spot overlooking Wrangell Narrows. There is a state float and boat launch ramp there and the entrance road is a riot of fireweed and other wild flowers in July. Kupreanof Island is only a few yards away. Papke's Landing is

An abandoned building overlooks Wrangell Narrows not far outside of Petersburg.

named for Herman Papke who homesteaded the site in 1903. "Ol' Man Papke" lived alone in his log cabin, raised a bountiful garden, and observed the happenings around him, which he recorded every day in his diary for some sixty years. He died in 1964—among the most beloved of men and definitely not forgotten.

At approximately mile 14, a planked forest service trail takes you a third of a mile across the muskeg to *Blind River Rapids,* a beautiful spot with excellent king salmon fishing in July, coho in late August and September, and cutthroat and Dolly Varden in late summer and fall. Two miles farther south, you will see a sign for the *Trumpeter Swan Observatory,* a simple blind situated to overlook Blind Slough. One of the northernmost wintering areas for swans, Blind Slough attracts 50 to 120 trumpeters during the period between late October and April. As well, an estimated 1,000 swans stop over during their southward migration to other wintering grounds along the northwest coast. The *Crystal Lake Hatchery* at mile 17.5 is the largest state-run hatchery in Alaska, producing over a million king salmon and hundreds of thousands of coho, chum, and steelhead annually in the outdoor rearing pens. Visitors are welcome.

You can have a close-up view of the aftermath of logging by taking the *Three Lakes Loop Road* that leaves Mitkof Highway to the north at mile 20 and loops around through hills and forest to rejoin the highway near Papke's Landing. This road is essentially a logging road, giving access to

The Beachcomber Inn is the site of a former cannery. Its restaurant specializes in fresh local seafood.

the lands being harvested in the Three Lakes region. The U.S. Forest Service maintains the road to provide recreational access into the region and provide a model for demonstrating the effects of clear-cutting. As you drive along the road, you will observe some areas that have been cut recently and others that were logged in the 1960s and 70s.

The area is named for three large freshwater lakes (Sand, Hill, and Crane lakes) that lie within a half-mile of the road. All are stocked with cutthroat trout. In winter, Petersburg residents frequent the lakes region for ice fishing, snowmobiling, and cross-country skiing. Three Lakes Loop Road winds you through some beautiful off-road country (not all of it has been logged) with vistas of spruce, hemlock, wild flowers, and water. Enjoy a picnic, or hike; take some photographs and watch the wildlife. Be forewarned that this is a working logging road—unpaved and extremely narrow in places. Go slowly and if you meet a logging truck, give way. Before you go, pick up a U.S. Forest Service brochure and map of the Three Lakes Loop Road at the district ranger's office (located in the Federal Building on Nordic Drive).

On your way back to town, consider stopping at the *Beachcomber Inn* for a meal of local seafood (especially Petersburg shrimp). Located on the waterfront at mile 4, the hotel and restaurant complex is the site of the former Scow Bay Packing Company cannery that closed in 1953. There is a boat and seaplane dock, and plenty to watch from the restaurant windows.

North of Petersburg, Mitkof Highway leads to the *Sandy Beach picnic area* (look for petroglyphs at low tide on the left) and to the garbage dump, where you might spot some scavenging bears.

The *Le Conte Glacier*, twenty-five miles east of Petersburg on the mainland, is the southernmost tidewater glacier in North America. It flows into Frederick Sound from the Stikine Ice Field in the Coast Mountains and is very active, producing a continuous crop of icebergs at the mile-wide face. Although the Le Conte is moving quickly, the glacier is in a state of equilibrium at the present time—neither advancing overall nor retreating. Boat, floatplane, and helicopter excursions to the glacier are readily available from Petersburg and are a good way to view some wildlife as well, as Le Conte Bay is home to two thousand harbor seals.

Petersburg is known throughout Alaska for the *Little Norway Festival* held every year on the weekend closest to 17 May, Norwegian Independence Day. Visitors from all over Southeast put everything aside on that weekend in order to get to Petersburg and enjoy the folk dancing, costumes, halibut-filleting contests, "Viking raids" that spirit the unsuspecting off to the *Valhalla*, and—best of all—the food that is prepared by all the good Norwegian cooks in town. The tables groan under the weight of fish cakes, fish puddings, gravadlox, lutefisk, and an incredible array of Norwegian desserts. There is also a salmon bake at Sandy Beach. If you can make the festival you will see Petersburg's Norwegian heritage in full sway. The *Petersburg Salmon Derby* is held over two weekends in June. The community salutes American Independence Day with an old-fashioned *Fourth of July*.

SITKA
Population 8,200

As a tourist destination Sitka enjoys an unfair advantage over other Southeast cities. The setting is unbelievably spectacular, from the countless forested islands that bob and weave upon Sitka Sound to the perfectly symmetrical cone of Mount Edgecumbe that rises to the west. Then there is the exotic Russian heritage, the fabulous totem park, and the attractive city center that corrals all of the important sights within easy walking distance of the harbor. Even the lodgings have a touch of the extraordinary. Where else but Sitka can you book a stay in an operational lighthouse on a private island?

The Sitkans have put their Russian pedigree to good advantage, from their widely acclaimed Russian dance troupe to tunicked bus drivers who meet the ferries. The Russian influence is most apparent in Saint Michael's Russian Orthodox Cathedral in the heart of town. Orthodox crosses in the old Russian graveyard and blackened cannons on Castle Hill are other

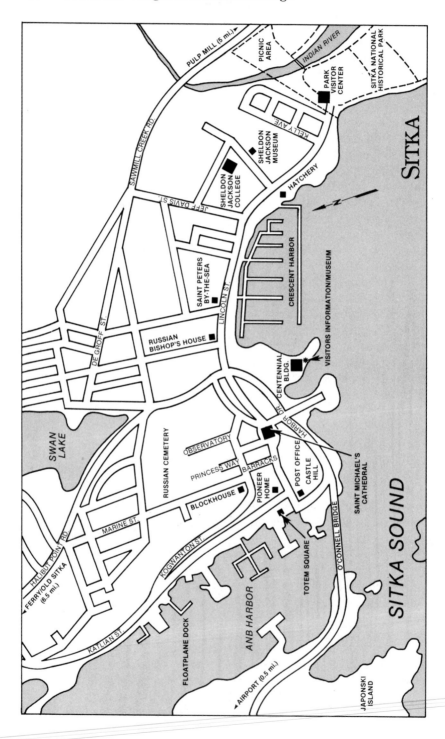

relics of a foreign heritage.

Sitka takes pride in being a cultural center and college town. There are two colleges, two museums, bookstores and galleries, and a national historic park containing one of the largest exhibitions of Tlingit and Haida totem poles in existence. The annual summer music festival unites outstanding musicians from all corners of the United States and abroad. The town is growing in an appealing manner, too. The ninety-seven-room Shee Atika Lodge constructed by the Sitka urban Native corporation (now a Westmark Hotel) dominates the downtown scene and is one of the brightest stars in the Southeast hotel galaxy with quiet rooms, plush furnishings, a good restaurant, and interior decor that takes advantage of Native motifs. (Do not let them put you in the leaky tomb of the "annex," though.)

BACKGROUND

Sitka is situated on the west coast of Baranof Island on Sitka Sound, a body of water that faces the open Pacific. The site of the Russian capital after 1804, the town is the oldest non-Native settlement in Southeast. Sitka was home to a community of Tlingit Indians prior to the Russian arrival. When Alexander Baranof, chief manager of the Russian-American Company, decided to move the Russian headquarters from Kodiak in 1799, he bargained with the local Tlingit chief for ground for a fort. The completed post, consisting of various outbuildings enclosed within a wooden stockade, was located six miles north of the present town and called Saint Archangel Michael.

The Tlingit grew increasingly hostile toward the Russians and the Aleut hunters they brought with them from Kodiak. Armed with guns and ammunition received from English and American traders in the area, they attacked the fort on a Sunday in June of 1802, burned the buildings, and killed all of the occupants except the few who managed to escape into the woods to take refuge aboard foreign trading vessels in Sitka Sound.

Baranof, who was away at Kodiak at the time of the massacre, immediately began making plans to retake Saint Archangel Michael. The battle was joined in September 1804, the Tlingit making their stand from a wooden stronghold near the beach at Indian River (the site of the present-day historical park), and the Russians bombarding with cannons. After several days of negotiations, interspersed with shelling, the Tlingit abandoned the site and retreated northward to Chichagof Island. The Russians built a new settlement where Sitka is located today, calling it New Archangel. By the following spring they had completed eight buildings within a wooden stockade and cleared land for gardens and livestock. Shipyards were established two years later.

The Sitka Indians were allowed to return to Baranof Island in 1821.

They rebuilt their homes around the Russian encampment, outnumbering the colonists about three to one. The Russians were in constant fear of another uprising, but their food supplies were low, and they depended upon the Tlingit to exercise their superior hunting skills and provide meat to be purchased for the table.

New Archangel reached the height of activity and stability in the 1840s and 1850s. Besides the fur business, the settlement bustled with ship-building and repair facilities, sawmills, a forge and foundry, salmon saltery, and even an ice industry that shipped blocks of lake ice to California markets. The colony expanded to include schools, a hospital, library, club-house, and Saint Michael's Cathedral. The crowning jewel was the gover-nor's residence built at the top of a hill overlooking the harbor. A seal oil beacon was kept burning in the cupola window, and a three-foot diameter reflector projected the light six miles out to sea to guide mariners into the harbor. This was the first lighthouse on the Alaska coast. The interior, fur-nished with fine European furniture, rugs, paintings and a library, was con-sidered a haven of culture and enlightenment for European traders who plied the barren waters of the North Pacific coast. Although rebuilt many times, the structure came to be known as Baranof's Castle and the hilltop site as Castle Hill. Today, Castle Hill remains a monument to the Russian colony, but the last castle burned down in 1894.

When the fur trade declined, the Alaska colonies became expensive to maintain. With both British and American traders threatening the Russian prerogative, the political situation was uncomfortable and renewal of the Russian-American company charter was in question besides. Russia de-cided to give up Alaska, and in October of 1867 the Russian flag was lowered from Castle Hill and the American flag raised in its place. The Americans changed the name of the community to Sitka, a derivation of the Tlingit word for their forested island by the sea.

The years following the Russian departure were lean ones for Sitka. Employment centered around the sawmill, which operated intermittently, and fishing. Sitka was the site of one of the first two salmon canneries built in Alaska in 1878 (the other was at Klawock on Prince of Wales Island). The plant folded after two years, however, and Sitka did not become a suc-cessful fish-processing center until after the turn of the century.

The gold rush caught up to the community at about the same time. Prospectors had been poking around Baranof Island, like other places, and there were attempts at lode mining in the vicinity as early as 1871. A rush to Sitka followed the discovery of gold-bearing quartz at Stewart Ledge on Silver Bay, slightly southeast of Sitka. In 1879, George Pilz built Alaska's first stamp mill on the Stewart claim. (Pilz would also finance the two vaga-bond prospectors who located the Juneau lode the following year.) In the years that followed, other mining efforts were made on nearby Chichagof Island. The two biggest Chichagof gold mines produced consistently until

World War II closed them down. Gypsum was also mined on Chichagof for a seventeen-year period beginning in 1906.

A mission school opened in 1878 under the auspices of the United Presbyterian church and evolved into an industrial trade school for Native students. The school continues today as Sheldon Jackson College, a private two-year institution specializing in fisheries management, forestry, wildlife management, and other Alaska fields of interest. The college is named for Dr. Sheldon Jackson who, as general agent for education in Alaska's infancy, is credited with establishing the state's school system. With the founding of Sheldon Jackson College, Sitka was on the way to reestablishing itself as a cultural center, but in 1906 the capital of Alaska was transferred to Juneau where the predominant gold-mining activity had centered.

The whaling industry moved onto Baranof Island in 1912 when the U.S. Whaling Company established a shore station at Port Armstrong on the south end of the island. Using a fleet of three modern "killing boats" with bow-mounted harpoons, the company harvested 314 whales the first year. The station processed the entire carcass, extracting oil and turning leftovers into fertilizer. When the whaling operation ceased in 1923, the Port Armstrong facility continued as a herring reduction plant.

The next surge of development came with the military in the late 1930s, when a U.S. naval air station was built on Japonski Island, across Sitka Harbor from the city. World War II brought an army fort as well, and suddenly Sitka was host to thirty thousand military personnel and seven thousand civilians. After the war the naval station was converted to the Bureau of Indian Affairs's Mount Edgecumbe boarding school to accommodate Native high school students from all over Alaska. Since 1972, the facilities on Japonski Island (which also include the Sitka airport), have been brought within easy reach by the 1,225-foot O'Connell Bridge from Sitka.

Today Sitka's economy is supported by two colleges (Sheldon Jackson College and Islands College), tourism, commercial fishing and fish processing, and timber. Besides housing a sizable commercial fishing fleet, the town has two fish-processing plants, the newest a cold storage facility built in 1980 to process salmon, black cod, herring, and halibut. The seventy-million-dollar Alaska Pulp Corporation mill was built six miles east of town at Silver Bay in 1960 to produce a high-grade dissolving pulp for industrial use. A small sawmill is in operation as well.

GETTING THERE

Sitka figures in most cruise ship itineraries. The vessels usually run down the outside coast of Baranof Island after visiting Glacier Bay and anchor in Sitka Harbor opposite town. Alaska state ferries dock at the Marine Highway terminal seven miles north of town near Old Sitka, the site of the first Russian settlement. Sitka is also serviced by jet aircraft on the Seattle to Juneau route. The airport is located on Japonski Island, across O'Connell Bridge from the downtown area.

TO SEE AND DO

Your first destination should be the *Sitka Visitors' Bureau* in the Centennial Building (overlooking Sitka Sound near the cruise ship embarkation point) for maps, brochures, and other information. While you are in the building, take a turn through the *Isabel Miller Museum*, which is devoted to items from local history. Of particular interest is an extensive scale model of Sitka that shows how the community looked during the Russian era. Exhibits from the Russian tenancy include ice saws that were used to cut blocks of ice from Swan Lake for shipment to San Francisco during the gold rush, and some tables and a desk handmade by Bishop Innocent Veniaminov who was head of the Russian Orthodox church in Alaska and responsible for building the original Sitka cathedral.

Representing the transfer from Russian to American ownership are copies of documents pertaining to the purchase agreement and a copy of the warrant for $7.2 million (the original is in the Smithsonian Institute in Washington, D.C.). Other displays feature enterprises of later years including fishing, logging, and gold mining (note the mold for forming gold bricks). Children will enjoy examining the extensive collection of Southeast seashells.

At the other end of the Centennial Building, members of the *Baranof Arts and Crafts Association* proffer a selection of recent work. Here is an opportunity to meet some Sitka artists and shop for local art. There is also a *wildlife display* of bald eagles, sea otters, fur seals, beaver, Arctic fox, and other fur-bearing animals and pelts. Outside the building is a fifty-foot ceremonial canoe carved by local woodworker George Benson for the Alaska Purchase Centennial commemoration in 1967. The canoe was hollowed from a single, seventy-foot red cedar log that was towed to Sitka from Port Renfrew, British Columbia, behind a fishing boat. The painted totemic designs represent Eagle and Raven. On one side of the canoe Eagle is on the prow and Raven on the stern. The order is reversed on the opposite side.

Leaving the Centennial Building with map in hand, take a stroll through town. The main thoroughfare is Lincoln Street. You pass an array of enticing gift shops and galleries. *Old Harbor Books, Impressions,* and *Artists' Cove Gallery* are especially worth your while. *Calico Cross Stitch* (223 Lincoln Street) sells counted cross-stitch and needlepoint patterns developed by Sitka residents Gail Sohornak and Sandy Greba, whose designs feature Southeast wild flowers and wildlife and other locally inspired themes. Check out the *Russian-American Company* in the Bayview Trading Company (407

Lincoln Street) for carved wooden toys, amber necklaces, wool shawls, lacquerware, and other Russian imports; then backtrack to *The Coffee Express* (327 Seward Mall, at the *back* of the building) for a restorative brew from the espresso machine, and perhaps a muffin (blueberry, peach, rhubarb. . .), sticky pecan roll, or sandwich.

Saint Michael's Russian Orthodox Cathedral, which straddles Lincoln Street, is a replica of the original cathedral that was built on the site between 1844 and 1848. In 1966 the old church was destroyed by a fire that swept through the business district. The townspeople rushed in and managed to save almost all of the precious icons and other furnishings that had been brought from Russia in the early days of the church. The cathedral was rebuilt in 1976 from original blueprints.

Saint Michael's is a cathedral built on a human scale—not for Sitka the echoing edifice of a Saint Peter's or a Notre Dame. The architecture is a mixture of bulbous onion dome and delicate spire, a combination of styles that was common around Saint Petersburg at the time of the Russian occupation. The interior walls are covered with natural-colored canvas (originally sailcloth). The dome is painted sky blue on the inside and the windows set around the top flood this artificial heaven with natural light.

The cathedral is a showcase of icons (sacred images or paintings) brought to Alaska from Russia. The two most prized are Our Lady of Sitka, familiarly known as the Sitka Madonna, and Christ Pantocrator (Christ the Judge or Christ Omnipotent) that flank the doors of the altar screen. Both paintings are attributed to Vladimir Borovikovsky, a leading eighteenth-century portrait artist and one of Russia's most revered masters. The Sitka Madonna, the oldest of the icons and thought to have been the gift of the Russian-American Company employees, is regarded by many faithful as a miraculous healer and protectress. At Saturday evening services, letters are read from faithful the world over petitioning the Sitka Madonna to intercede on their behalf. The painting, of a gentle-faced madonna holding the Christ Child, is oil on canvas overlaid with a heavy silver gilt *riza*. The *riza*, or metal overlay, became common in seventeenth-century Russia as a means of honoring and protecting the sacred image. In some cases the beautiful carved and sculpted *riza* is so extensive that the painting underneath is all but obscured. Another famous icon is Saint Michael the Archangel, patron saint of the cathedral. This icon was brought to Sitka in 1816 by the first ordained priest.

Besides the fine collection of icons, the cathedral contains other objects of interest to visitors. The carved and painted doors in the altar screen are from the original church. Also note the silver gilt wedding crowns dating from 1866, Bishop Innocent Veniaminov's pearl-encrusted miter, gospels encased with silver and other metals and studded with clear Siberian topaz, and the silver gilt tabernacle modeled after the cathedral. The tabernacle, thirteen inches high with cloisonné cupola and steeple, was presented to

Sitka's Saint Michael's Cathedral is a prominent reminder of the Russian influence.

The carved doors of the altar screen are part of the original furnishings brought from Russia.

the church in 1904.

Saint Michael's Cathedral is the seat of the Russian Orthodox church in Alaska; the bishop travels from Sitka to parish churches throughout the state. The cathedral is a working church with regular services, to which visitors are always welcome.

Continuing along Lincoln Street, you will come to *Castle Hill* overlooking Sitka Sound to your left. A path beside the post office leads to the top. Castle Hill was the site of a Tlingit Indian village when Alexander Baranof reestablished the Russian fort in 1804. The Russians destroyed the Indian houses and built their own quarters with the manager's residence at the top. In time the residence came to be known as Baranof's Castle and the hilltop site as Castle Hill. The castle was rebuilt twice before fire destroyed the structure completely in 1894.

On 18 October 1867, Castle Hill was the site of transfer ceremonies between Russia and the United States as the Russian flag came down and the Stars and Stripes was raised in its place. The transfer is reenacted at the site every 18 October as part of the Alaska Day celebration. Several Russian cannons still guard the hilltop (note the double-eagle insignia) and historic markers explain the significance of Castle Hill. It is well worth making the short trek to the top for the sweeping view over Sitka Sound.

Across Lincoln Street is the handsome red-roofed *Pioneer Home*, a state-supported residence and medical care facility for Alaska's longtime residents. There are several Pioneer Homes in the state. Sitka's, built in

1934, was the first. The thirteen and one-half-foot bronze statue of a prospector in front of the home was created by Alonzo Victor Lewis in 1949.
The residents and staff of the Pioneer Home welcome visitors. They are
especially proud of their gardens, which are devoted to native Alaska
plants, and a basement shop, which features handicrafts made by residents. *Totem Square*, an expanse of park across Katlian Street from the
Pioneer Home, contains a Russian cannon and three old anchors recovered
from the Sitka vicinity in 1950. They are believed to be of English origin
prior to 1800 and probably were lost by early British or American explorers. The totem pole, designed by local carver George Benson in 1940,
displays the double-headed eagle of Sitka's Russian heritage.

Angling to your right along the waterfront, you come to one of Sitka's
several commercial boat harbors. Continue on Katlian Street to *Taranoff's
Sitkakwan Shop* to shop for Alaskan art and craft items and unusual finds
such as antique Russian necklaces, plus a look at Taranoff's private collection of Northwest Indian artifacts. Larry Taranoff is a master silversmith
producing bracelets and rings of distinctive design. His production is
limited but he will take your order for future delivery. Along the same
street, which winds through the old Indian village, you will find *The Observatory*, specializing in old and new Alaska books, maps, and prints.

Tucked back among the fish-processing plants and marine supply
stores that line the harbor you will find *Compass Rose Maps,* which stocks
charts of the local waters, and *The Fresh Fish Company,* selling gift packs
of canned smoked salmon and halibut in addition to a variety of fresh,
frozen, and vacuum-packed local seafoods. Another five minutes of walking takes you to an excellent meal at *Wild Strawberry* (724 Siginaka Way—
behind the forest service building), where a typical dinner menu includes
Parmesan rockfish or chicken with apricots and currants.

Other Russian sights in the city include a replica of a wooden *blockhouse* of a type the Russians built to guard their stockade. Originally three
such blockhouses stood sentry along the wall (which extended roughly
from the site of the Sheffield House to Swan Lake) separating the Indian
village from the Russian community. The blockhouse is adjacent to the
Russian cemetery where you will find old headstones and Orthodox crosses.
The only original Russian building still standing in Sitka is the *Russian
Bishop's House* on Lincoln Street at the opposite end of town from Totem
Square. The Bishop's House—the oldest building in Alaska that has not
been significantly altered and one of the few remaining Russian log structures in Alaska—was built in 1842 by the Russian-American Company to
house the first bishop of the Russian Orthodox church. The church continued to use the facility until 1972. Now owned by the National Park Service, the Bishop's House is undergoing thorough restoration as part of
Sitka National Historical Park. When complete, the structure will house a
museum pertaining to Russia's presence in Alaska. Visitors will also be

The red-roofed Sitka Pioneer Home was the first of Alaska's state-supported care facilities for longtime residents.

able to tour the Bishop's office, private apartments, chapel, and other rooms, restored to their 1850s appearance.

A grassy esplanade takes you the short distance along Crescent Boat Harbor to Sheldon Jackson College and the main portion of Sitka National Historical Park. Just past the Russian Bishop's House you will come to the stone and brown-shingled *Saint Peters-by-the-Sea* Episcopal Church. The parish church was built by the Right Reverend Peter Trimble Rowe in 1899. A few more steps bring you to the college campus. The octagonal *Sheldon Jackson Museum* was built in 1895 as a repository for the articles that Dr. Sheldon Jackson collected in remote areas of Alaska during his travels as general agent for education. The collection of Alaskan Indian, Eskimo, and Aleut artifacts is one of the most important in the world. When you walk through the door, look up. On top of the display cases and suspended from the ceiling are examples of all the different kinds of sled and boat used in Alaska, from dogsleds and reindeer sleds to kayaks, umiaks, and canoes.

The Eskimo and Aleut exhibits are to your left as you enter the museum. If time is limited, I would recommend you start here as they include many items you will not see elsewhere. Some of the most intriguing are ceremonial masks, including finger masks that the women used for dancing; fishing flies made of stone, bone, and sinew or baleen; bentwood sunshades for kayaking; waterproof clothing of walrus intestine and salmon skin; and a man's ivory-decorated workbox with a set of tools for making nets.

To the right of the entrance are Tlingit and Haida exhibits, among them a notable collection of argillite carved by the Haida, a display of Tlingit feast dishes, beautiful bentwood boxes, baskets of every type, and an old Chilkat blanket and pattern board. A truly one-of-a-kind item is the Raven's head helmet worn by Sitka Chief Katlean during the battle with

The Sheldon Jackson Museum has a rich collection of Native artifacts, including carved wooden masks.

the Russians in 1804.

Other exhibits feature items from Russian-America, and two of the oldest totem poles left in Alaska. If you have time left, open some of the special display drawers, which contain some of the little charmers from this extensive collection, such as ivory sewing implements, jewelry, pipes, and lip labrets.

Across Lincoln Street from the museum is the *Sheldon Jackson College Salmon Hatchery*. This nonprofit hatchery was established in 1975 as part of the college aquaculture technology program. The facility releases up to fifteen million pink and chum and two hundred thousand coho salmon a year to the surrounding waters (tours available).

The fifteen totem poles in *Sitka National Historical Park*, at the end of Lincoln Street, are spaced along a forested path beside the sea. The 107-acre park is the site of the Tlingit and Russian battle of 1904. The original collection of totem poles was gathered at the instigation of District of Alaska Governor John Brady, who had a deep and abiding interest in preserving Alaska Native culture. The poles—most from Prince of Wales Island near Ketchikan—were displayed at the 1904 Louisiana Purchase Exposition in Saint Louis. After the fair they were returned to Alaska for placement in the Sitka park. During the 1930s, the poles were repaired by the Civilian Conservation Corps as part of their totem restoration project. All but one of the original poles have since been replicated (the life of a totem pole is eighty to one hundred years), the exception being the Raven Crest pole (number nine in the booklet—see below).

Before starting out along the path, spend a few minutes at the park visitors' center viewing the exhibits on Tlingit culture, including old houseposts from the Sitka area, Chilkat blankets, and a brief slide-tape presentation on the history of Sitka and the battle of 1804. One wing is devoted to workshops and demonstrations of Native wood carving, silver-work, bead- and button work and other crafts. You might want to purchase a copy of *Carved History, The Totem Poles and House Posts of Sitka National Historical Park* by Marilyn Knapp (Alaska Natural History Association and

Eskimos commonly engraved hunting scenes on their ivory pipes. This pipe is on display in the Sheldon Jackson Museum.

The middle figure of the Bicentennial pole depicts the arrival of the white man with his rifle and religion.

National Park Service). This excellent booklet describes all of the totem poles in the park. I will point out here only the two plain mortuary and memorial columns that stand out in contrast to the more complicated poles. One pole is topped by Cormorant and the other by Raven. There are more than two miles of established trails within the park, although you do not have to walk that far to see the totem poles. If it is a nice day, bring a picnic lunch with you. There is a picnic shelter across Indian River from the totems and a path that follows along the riverbank to a Russian memorial.

The New Archangel Russian Dancers put on an authentic performance for Sitka visitors. (Alaska Division of Tourism)

One of the totem poles in front of the visitors' center is a new pole that was created for the nation's Bicentennial celebration in 1976. The Bicentennial pole, carved by Duane Pasco, depicts new concepts in a traditional style. The topmost figure represents the Northwest Coast Indian of today holding two staffs, one symbolizing the rich heritage of the past and the other the unknown future. The second figure recalls the arrival of the white man (note beard and dress) with his rifle, religion, and paper treaties. Raven and Eagle are below him, and on the bottom the Northwest Indian in precontact days, holding a wooden halibut hook and rattle.

For entertainment in Sitka, the best show in town is the Sitka *New Archangel Russian Dancers*, an all-women dance troupe that has entranced visitors and local audiences with authentic Russian folk dances for sixteen years. The bright peasant costumes and the swirling, leaping dances are a splendid antidote to the bad-weather blues. Check out their performance schedule at the Centennial Building. For evening relaxation, take a *harbor cruise* aboard the blue and white *Saint Nicholas* or *Saint Aquilina*. The ships depart from Crescent Harbor by the Centennial Building for a two-and-one-half hour scenic, wildlife, and historical tour of Sitka Harbor and Silver Bay. Or, book a daytime naturalist cruise to *Saint Lazaria National Bird and Wildlife Sanctuary.*

The annual *Sitka Summer Music Festival* is held during three weeks in June. Performing artists from all over the world gather in this seaside setting for daily instructional workshops and twice-weekly evening concerts in the Centennial Building. The festival dates from 1972 when some protégés of Jascha Heifetz and Gregor Piatigorsky put together an informal concert in Sitka. The event has proved so popular that there are standing-room-only crowds for the Tuesday and Friday evening performances (there may be some special Saturday concerts, too). If you want to attend one of the concerts, write ahead for reserved seats to *Sitka Summer Music Festival, Box 3333, Sitka, Alaska, 99835*; telephone *(907) 747-6774*. Rehearsals are open to the public as well and are usually free.

Other local events include the two-day *All-Alaska Logging Championships* over the last weekend in June, in which loggers from all over the Pacific Northwest compete in traditional loggers' contests such as ax throwing and powersaw bucking. The *Alaska Day Festival*, October 16–18, commemorates the Alaska Purchase with a reenactment of the transfer ceremonies on Castle Hill. There are period costumes, a costume ball, and parade. The Sitka *Salmon Derby* takes place over two separate weekends in the summer. Write ahead to the visitors' bureau for information.

JUNEAU
Population 29,400

After you have visited the other communities along the Inside Passage, Juneau seems like a big city. It is not simply the imposing physical plant associated with the state capital that gives this impression, but the cosmopolitan atmosphere that comes with an affluent, well-educated, well-traveled population. How many other communities of twenty-nine thousand support a genuine French pastry shop and a foreign-films theater? For those of us who make this city our home, though, the small-town traits of Juneau are the most endearing. We still recognize most of the people we pass on the narrow, hilly streets; know local shopkeepers by their first names; and leave Christmas cookies in the mailbox for the postman. It was not so very long ago that we also left the keys in the car as a matter of course and locked our homes only if we were going on a long trip and happened to remember where we put the keys. This, alas, has changed.

As Alaska's state capital, Juneau bustles twelve months of the year, but especially during the winter legislative session when the town fairly explodes with elected officials and their staffs, concerned citizens, lobbyists, and the usual political hangers-on. By the time that lot retreats to their own districts in May or June, the big tour boats are coming into port—on some days five and six at a time—and unloading thousands of eager tourists into the city streets.

Until very recently, visitors spilled out of the cruise ships onto uneven sidewalks bordered by sagging buildings seemingly held in place by a rat's maze of overhead wires. Today, after a massive multi-year face-lift, the downtown historic district boasts broad pedestrian walkways outlined with

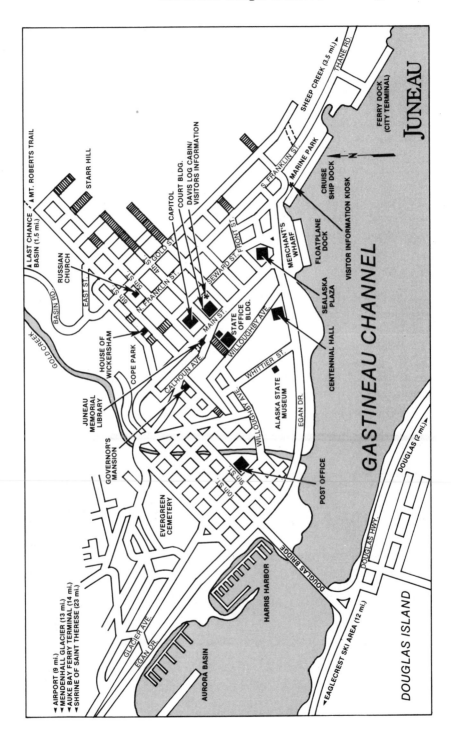

JUNEAU

GASTINEAU CHANNEL

DOUGLAS ISLAND

FERRY DOCK (CITY TERMINAL)

THANE RD.

SHEEP CREEK (3.5 mi.) ▶

CRUISE SHIP DOCK

MARINE PARK

S. FRANKLIN ST.

VISITOR INFORMATION KIOSK

FLOATPLANE DOCK

MERCHANT'S WHARF

SEALASKA PLAZA

CENTENNIAL HALL

DAVIS LOG CABIN/ VISITORS INFORMATION

COURT BLDG.

CAPITOL

FRONT ST.

SEWARD ST.

STATE OFFICE BLDG.

WILLOUGHBY AVE.

WHITTIER ST.

ALASKA STATE MUSEUM

EGAN DR.

POST OFFICE

MAIN ST.

N. FRANKLIN ST.

GOLD ST.

▲ LAST CHANCE ↗↗ ▲ MT. ROBERTS TRAIL
BASIN (1.5 mi.)

STARR HILL

RUSSIAN CHURCH

EAST ST.

BASIN RD.

GOLD CREEK

HOUSE OF WICKERSHAM

COPE PARK

JUNEAU MEMORIAL LIBRARY

GOVERNOR'S MANSION

CALHOUN AVE.

WILLOUGHBY AVE.

9TH ST.

10TH ST.

EVERGREEN CEMETERY

GLACIER AVE.

EGAN DR.

HARRIS HARBOR

AURORA BASIN

DOUGLAS BRIDGE

DOUGLAS HWY.

DOUGLAS (2 mi.) ▶

EAGLECREST SKI AREA (12 mi.) ▶

▼ AIRPORT (9 mi.)
▼ MENDENHALL GLACIER (13 mi.)
▼ AUKE BAY FERRY TERMINAL (14 mi.)
▼ SHRINE OF SAINT THERESE (23 mi.)

brilliant banners and twin-globe streetlamps, buried utilities, renovated shopfronts, and flowers, flowers, flowers. While parts of South Franklin Street still suffer from the ill effects of too many bars, the new old-Juneau is a very pleasant place.

There are first-class galleries and gift shops, good hotels, a wide choice of passable but expensive restaurants, a superb community theater, and on any given night, summer or winter, a hefty roster of activities and entertainment from which to choose. If you are of the outdoors set, you can enjoy both cross-country and downhill skiing in winter plus a myriad of hiking trails and other outside activities. (Hikers should pick up a copy of *Juneau Trails*, free from city visitors' centers. Other excellent trail guides are Isabel McLean's *Exploring Trails Around Juneau* and Mary Lou King's *Short Walks Around Juneau,* available at local bookstores.) Whatever your interests, Juneau can keep you busy for at least a couple of days.

BACKGROUND

What we commonly refer to as Juneau is in reality a number of geographically and historically distinct communities interconnected by highway and bridge. Juneau proper is snuggled up against the flanks of thirty-six-hundred-foot Mount Juneau on the Southeast mainland, nine hundred air miles north of Seattle. The residential communities of Thane, the Mendenhall Valley, Auke Bay, and others stretch north and south of Juneau along the coast. Across Gastineau Channel by bridge is the small city

Galleries and shops entice visitors to Juneau's downtown historic district.

Constructed in 1894, Juneau's Saint Nicholas Orthodox Church is the oldest original Russian church in Southeast Alaska.

of Douglas and neighboring developments on Douglas Island. Together these communities and surrounding lands make up the 3,108-square-mile city and borough of Juneau.

The story of Juneau and the surrounding communities begins with the discovery of a vast treasure trove of gold-bearing quartz. The Gastineau Channel area was a fishing ground for local Auk Tlingit in the late 1800s when prospectors began scouring the hills and gullies of Southeast Alaska and Canada for signs of gold. One man set about locating potential gold-bearing properties more efficiently than the rest. George Pilz, a German-born mining engineer in charge of the Stewart Mine near Sitka, offered a substantial reward ("100 pair of Hudson's Bay blankets and work for the tribe at one dollar per day," he later recalled) to any local Indian chief who could lead him to gold-bearing ore in minable quantities. When samples began coming in from up and down the coast, Pilz sent his men out in teams with Indian guides to investigate the prospects.

Chief Kowee of the Auks brought samples of ore from Gastineau Channel to Pilz in 1879. To investigate the body of ore, Pilz selected Richard T. Harris and Joseph Juneau, a pair of down-and-out prospectors recently returned from the Cassiar. Harris and Juneau left Sitka in July of 1880 and explored several likely looking sites before reaching Gastineau Channel in mid-August. They followed Gold Creek inland, getting good color in their pans and deciding the place was the best prospect so far (which is why they named it Gold Creek), but went back to Sitka without tracing the gold to its source. Pilz was not terribly impressed with their results and Kowee was extremely put out. The chief carried more samples to Sitka and insisted that Harris and Juneau would have found what Pilz was looking for had they only continued up Gold Creek. When Pilz sent the pair back again, Kowee made sure they reached the mother lode.

On 3 October Harris and Juneau climbed Snow Slide Gulch, where they had stopped the first time, and looked down over Silver Bow Basin and Quartz Gulch which, Harris later recalled, "I named from the fact that it contained the most gold-bearing quartz I had ever seen in one gulch." The quartz outcroppings were shot through with streaks of gold, and "little lumps as large as peas or beans." Inspired by this splendid sight, Harris and Juneau fell to work. Harris wrote out a code of local laws governing the staking of claims in the Harris Mining District (this his legal prerogative according to the Mining Act of 10 May 1872, which allowed miners to make regulations concerning claims in their district), and they set out claims throughout Gold Creek Valley for themselves, Pilz, and several creditors and friends. On 18 October they staked a 160-acre townsite on the beach along Gastineau Channel, naming it Harrisburgh.

In November, the first shiploads of prospectors left Sitka for the new strike location on Gastineau Channel. Forty or so miners spent an uncomfortable winter in Harrisburgh, clearing land to build rough cabins, hacking a pack road to the diggings, and sawing planks to build flumes when the ground thawed in the spring. In February 1881, the miners voted to change the name of the mining camp to Rockwell, for Lieutenant Commander Charles H. Rockwell who had been sent with a party of men from the naval vessel USS *Jamestown* to keep an eye on developments.

When spring came, the banks of Gold Creek crawled with prospectors working their claims while others, recently arrived by steamer from the south, looked for places to drive in their stakes. In May, Lieutenant Commander Rockwell returned to Rockwell with a detachment of marines. His instructions were to establish a military post and preserve order, especially between the miners and the estimated 450 Auk and Taku Tlingit who had taken up residence in the town. The marines put up some small buildings on a ridge overlooking the town, but by December things had simmered down to the extent that the post was closed. Rockwell turned the buildings over to the postmaster and eventually a federal courthouse was built on the site. Meanwhile, the town residents decided to change the name of their community again—to Juneau City after Joe Juneau. The post office dropped the city part and the miners had to be satisfied with just Juneau.

Across the channel on Douglas Island, the ground proved equally rich. The first gold taken out of the entire Gastineau region came from the "Ready Bullion boys," who recovered twelve hundred dollars of gold by the spring of 1881 from their claim on Ready Bullion Creek at the southern end of the island. In September of 1881 a piece of property close to the Ready Bullion claim passed auspiciously into the hands of John Treadwell, a carpenter-cum-miner who had been sent into the area by a group of San Francisco investors to check out the new strike. After ore samples from Treadwell's claim were tested, Treadwell hastened back to Juneau to acquire more property for the newly established Alaska Mill and Mining Company. Their 5-stamp mill, established in May of 1882 and replaced by a 120-stamp mill the following year, was the beginning of the great Treadwell mining complex that would produce more than seventy million dollars in gold.

In the ensuing years, Gastineau Channel would become a center for large-scale, hard-rock gold mining. Initially, lone prospectors took what they could from their claims with shovel and sluice box and drifted on to other strikes. (Among them was Joe Juneau, who went on to the Klondike and died at Dawson in 1899. Richard Harris mined in Juneau for several years until he lost his claims in a suit brought by one of his original backers. He died in a sanitarium in Oregon in 1907. Both are buried in Evergreen Cemetery in Juneau.) Harvesting the Juneau lode, however, was really a job for organized mining companies with the resources to tunnel deep within the earth and mill thousands of tons of ore per day. Companies formed, consolidated claims, and grew larger. On the Juneau side of the channel there were the Perseverance and Alaska Juneau mines in Silver Bow Basin, Jualpa at Last Chance Basin, and Ebner Mine on Gold Creek. Across the way were the Ready Bullion, the Mexican, the Seven Hundred Foot Mine, and the Treadwell. Around the mine and mill sites grew the stable communities of Juneau, Douglas, Treadwell, and Thane, peopled by mine and mill employees and their families. The mines and the businesses that served them functioned twenty-four hours a day.

The Treadwell mines reached the peak of production in 1915 with 960 stamps crushing five thousand tons of ore daily, a world record. Two years later, a cave-in at the edge of Gastineau Channel flooded all of the Treadwell workings except the Ready Bullion. That mine shut, too, in 1922 for lack of quality ore, bringing to a close one of the greatest mining efforts ever. Over in Juneau, the revolutionary Alaska-Gastineau mill at Sheep Creek, patterned after a dry-ore copper mill in Utah, surpassed the Treadwell record by grinding twelve thousand tons of ore per day until 1921 when costs became prohibitive. The last of the big mills, the Alaska-Juneau, constructed in 1916, was closed down by the war in 1944, but not before producing $80.8 million in gold. Together these three industrial giants produced $158 million worth of gold at values of twenty to thirty-five dollars per ounce.

The visible remains of the three great plants are awesomely insignificant. The burned-out shell of the Alaska-Juneau mill is little more than a scar above Gastineau Channel on the approach into town. The Gastineau mill was dismantled and shipped south when the company folded. As for the Treadwell—that wondrous complex of mills, mines, wharves, piers, shops, warehouses, trams, and a town full of people—nothing remains except a few ghostly pilings in the channel and the occasional crumbled foundation that has been spared the advance of the undergrowth.

But by the time the last mine had closed, the surviving communities of Douglas and Juneau had managed to diversify their interests. The governor's office had been transferred from Sitka to the thriving mining town of Juneau in 1906, establishing Juneau as the capital city. The governor's mansion was built in 1912 and the capitol building in 1930. When statehood was awarded in 1959, Juneau remained the focal point of state government activity and continues so today, despite repeated campaigns to relocate the capital of Alaska nearer the northern population centers of Anchorage and Fairbanks.

Government—federal, state, or local—employs one out of every two workers in Juneau today. Fishing is an important industry here as elsewhere in Southeast, with a sizable fishing fleet and a small cold storage operation. Tourism plays an integral role in the local economy, the capital city being a destination or transfer point for most tour ships plying the Inside Passage. And, gold mining might not be relegated to the past—a Canadian firm is actively sampling the remaining ore body to test the viability of reopening the Alaska Juneau Mine.

GETTING THERE

Access to Juneau is by air and water only. Several flights a day from Seattle, Anchorage, and the communities between, land at Juneau International Airport, nine miles north of the city center. Alaska state ferries normally dock at the Auke Bay Terminal, fourteen miles north of Juneau (the

The Juneau waterfront encompasses cruise ships, fishing boats, and government office buildings.

downtown ferry terminal is used only rarely). Most cruise ships tie up at either the downtown ferry terminal or Alaska Steamship Dock, but some anchor in Juneau Harbor. If the latter, passengers are lightered ashore and disembark at the lightering dock at Marine Park on the downtown waterfront.

To See and Do

If you are fortunate enough to approach Juneau from the water, your first glimpse of the capital city will be the one that stays with you. Gliding slowly up the narrow reaches of Gastineau Channel, you will pass the remnants of the Treadwell wharves off Douglas Island to your left, while ahead looms the towering profile of Mount Juneau. At the bottom and insignificant in comparison, the buildings of Juneau cling to their shelf between mountains and sea.

As you pull into port, you will see *Merchant's Wharf*, a former seaplane hangar, now offices and shops, and the *seaplane float* where excursion flights depart for the Juneau Ice Cap. *Marine Park*, where cruise ship passengers alight, is a popular gathering spot for local residents on sunny days. Bright-colored banners mark the location of picnic tables and covered shelters where you can enjoy a lunch or snack from one of the street vendors that set up shop on the downtown streets. There is an information kiosk staffed by volunteers who dispense maps, brochures, and answers to your questions. Pick up a map of the *Juneau Walking Tour* which will guide you to the major attractions around town. (Or, let a Clydesdale do the walking and ride around the city center with the Juneau Carriage Company.)

Many downtown buildings have retained their original facades, due to the fact that Juneau has been spared the sort of major fire that ravaged Douglas and Wrangell. A stroll along South Franklin, Front, and Seward streets will carry you back in time. South Franklin (all the way to the old ferry terminal) is the place for gift and curio shops—and taverns, including the landmark *Red Dog Saloon*, an old-fashioned, sawdust-on-the floor establishment that draws residents and visitors alike. The recently restored *Alaskan Hotel* (since 1913) is a current local favorite for after-hours cocktails. The turreted *Alaska Steam Laundry Building* on the opposite side of the street is another Juneau landmark, dating from 1901. Today the building connects with the Emporium Mall on Shattuck Way. You will find several specialty shops and stores, including a fast-photo film developing service.

Art galleries on or near Franklin Street include *Rie Muñoz Ltd. Gallery* (on Ferry Way), *Cha, Objects of Bright Pride,* and *Artwork Unlimited.* Also try *Kaill Fine Crafts* (on Front Street near Franklin), which specializes in unusual gift items with or without an Alaska theme. The restored *Senate Building* houses a host of attractive shops (Christmas ornaments, toys, and Irish, Russian, and Scandinavian imports), as does *Marine View Center* (check out the *Alaska Smoked Salmon Co.).* Turning to practical matters, hook up with *The Connection* (275 South Franklin Street) to place your phone calls to the Lower 48 or overseas from comfortable, private indoor booths.

At Third and Seward streets, the *Juneau Visitors' Information Center* is housed in a small log cabin with a bell tower, a replica of the Presbyterian log church that stood in Juneau in the early days. The new structure, known as the Davis Log Cabin, was built in 1980 for Juneau's Centennial celebration. The visitors' center also features exhibits pertaining to the city's rich and varied past.

The most photogenic sight in town is the tiny, octagonal *Saint Nicholas Russian Orthodox Church* (Fifth Street between Franklin and Gold). Although constructed in 1894, nearly thirty years after Russia sold the Alaska colony, Saint Nicholas is the oldest original Russian church in Southeast Alaska. The postage-stamp-sized Cathedral Park next door was recently renovated for tots, but offers a comfortable adult-sized bench for resting your feet. While you are on Fifth Street, continue two blocks toward the mountains, and you will find yourself looking up at a long set of stairs. This is *Starr Hill,* one of the oldest and most colorful residential neighborhoods in Juneau. Many of the houses were built for employees of the nearby mines. Behind Starr Hill, Mount Roberts rises 3,819 feet (there is a steep but easy trail to the top; allow three hours round-trip). The flight of steps from Fourth Street is even more of a challenge than the Fifth Street stairs.

The state government complex is centered at Fourth and Main. The six-story *Capitol* was built as the Federal and Territorial Building in 1930, when Alaska was not yet a state. Local marble from Tokeen, near Prince of Wales Island, was quarried for the front columns and interior paneling. The Alaska Senate and House of Representatives meet in the building, which houses the governor's office as well. Tours of the Capitol are available in summer (check at the tour desk in the lobby or contact the Legislative Information Office at (907) 465-4648 to find the time of the next tour departure). During the legislative session (approximately January to May), you can request a special tour by contacting the House of Representatives sergeant-at-arms at (907) 465-3869.

Of course, you can also look around by yourself. The front doors of the Capitol remain open during weekday office hours (8 A.M. to 4:30 P.M.). At least look into the ground floor lobby which recently has been restored to the original blue and gilt decoration. The legislative chambers are on the second floor and are always open during the session. Spend a few minutes in the visitors' galleries for a view of politics Alaska-style. If no one is using them, you might try to peek into the house speaker's conference room (second floor) and the finance committee rooms (fifth floor), which have also been renovated.

The governor has only a short walk from office to home. The *governor's mansion* is a couple of blocks away from the Capitol on Calhoun Avenue. The white-pillared colonial, completed in 1912, could just as easily

Rare sunny days find Juneau office workers at Marine Park during the lunch hour. Colorful banners mark the spot.

be situated in Massachusetts or Vermont, were it not for the dramatic totem pole in front. The Governor's totem, carved in 1940 by Tlingit Indians from Klukwan and Saxman, represents several Tlingit legends, among them the origin of the mosquito, pictured as the fourth figure from the top. The mansion is not usually open to view. Contact the governor's office in advance (write P.O. Box A, Juneau, Alaska, 99811-0101) if yours is a special request, such as for a group of visiting schoolchildren.

Recent additions to the state government complex include the bunker-like *State Office Building* (which Alaskans quickly dubbed the "S.O.B.") completed in 1974 and the high-rise Alaska *Court Building* built in 1975. The vast open foyer of the S.O.B. stretches four stories above the lobby floor and the surrounding tiled terraces offer a marvelous view of Gastineau Channel and Douglas Island. The *Old Witch totem pole* displayed in the foyer came from a Haida village on Prince of Wales Island and was carved in the 1880s. The pole recalls the Haida version of the "old witch" or mother-in-law story of Gonakadet, who assumes the identity of a lake monster in order to provide fish for his abusive mother-in-law. A brown-baggers' concert takes place every Friday noon on the 1928 Kimball theatre organ housed on the lobby floor. There is a small snack bar where you can buy a sandwich.

The *Friendship pole* displayed in the lobby of the nearby Court Building is one of several large-scale copies of a twenty-eight-inch totem pole that has special significance for Chilkat Tlingit of Klukwan, near Haines. In the late 1920s, the Indians presented the original pole to Steve Sheldon of Haines, a U.S. deputy marshal who was instrumental in restoring good will between conflicting clans. The Friendship totem symbolizes peace by representing both Eagle and Raven moieties on the same pole. From top to bottom the primary figures represent: Eagle, Raven, Hawk, Bear, Frog, Wolf, and (very small) Eagle. This pole was carved by Alaska Indian Arts, in Haines.

Juneau has many treasures tucked here and there about town. The forty-five-foot *Four-Story totem* at the top of Seward Street was carved in Hydaburg in 1940 and represents four Haida legends. Another pole, outside the Juneau Memorial Library (Fourth and Main), was carved for Alaska's Centennial celebration in 1967 by Amos Wallace. If art is one of your enthusiasms, duck into Juneau Memorial Library to see the modernistic *stained glass window* designed by well-known Juneau artist Rie Muñoz. A *tapestry* designed by the same artist and woven in Aubusson, France, is on display at the Bank of the North at Sealaska Plaza. Also stop at the plaza lobby, for an exhibit of *Chilkat blankets*, a small Haida canoe, and other Native artifacts.

If your energy level starts to wane, drop in to *Le Petit Paris* on North Franklin Street, one block uphill from the Baranof Hotel, for an authentic croissant or cream-filled flaky pastry and a cup of cafe au lait. Pastry chef

Tom Loatman was trained in Paris. Equally fattening results can be obtained at the *New Orpheum Theater-Gallery-Cafe* near Marine Park (go to the Orpheum in the evening, too, for foreign and art films).

Plan to spend a minimum of one hour at the *Alaska State Museum*. To get there on foot you can walk along Egan Drive to Whittier or take a shortcut through the State Office Building: pass through the foyer and bear right to the rear bank of elevators leading to the parking garage and exit at P2. You will emerge onto Willoughby Avenue, a long block from the museum. (Willoughby follows the original shoreline of Gastineau Channel. The waterfront was extended by tailings from the Alaska-Juneau Mine.)

The museum has gained a reputation for its eagle nesting tree. This unusual exhibit replicates a bald eagle nest in a tall spruce tree, complete with eggs and lifelike (but stuffed) eagles in various stages of development. As you follow the gently spiraling ramp to the second floor, you circle the tree to look down upon the nest and its occupants. The totem poles at the base of the tree are actually three segments of a Beaver totem pole that once stood in front of a Wrangell house. The pole represents several Tlingit legends.

The complex Thunderbird screen from Yakutat (just inside the entrance) dates from 1905. The painted and carved screen depicts the mythological Thunderbird, creator of thunder and lightning, emerging from the storm clouds (represented by small faces). The story that inspired the screen concerns a small boy who became lost on a canoe trip down the Alsek River and was subsequently found by Thunderbird. The parents located the boy as he was about to be changed into a bird. Thunderbird agreed to return the child if the family put up a screen in a Yakutat house.

A prominent exhibit on the ground floor is a thirty-eight-foot walrus skin umiak that was assembled in the museum in 1971 by Eskimos from Saint Lawrence Island. The driftwood frame came from the village of Wales on the Seward Peninsula, where it had been made at the turn of the century. Do not miss the fine exhibit of Eskimo masks or the Aleut waterproof clothing.

Another major exhibit is a model of a Tlingit community house that has been constructed in authentic fashion without nails from hand-adzed boards. The painted screen at one end is a replica of a well-known rain screen from Klukwan (near Haines). The famous Lincoln totem pole is also exhibited here. This weathered form strikes an amazing likeness to the bearded-American president and originally was positioned atop the Proud Raven pole on Tongass Island. As the story has been pieced together, the chief of the Raven clan commissioned the pole in the late 1800s to commemorate the clan's first contact with a white man (who had likely been one of the early explorers). Needing something from which to work, the carver apparently obtained a photograph of Lincoln from an army post that was located on Tongass Island from 1868 to 1870. A replica of the Proud Raven pole is at

Among the Aleut items in the Alaska State Museum is this waterproof gut parka. (Alaska State Museum, Alfred A. Blaker)

Saxman Totem Park in Ketchikan. Before leaving the Tlingit exhibits, notice the beautiful carved wooden feast dishes, carved argillite, ringed potlatch hat, and four houseposts from the Frog House in Klukwan.

The upstairs floor is devoted to Alaska state history. The Russian heritage corner has icons, gospel books, a fascinating collection of trade beads of different shapes, colors, and sizes, plus the ubiquitous samovar. There is also a brass double-headed eagle of the Russian imperial crest. Russian explorers used such crests as territorial markers along the North American coast, but this is one of the few known to have been recovered. Other exhibits feature equipment from the A-J Mine and the original French-made lens (circa 1900) from the Cape Spencer lighthouse.

An excellent spot for lunch or afternoon tea near the museum is the *Fiddlehead Restaurant* (walk down Whittier Street to Willoughby and turn left) which leans toward natural foods but serves terrific hamburgers on homemade buns. Pick up a loaf of bread or some cookies from the Fiddlehead Bakery to enjoy later on. If your visit is on a weekday, try to arrive early or late to avoid the crush of the state office lunch crowd. Also near the museum—just one block away on Egan Drive—is the *U.S. Forest Service Information Center* in Centennial Hall. There are wildlife films, informative exhibits, and plenty of soft chairs. Rest your feet awhile!

Still being developed is the *Wickersham State Historic Site*. This fine house on Seventh Street, overlooking the city and down-channel view, was built around 1899 for one of the early mine owners. The residence was later owned by Judge James Wickersham, who came to Alaska in 1900 and played a prominent role in shaping Alaska's body politic. As Alaska's voteless delegate to Congress, Judge Wickersham worked tirelessly to achieve territorial status and followed that victory of 1912 with the first statehood bill four years later. He died twenty years before that goal was finally achieved in 1959. Recently acquired by the State of Alaska, the Wickersham House is still undergoing renovation and restoration. So far, visitors can view the main floor rooms, which are furnished as Judge Wickersham enjoyed them, with his 1904 gramophone and his Chickering concert square grand that the Russian government installed in Sitka in the 1850s. Some of Wickersham's vast collection of Alaskan artifacts and mementos spanning his thirty-nine years in Alaska also are on display.

One of the nicest museums anywhere, the *Juneau-Douglas City Museum,* is currently without a permanent home. When the Juneau public library moves into its new quarters atop the downtown parking garage, this fascinating and artfully displayed collection of equipment and curiosities from the gold mining era (miners' helmets, carbide lamps, and lunch pails; assaying and surveying gadgets; pneumatic drills) will be housed in the present library building at the corner of Fourth and Main streets. In the meantime, the museum bumps from one vacant spot to another—you will have to ascertain its current address from the visitor information center. It is worth finding.

Gold is also the theme of the *Lady Lou Revue,* a fun-packed quality musical staged by *Perseverance Theatre.* Loosely based on Robert Service's ballads about the Klondike gold rush, the plot unfolds around Dan McGrew, Sam McGee, and the delectable lady whose name was Lou.

All through the year "Juneauites" pile children, dogs, lunches, and—depending upon the season—fishing poles, berry pails, or cross-country skis into the car for a drive "out the road." The destination can be just about anywhere that is pretty to look at and possesses the desired habitat: Fritz Cove for blueberry picking, Auke Bay for picnicking, or Eagle River Beach for Dolly Varden fishing. Consider renting a car for a day or two to explore some of the local haunts. Outside of downtown Juneau, Egan Expressway extends northward along Gastineau Channel past two boat harbors and the bridge to Douglas Island. During very low tides you can walk across the channel at the narrowest points, but be prepared to come back another way. As you drive out the expressway near the airport, look for Canada geese on the *Mendenhall Wetlands State Game Refuge,* the saltwater marsh area that borders Gastineau Channel. These tidelands—green in summer and straw gold in fall—are a feeding station for migrating waterfowl. There is a turnout and viewing platform on the channel side of the highway at mile 6. The Canada geese are present year-round in the Juneau area, but you will see huge flocks of them in early summer and fall.

Foremost among the sights out the road is the *Mendenhall Glacier,* a twelve-mile river of ice that descends to sea level from a fifteen-hundred-square-mile ice field in the Coast Mountains behind Juneau. Located just thirteen miles north of the city center via the expressway and Mendenhall Loop Road, the Mendenhall is rightly called the most accessible glacier in North America. I call it Juneau's drive-up glacier because you can enjoy a splendid view of the mile-and-a-half face without ever leaving your car. You should get out, though, and walk to the visitors' center and glacier overlook (a half-mile from the face) where U.S. Forest Service representatives are prepared to answer your questions with the aid of a topographical model of the Juneau Ice Field that feeds the glacier.

The Mendenhall Glacier was formed during the Little Ice Age that peaked in the seventeenth and eighteenth centuries, and has retreated 2.5 miles in the last 230 years. The glacier terminates in Mendenhall Lake, which reaches depths of 200 feet. Chunks of ice are continually falling from the glacier with a resounding crack!—leaving a deep blue rent in the face. A brochure outlines a self-guided exploration along the "trail of the glacier." You need about forty-five minutes to walk the path and observe the telltale signs of a receding glacier, such as grooved bedrock, kettles or depressions in the soil made by blocks of melting ice, and a glacial moraine. More rigorous trails are mapped out for serious hikers seeking a closer look at the terrain. In winter, a level trail near the glacier is inviting to cross-

Just thirteen miles from Juneau is the Mendenhall Glacier, a twelve-mile river of ice that originates in the Coast Mountains.

country skiers.

Steep Creek, near the glacier parking lot, is one of the best places in Southeast to observe spawning salmon. From July through December, sockeye, coho, and chum salmon enter the creek from salt water and swim upstream to spawn near Mendenhall Lake. A roadside exhibit points you in the right direction.

When you leave the glacier, continue north on the expressway (it becomes Glacier Highway at this point) for *Brotherhood Bridge* over the Mendenhall River, which affords a stupendous view over fields of wild flowers (especially lupine, wild iris, and Alaska cotton) and the glacier beyond. Be sure to bring color film. There is a turnout from the highway. Another scenic wayside one and one-half miles farther along gives you a view of *Auke Lake*. In summer the lake is a place for a quiet paddle in a canoe or kayak and you will see sockeye salmon there late in the season. In winter the scene turns to ice and glittering snow. (Inquire about kayak and canoe rentals at *Alaska Discovery,* 369 South Franklin Street.)

Past a small lily pond at the edge of Auke Lake there is a turnoff for the lakeside campus of the *University of Alaska*, which offers associate, bachelor, and master's degree programs in education, fisheries management, business administration, and several other fields of study. You would be hard put to find a more dramatic setting for a college campus. As you leave the campus, visit the log-and-shingled *Chapel by the Lake*. The outside of the building—constructed of forty-eight-foot spruce logs and hand-split shakes with a belfry on top—has considerable charm, but go on inside. The simple, varnished logs are a perfect foil for the grandeur framed within the front window. The Presbyterian chapel was completed in 1958.

From Auke Lake, Glacier Highway stretches northward for another thirty miles to terminate near Berners Bay. If you have time, by all means make the entire drive. The road is good and offers exceptional views of water, mountains, forest, and wild flower strewn fields. Side roads lead from the highway to waterfront residential neighborhoods. Among the most scenic are *Fritz Cove* and *Point Lena Loop* roads and *Amalga Harbor. Auke Bay*, twelve miles from town, is a small commercial community and boat harbor with a grocery store to fix you up with a cold drink or snack. In the fall, crab boats come into Auke Bay and you can buy king crab at the dock.

The *Auke Village Recreation Area*, a short distance beyond the boat harbor, was for centuries the site of a winter village of the Auk Tlingit. Mining activity in Juneau drew the Indians into town where the jobs were and the village was mostly deserted by 1900. Today the site is again populated—with picnickers, campers, fishermen, and boaters who revel in the gentle beach and glorious view. Covered shelters guarantee a pleasurable outing even on liquid-sunshine days, and there is a campground nearby. The unusual totem pole opposite the site on the highway is the *Yax-te pole,* which was set in place in 1941 to commemorate the old village site. The Yax-te—what we call Ursa Major or the Big Dipper—was a crest of a clan of Indians near Klawock on Prince of Wales Island. After a battle, the crest was given to one of the Auk chiefs who adopted it for his clan. The top figure on the pole is Raven. Below him several tiny faces peer out from the wood. They represent different birds that assisted Raven in his adventures, except for the bottom face which represents an Auk princess. The last figure on the pole, resembling a bear, is Yax-te.

Another scenic chapel is the Roman Catholic *Shrine of Saint Therese* at mile 23. A gravel causeway leads out to a small island where a stone church is tucked into a wooded path on the sea. The interior is plain. The shrine was built in 1938 and, like the Chapel by the Lake, is in great demand for weddings.

South out of Juneau, *Thane Road* begins at South Franklin Street and continues for five miles beyond the old state ferry terminal. First, uphill on the left, you will pass the shell of the Alaska-Juneau mill and, on your right, the tailings from the A-J Mine. Several years ago, Juneau residents played a form of golf on this "million-dollar golf course." Thane is strictly residential today, but in former years quite a community of warehouses, shops, offices, boardinghouses, and even a school grew up around the great Alaska-Gastineau mill at Sheep Creek. You can view a small *fish hatchery* at Sheep Creek. Nearby, the *Thane Ore House* (mile 4) serves grilled salmon, deep-fried halibut, and barbecued ribs at their "Miner's Cookhouse" on the beach.

Across the Douglas Bridge you turn left for a two-mile drive to Douglas. (You will pass an old Tlingit cemetery on the left.) Try to take in a theatrical performance at Douglas's award-winning *Perseverance Theatre* on Third Street. At the end of town the road angles left to the boat harbor and *Sandy Beach* in Savikko Park. Bring the family here for a picnic (covered shelters with fireplaces), softball game, tennis match, or walk on the beach.

In the other direction, Douglas Highway extends a dozen miles to the north end of Douglas Island and *Eaglecrest* downhill ski area, which has dominated the winter recreational scene since its opening in 1976. Facilities include a beginner's tow and two chair lifts, equipment rental shops, and a day lodge and snack bar. There are established cross-country ski trails, too, although good cross-country skiing (and snowshoeing) is readily available in the muskeg meadows that border Eaglecrest Road. Eaglecrest is a municipal ski resort. Lift tickets are reasonably priced and there are no lift lines—yet. Skiing usually starts by mid-December, but in this region snowfall, unlike rainfall, is never guaranteed. Some winters provide excellent skiing and others almost none.

I have saved this final excursion for last because it is my own favorite, my personal restorative when I have been too long at my desk or too heavy in my mind. *Basin Road* begins at the intersection of Sixth and East streets in Juneau, curves up and around a tree-covered knoll, then follows Gold Creek into Last Chance Basin. Houses rim the first section of the road, before the pavement ends, and then a wooden bridge hangs high above the tumbling waters of Gold Creek. On the opposite side of the creek an old avalanche scar grows brilliant green with the advance of summer. Sometimes you can spot black bears there, testing the new vegetation. You can

This is not Soapy Smith's gang down from Skagway, but a makeup class at Douglas's Perseverance Theatre.

A Mendenhall River float trip combines a river ride with a closeup look at the glacier. (Alaska Travel Adventures)

drive to this spot but it is a much better walk, and an easy one after the first few uphill yards.

The gravel road continues for nearly a mile and a half through Gold Creek Valley. Mountains rise on every side, Mount Juneau on the left, Mount Roberts on the right, white on top, dark green below. This is gold country and it looks like it. Prospectors cut this road through the mountains in the winter and spring of 1881. The valley opens up into Last Chance Basin and some old mine buildings come into view. Ahead is Snowslide Gulch. Joe Juneau and Richard Harris labored to the top and looked down into the promised land of Silver Bow Basin (trails lead there for the more adventurous). I never walk this road without thinking of the events of 1880 and 1881 and of the gritted-teeth determination of the men who passed this way.

Now if you make this walk in the late afternoon you can stay in Last Chance Basin for dinner at the *Gold Creek Salmon Bake*, which is one of the most enjoyable dining experiences in Southeast Alaska. The salmon is liberally coated with a brown sugar glaze and grilled over an alder fire. There is a salad bar, bread, beer, and toasted (by you) marshmallows for dessert. You sit at wooden tables and benches under the protective shelter of a geodesic dome. Local musicians entertain for tips. The salmon is very good and ambience great, but the setting is spectacular. Gold Creek rushes along by your feet, and gold pans are provided if you care to try your skill. Across Gold Creek, you can walk uphill to the former tram yard of the Alaska-Juneau Mining Company with adjacent locomative repair shop and compressor building. (Those who do not care to walk or drive can be collected by the Salmon Bake's yellow school bus.)

Excursions out of Juneau are available by plane or boat. On sunny or near-sunny days, you can schedule a floatplane flight over the *Juneau Ice Field* for a look at the world of permanent ice and snow. Or, board a Temsco helicopter for a tour over Mendenhall Glacier—you'll touch down on the glacier floor. A floatplane ride to *Taku Glacier Lodge* takes you over the ice field on your way to a wilderness lodge for a salmon bake dinner. There is a dinner cruise to twenty-five-mile-long *Tracy Arm*, a deep fjord about fifty miles south of Juneau where two glaciers descend to the sea. (This is a good place to spot whales, sea lions, seals, and porpoises, too.) Excursions to *Glacier Bay National Park and Preserve* are available from Juneau. Juneau (Auke Bay Terminal) is also the departure point for smaller ferries to Hoonah, Angoon, Tenakee Springs, and Pelican. A miniexcursion that is good fun for all is Alaska Travel Adventure's *Mendenhall River float trip*, with a midfloat snack on the riverbank.

Local celebrations in the Juneau vicinity include parades and fireworks on the Fourth of July and the three-day *Golden North Salmon Derby*, usually held in August. And what do locals celebrate with? Our own great beer, *Chinook Alaskan,* brewed right here at Lemon Creek and bottled every Thursday. Ask for it!

HAINES
Population 1,800

On a cold, clear day when the mountains are out, it is hard to imagine a setting more stereotypically Alaskan than that of Haines. The jagged Cathedral Peaks of the Chilkat Mountains are massed behind the town, raw-edged reminders that an ungentle spirit is abroad in this far-northern land. Salt water is also close to hand in frigid, salmon-filled Chilkoot Inlet on the upper reaches of Lynn Canal.

Haines was the only sizable Southeast port city with highway connections to the outside until 1978 when the Skagway-Carcross leg of the Klondike Highway opened the way to Whitehorse and the Alaska road system. A steady stream of traffic and freight still passes through the community en route between the Alaska state ferry terminal and the Haines Highway.

If you have the luxury of a leisurely schedule, especially if you are driving or camping, I highly recommend a few days in Haines. There are three state campgrounds from which to choose, each more beautiful and isolated than the last, and plenty of RV parking. The fishing is superb. The art community is one of the more flourishing in Southeast. All of these things can be found to a greater or lesser degree in any community along the Inside Passage, but Haines has a come-hither quality that reaches out to the visitor and says, "Welcome."

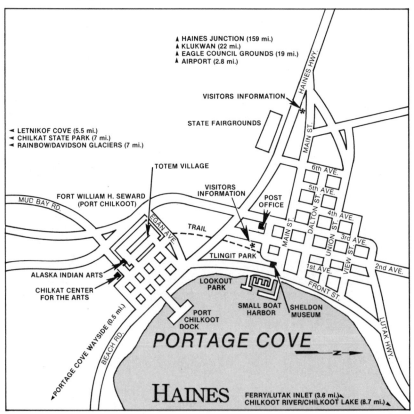

If you spend one day in Haines you will enjoy the sight-seeing opportunities presented by Port Chilkoot, Alaska Indian Arts, and the Sheldon Museum. At night there is the salmon bake at the Totem Village Tribal House. If you spend two days you can take in some of the spectacular wilderness scenery along the way to Lutak Inlet or Chilkat State Park and, if your timing is right, catch a performance of the Chilkat Dancers or the Lynn Canal Community Players. If your stay extends to three days, you will start greeting people you pass on the street by name, having discovered that the personable artist you chatted with at a Port Chilkoot studio is the same person playing Jack Dalton in *Lust for Dust*, the Haines Revue melodrama; the live-wire lady at the travel bureau is one and the same with the driver of the minibus that met your ferry; and so forth.

If you stay four days look out, because you are liable to find yourself in costume and up on the stage, too. Haines is like that; it reaches out and grabs you and will not let go.

BACKGROUND

Lynn Canal, one of the longest and deepest fjords on the North American continent, terminates at the northern end in two narrow fingers of

"Jack Dalton" and his lady stroll out to greet a visiting tour ship at the Port Chilkoot dock.

water: Chilkat Inlet on the left and Chilkoot Inlet on the right (these two words, Chilkat and Chilkoot, will have you horribly confused before your stay in Haines is over). Between them, on the Chilkoot side of the eleven-mile Chilkat Peninsula, lies Haines, approximately seventy-five miles northwest of Juneau and only fourteen nondrivable miles south of Skagway.

At the time of the first European contact, all of this territory was inhabited by the powerful and wealthy Chilkat Tlingit who lived in several villages in the area, of which the principal village was and continues to be Klukwan on the Chilkat River. The Chilkat controlled the passes leading through the Coast Mountains to the Alaska and Canadian Interior, trading the coveted eulachon oil to the Athapaskans in exchange for valuable hides from moose or caribou. The Chilkat were respected throughout the Tlingit nation for their wealth and strength and were particularly renowned for their skill at weaving Chilkat blankets.

The present settlement of Haines got its start in 1879 with the arrival of S. Hall Young, a Presbyterian missionary, with his naturalist friend John Muir. Muir was studying the surrounding wilderness, but Young was looking for a site to establish a mission. The two had journeyed from Wrangell in an open canoe in late October, which is a feat few would attempt today. The Tlingit chiefs offered Hall a site on Portage Cove, on a well-used portage trail between the Chilkat River and Chilkoot Inlet. The Tlingit name for the place was Dei-shu, or "End of the Trail." The mission school opened the following year. The settlement was named Haines for Mrs. F. E. Haines, secretary of the Presbyterian home mission board that had raised funds for the mission.

Hard on the heels of Haines Mission came the canneries. Several operated in Chilkat and Chilkoot inlets starting in 1882, but only one, Haines Packing Company at Letnikof Cove, was a long-term success. Haines Packing Company continued operations as a cannery until 1972 and still runs a fish tender out of Letnikof Cove to a cannery on Excursion Inlet, making it Haines's oldest continuously operated business.

Haines next found itself caught up in the gold rush. In 1897, Jack Dalton, a shrewd business man and sawed-off-shotgun-toting Wild West type who had come to Alaska in 1890, began driving livestock and pack horses over a trail to the Interior to stock the mining camps that had sprung up in Yukon Territory. The price was $2 a head for cattle and $2.50 a head for horses. The Dalton Trail, in reality a toll road, led from Pyramid Harbor on Chilkat Inlet to the vicinity of Whitehorse, some three hundred miles distant. Today's Haines Highway follows the route of the trail quite closely.

The Dalton Trail was heavily used as a pack route into the Klondike, a longer but easier alternative to the Chilkoot and White Pass trails, until the White Pass and Yukon railroad out of Skagway was completed in 1900. In 1898 a stop on the trail about thirty-five miles from Haines turned into a bonanza itself: Porcupine became the center of a rich mining district that

The fishing fleet awaits the season opening at the Haines Packing Company dock at Letnikof Cove.

produced gold until the mid-1930s, and Haines was the supply depot.

In 1903 the army stepped in with the construction of Fort William H. Seward at Port Chilkoot, one-half mile south of Haines Mission. Fort Seward housed two companies of soldiers. By 1904 Haines counted three hotels, two restaurants, several stores, and more than four hundred residents. Between 1922 and 1939, Chilkoot Barracks, which the post had been renamed in 1922 in commemoration of the famous trail to the Klondike, and to avoid confusion with the town of Seward, was the only army post in Alaska. The post served as an induction and rest camp during World War II, but closed in 1946 in favor of other military installations that had been built in Alaska. The property was purchased by a group of World War II veterans who established the community of Port Chilkoot, later merged with the city of Haines. The handsome white frame buildings of the old army post, ringing the grass parade grounds, are a serene sight today. Most have been restored for use as private residences or commercial enterprises. The post was designated a national historic site in 1972, reverting to the original name Fort William H. Seward.

Two great transportation links were forged out of Haines in the 1940s. The 159-mile Haines Highway was built by the military during World War II to provide access from the Interior to tidewater. Approximating the route of the old Dalton Trail, the all-weather road extends from Haines to Haines Junction to link with the Alaska Highway, giving access to Anchorage, Fairbanks, and the Yukon Territory in Canada. The present Alaska Marine Highway System also had its birth in Haines as the brainchild of Steve Homer, one of the purchasers of the Port Chilkoot post. Homer envisioned a ferry system that would transport both passengers and freight between Southeast ports and connect them with the Alaska Highway through Haines. He purchased a landing craft, named it the *Chilkoot*, and in 1948 initiated the first ferry service between Haines, Skagway, and Juneau. After three successful years, Homer sold the *Chilkoot* to the territory of Alaska. The system proved so popular that a special ship, the *Chilkat*, was commissioned, the first vessel of the Alaska Marine Highway fleet. The *Chilkat* is still in service, usually handling the runs between Ketchikan, Annette Island, and Prince of Wales Island.

Today Haines relies primarily upon tourism and transportation to keep the economy fueled. Fishing has always contributed to the economy, and there is a small lumber mill four miles north of town. With noticeably drier weather than most parts of Southeast, striking wilderness scenery, excellent fishing, a magnificent new state park, year-round highway and water access, and the world's largest gathering of bald eagles in residence October through January each year, Haines seems poised to become a major recreational destination in Southeast. If I were a betting person, I would put my money on Haines.

GETTING THERE

You can reach Haines year-round by road via the 159-mile Haines Highway that links with the Alaska Highway at Haines Junction. U.S. and Canadian customs and immigration offices are located at mile 42 on the Haines Highway. Be sure to find out in advance how late they stay open (it has previously been until midnight only). Also check into Canadian regulations concerning such matters as car insurance, cash requirements, pets, and firearms before setting out for the border from Haines.

Alaska state ferries stop regularly at Haines en route between Juneau and Skagway. The ferry terminal is located at Lutak Inlet, 4.3 miles north of Haines (transportation to town is available). Scheduled air service into Haines is offered from either Juneau or Skagway, but on small prop planes, not jets. Only a few of the large cruise ships currently call at Haines, but the smaller "exploration class" ships (such as the *Great Rivers Explorer* and *North Star*) are taking advantage of the community's hospitality to dock at the Port Chilkoot wharf. With new ships traveling the Inside Passage every year, the tour ship scenario changes constantly. Write the Alaska Division of Tourism or Haines Chamber of Commerce to find out which ships might be stopping in Haines.

The passage up Lynn Canal has some of the most diverse views along the entire Inside Passage route, beginning with the boat traffic around Auke Bay. Besides dozens of pleasure craft, you will see fishing boats, crab boats, and the occasional tug and barge. Farther north, nearing Haines, your progress may be completely blocked by gill-net fishermen, should your trip coincide with a gill-net opening. The white floats that suspend the nets look like strings of pearls cast upon the water.

You will pass two lighthouses in Lynn Canal, Sentinel Light and the octagonal Eldred Rock (look for the weathered remains of the Comet gold mine on your right as you near Eldred Rock). The discoloration of the water as you enter Chilkoot Inlet is silt from the Katzehin River. Occasionally, you can see moose on the sandy flats at the river mouth. Across the way, you will see Davidson Glacier flowing toward Chilkat Inlet and Rainbow Glacier, a hanging glacier that cascades over a cliff, a little farther beyond.

To See and Do

Haines has two *Visitors' Information Centers*. If you arrive by car on the Haines Highway, you'll find an information office on your way into town (about one mile from Haines center). A second visitors' center is handily located at Second and Willard streets in downtown Haines. Both centers have lots of parking available, even for the largest motorhomes, and the coffeepots are always on. Pick up *walking tour maps* for Haines and Fort Seward.

The greatest attraction in Haines is historic *Fort William H. Seward* at Port Chilkoot, only a few minutes walk from the town center. The sight is an anomaly in Southeast Alaska: a great expanse of close-cropped green bordered by stately, white-painted and pillared frame houses. Were it not for the mountain peaks, you would think you had stumbled upon a Southern plantation.

The site, locally known as Port Chilkoot, was once an active army base—the only one in Alaska for nearly twenty years following World War I. The buildings are now in private hands, the entire post having been purchased by a group of war veterans when the army shut it down after World War II. A walking tour of the fort has been mapped out and the buildings are identified with small plaques. The large houses at the top of the parade grounds originally constituted officers' row, where captains, lieutenants, and their families were housed. The buildings—all painted white with varying trims

Officers' quarters face the parade grounds at Fort William H. Seward. The premises now house the Hälsingland Hotel.

of gray, blue, red, and green—have been turned into private residences, rental condominiums, small shops, and a Bed and Breakfast. Notice the beautiful oval windows in the gables.

On the right side of the green as you face uphill were the bachelor officers' quarters, captains' quarters, and commanding officers' quarters. Today these buildings are all a part of the Hotel Hälsingland, which offers gracious accommodations with a flavor of the past. Directly across the parade grounds from the hotel is the former post hospital, which now houses the workshops of Alaska Indian Arts, Inc. (see below). The shingled, barnlike building behind the old hospital is a convention hall and theater where local performances of the Chilkat Dancers and Lynn Canal Community Players take place. This building dates from the 1890s but not on this site. It was built originally as a cannery warehouse at Pyramid Harbor. The army dismantled the building and moved it to the present location in 1919 as the E & R (Education and Recreation) hall. The building was renovated in 1967 as the *Chilkat Center for the Arts*. The center also houses the Haines public radio station.

Be sure to stop in at *Alaska Indian Arts*. This nonprofit organization is dedicated to the furtherance of traditional Northwest Coast Indian arts. Artists are at work every weekday carving totem poles, masks, silver jewelry, or other items. The surroundings are pleasantly casual. The artists do not seem to mind if you peer over their shoulders and ask foolish questions while they work. Take a moment to look at the special tools they use, too.

One morning when we walked over to take some photographs, some of the carvers were just starting to outline the figures on a new totem pole.

Alaska Indian Arts artisans have produced totems for clients all over the world (and many in Alaska). They carved Alaska's tallest totem pole (132.5 feet) for Japan's Osaka World's Fair in 1970. The pole now stands in the village of Kake on Kupreanof Island. Alaska Indian Arts is open every weekday except over the noon hour and visitors are welcome. There is a showroom where you can purchase some of their works.

Alaska Indian Arts was founded by Carl Heinmiller, a retired army major and one of the purchasers of the Port Chilkoot post. His son Lee Heinmiller is the present director. Another of Carl Heinmiller's achievements was the formation of the *Chilkat Dancers* that give scheduled evening performances in the Chilkat Center for the Arts. Searching for a way to involve the local youth in constructive projects, Heinmiller drew upon the knowledge of the local Tlingit population in Haines and Klukwan to help recreate tradi-

Charles Jimmie works on a halibut design at the Alaska Indian Arts workshop. Visitors are welcome.

Lee Heinmiller explains Chilkat blanket design during a performance of the Chilkat Dancers.

tional Tlingit dances, complete with authentic costumes and masks. All children were encouraged to participate—Tlingit, Caucasian, old, young, boy, or girl. Gradually the idea took shape until today, over twenty-five years later, the Chilkat Dancers of Haines are known throughout the world for their stirring performances. Do not miss the opportunity to see them. You will enjoy the fantastic carved wooden masks, elaborate Chilkat blankets, er-mine headdresses, beaded dance shirts, and button blankets. Take your camera (with flash), as photographs are permitted. The program is narrated, so you will know the background of each dance.

Totem Village, located on the parade grounds of Fort William H. Seward, is also the work of Alaska Indian Arts. The most important feature is the Raven Tribal House, a replica of a traditional Native community house. A *salmon bake* takes place here every evening in the summer with fresh salmon grilled over an alder fire. The totem poles in and around the house were some of the first ever carved by Alaska Indian Arts and it is interesting to compare these early efforts with some of the later ones. The two corner posts at the front were carved in the late 1960s and while the carvers can point out flaws in design and execution, I think the posts have considerable charm. The top figure is Bear, with a small Frog on his chest. The center figure is Sea-Bear (with fins instead of legs), holding Halibut in his mouth. On the bottom is Bear again, holding a tinneh, a shield-shaped copper plate that was used as a form of currency by Southeast Natives in earlier days. In the carving, the tinneh symbolizes wealth.

The freestanding pole at the front and to the left of the house was one of the first carved. From top to bottom the figures are Raven, as the founder of the world, Bear holding a tinneh, and Beaver holding the traditional stick (the staff of authority of a chief of the Beaver clan) but, untraditionally, in a vertical position. The lone face is the sun, and the bottom figure is a Whale, with the tail curled in front.

The back corner posts show a potlatch chief at the top, holding a staff and wearing his ringed potlatch hat. Raven is below him, easily identified by the wings and long, straight beak. The head at the bottom is Frog, because of the wide mouth with protruding tongue. The tall center totem in back of the house is one of several copies of the small Friendship pole that can be seen in the Sheldon Museum (see below). The original pole, only twenty-eight inches high, was presented to Steve Sheldon of Haines in the 1920s by Chilkat Tlingit from Klukwan. Sheldon, a U.S. deputy marshal, had been instrumental in restoring good will between conflicting clans and the totem symbolizes peace by representing both Eagle and Raven moieties on the same pole. From top to bottom the primary figures are: Eagle (wearing hat), Raven (diving), Hawk, Bear, Frog, Wolf, and (very small) Eagle. Alaska Indian Arts carvers have produced two other copies of the original pole. One is displayed in Juneau in the foyer of the Alaska Court Building. A more recent pole, completed in 1977, stands before the Main Street school in Haines. If you have time and have an interest in totem design and carving techniques, walk over to the school and compare the superb design and craftsmanship of the later pole with the earlier model shown here.

There are carved houseposts within the tribal house, too. Inside the door to the right you will recognize the figure of Beaver from his crosswise stick and crosshatched tail with a small face in the tail joint. Hawk is below him and Frog is on the bottom. Inside the door to the left is Raven on top with a protruding beak and odd, elongated feet. On the rear wall on the right is a special pole honoring Carl Heinmiller and his Tlingit name Ka Woosh' Gaaw, which he translates to mean the "sound of the Raven's wings." The diving Raven figure is dramatic on this post. The pole on the left was raised in honor of Heinmiller's daughter, Judy Heinmiller Clark. It is called "Looking in the Water," and, according to Heinmiller, was named for her "big, blue eyes." The pole recalls the story of Raven who looks in the water, sees his own image, and fears that he represents all of the evil in the world. The top figure is Raven with a long bill, almost like a mosquito's. In the middle is an inverted figure with arms, representing imagination. On the bottom, the inverted figure of Raven represents his image reflected in the water.

One of the most recently carved poles has been erected outside the Chilkat Center for the Arts. The artists are pleased with this unusual pole, called *Raven: Guardian Spirit of the clans.* Each of the figures was carved by a different person. From top to bottom the figures include: Raven, with open wings. Notice the U-forms and split-Us painted on the wing tips. (Carved by Greg Horner.) Strong Man, holding Whale by the tail (the blow-hole is represented by the tiny face above Whale's head). Usually the figure in the Strong Man story is a sea lion, but the carvers wanted to work on Whale. (Carved by Dave Svenson.) Bird figure, emerging from Whale's mouth. (Carved by John Hagen.) Beaver, note the striking crosshatch tail. The artist departed from convention by substituting another design for the traditional face in the tail joint to avoid detracting from the central figure. This figure had distinct incisors and holds the usual stick. (Carved by Edwin Kasko.) Man holding tinneh. Note that the human figure has no ears, but has human arms and legs. (Carved by Clifford Thomas.) Frog, head downward. Note the absence of teeth. Frog has only the protruding tongue in a wide mouth. (Carved by Charles Jimmie.) The pole is thirty-seven feet tall and supported by a steel post. It was completed in 1980.

Before leaving Totem Village, drop into Tresham Gregg's sculpture studio, the *Sea Wolf,* for a look at the original designs in wood and metal sculpture with a Tlingit theme. The *Art Shop,* located in the former post telegraph office, features the work of several Haines artists.

From Port Chilkoot, it is a short walk along Beach Road, following the water to the north, to arrive at Haines proper. The new *Lookout Park* overlooks the Haines waterfront and small boat harbor, with benches, picnic areas, circular viewing platforms, and a beautiful new totem pole carved at Alaska Indian Arts. A topo sign identifies mountain peaks, glaciers, and other natural features in the vicinity. There is also a Rube Goldbergian steam mining drill that was used in the Chilkat Valley around 1900. The *City Boat Harbor* is home port for a sizable Haines fishing fleet. You might see the gill-net fishermen spreading their nets on the dock to dry, or making repairs.

Across Beach Road from the harbor is the *Sheldon Museum,* which houses an extensive local history collection. The museum is named not for Sheldon Jackson, as is the Sitka museum, but for Steve Sheldon, who adventured his way through Alaska at an early age and wound up in Haines, where he and his wife operated a series of businesses. He later became a U.S. deputy marshal and a U.S. commissioner. The Sheldons were enthusiastic collectors of Indian artifacts and other items of historical or artistic significance, and it is their collection that forms the nucleus of the Sheldon Museum. The collection is managed by one of the two Sheldon daughters, Elisabeth Hakkinen, of Haines. If you visit the museum, you will very likely encounter Mrs. Hakkinen bringing local history to life with her accounts of early-day Haines or offering a cup of Russian tea from the urn upstairs.

The museum takes up two floors. Upstairs you will find a model Chilkat clan house and exhibits on Tlingit-style fishing, basketry, beadwork, and dance. There are some fine examples of Chinese camphorwood trunks. These colorful trunks, covered with pigskin and painted bright red, green, or blue with floral designs, were brought to Alaska by early traders.

A special case houses the original lens from the Eldred Rock lighthouse (twenty-four miles south of Haines in Lynn Canal). Made in Paris, the lens was in place from 1906 to 1973 when the station was automated. The octagonal lighthouse, which you pass on the ferry route to Haines and Skagway, was one of twelve manned lighthouses originally established to watch over the Inside Passage.

Downstairs features natural history (children will enjoy the wildlife exhibit, including a black bear in the usual blue or glacier color phase) and early-day Haines. Missionaries, canneries, gold prospecting, pioneer life, and the military are the focus for several displays.

A corner of the room is devoted to Jack Dalton, who operated a toll road to the Interior and later built a hotel and saloon in Haines. There are photos of Dalton, along with pack saddles, yokes, and other equipment used on the Dalton Trail. The most romantic period piece is the sawed-off shotgun Dalton kept loaded with rock salt behind the bar of his saloon. Other photo exhibits show the *Chilkoot*, the landing craft acquired by Steve Homer that was the predecessor of today's "Blue Canoes" of the Alaska Marine Highway fleet, and early views of the army post at Port Chilkoot.

Leaving the museum, you are in perfect position to start the *Haines Walking Tour*. The 1.6-mile route from the museum to Lookout Park is easy walking, mostly on level ground. The tour is based on an historical building survey and provides an insider's look at past and present Haines. Count on spending forty-five minutes to one and one-half hours on your walk. While in town, consider a meal at the *Lighthouse Restaurant* overlooking the City Boat Harbor. The menu is not out of the ordinary, but the stop affords a view of fishermen putting to sea or returning. A local favorite is the *Chilkat Bakery and Restaurant* off Main Street on Fifth Avenue (opens at 7:00 A.M.—try the apricot bearclaws!). Just around the corner from the bakery, the *Trading Post* specializes in furs and fur products from Alaska and the Yukon, including red fox and wolverine from the local Chilkat Valley; also lovely hats, mittens, slippers, and gloves made by Lois Wiggins, a Haines resident. At the shop, you are likely to find Daisy Phillips at work on the beaded earrings and moccasins she is known for. Before leaving the Haines city center, browse through the *Whale Rider, Northern Arts,* and *Chilkat Valley Arts* galleries. Located near the downtown Visitors' Information Center, they all feature Haines artists.

If you are returning to Port Chilkoot after the tour, take the footpath through *Tlingit Park*. The trail leads from Main Street in back of the museum, crosses the park alongside an old tree-shaded cemetery, and emerges not far from the Hotel Hälsingland at Fort William H. Seward. Continuing down Beach Road one-half mile in the other direction from the fort, you come to the state-operated *Portage Cove Wayside* with tent sites, rest rooms, and a view of the passing ship traffic on Lynn Canal. A gentle trail follows the shore beyond the campground for about two and one-half miles. Beach Road cries out for camera or sketch pad. Haines seems to be a magnet for derelict fishing boats that beach themselves on the shore. Another scene for your viewfinder is the grayed timber warehouses on the Port Chilkoot wharf.

Out-the-road touring from Haines can take you in three different directions. You can easily rent a car. Follow *Lutak Highway* to the north along Chilkoot Inlet to reach the state ferry terminal. You will pass the Haines Tank Farm, southern terminus of an old oil pipeline to military installations in Fairbanks. The highway leads to the wide *Chilkoot River* that tumbles madly over stumps and boulders in its rush to the sea. You can easily imagine brown bears standing in the shallow water and scooping out the salmon that struggle upstream to spawn in *Chilkoot Lake* (mile 9.7 at the end of Lutak Road). There is a fish weir on the river to count the salmon as they travel upstream. The daily tally is noted on a blackboard alongside the road. "They're way up," someone said as we passed by. "The salmon are here today!"

At a fork in the road go left to reach the state campground and Chilkoot Lake, where there is good fishing for Dolly Varden and salmon. There are campsites, picnic shelters, rest rooms, and a boat launch. A Florida couple was casting serenely into the lake during a slight drizzle when we arrived. They had camped there the previous summer and could not wait to drive all the way across the country and up the Alaska Highway in their camper in order to come back. The right fork in the road takes you across the river to a residential road on Lutak Inlet. Drive *slowly* (walking is even better) if you want to see some Haines-style waterfront homes.

Driving south out of Haines on *Mud Bay Road* you will be following the shore of Chilkat Inlet. The gravel road is good; you will be rewarded with views of the Chilkat Mountains, the Chilkat River, and at least two glaciers. At *Letnikof Cove* are two small-craft floats and the red cannery buildings of Haines Packing Company. Fishing vessels may be roped together out front near the *Pacific Queen*, the Haines Packing fish tender. The cannery has been shut since 1972 but the buildngs still provide storage and overhaul facilities for the fleet. There is a postage-stamp-sized store where you can buy everything from a can of beans to a set of oilskins. More to the point, you can find a cold drink. There are many worthwhile photo subjects here, from the old cannery buildings and equipment to the fishing nets coiled on the dock.

A well-worn Haines gill-netter submits to a preseason overhaul at Letnikof Cove.

A right turn off Mud Bay Road at mile 7 (follow the signs) takes you to *Chilkat State Park* with campsites, rest rooms, and a hand-hewn ranger cabin that was built in Nenana (near Fairbanks in the Interior) of white spruce, disassembled, and trucked to the site. Go out on the front deck of the cabin (you can do this even if the station is closed). Almost within touching distance are the jagged peaks of the Chilkats, two glaciers (the hanging Rainbow Glacier to the right and Davidson on the left), and the ice blue waters of Lynn Canal. Back on Mud Bay Road, continue straight to reach Mud Bay on Chilkoot Inlet. There is a place to stop your car and get out to look at the view. Beach peas bloom here in summer, with lupine and wild roses.

The third road you can take out of Haines is the *Haines Highway*, which leads eventually to the Alaska Highway. The road follows the *Chilkat River*, which is wide and shallow with many islands and lined with cottonwood trees. There is an Indian graveyard on the right at about mile 3.5. On the river flats near mile 19 are the famous *Eagle Council Grounds* where an estimated thirty-five hundred bald eagles gather in the cottonwoods along the river from October through January every year to take advantage of a late run of spawning chum salmon. In 1982 the state of Alaska set this area aside as the forty-nine-thousand-acre Chilkat Bald Eagle Preserve to protect the birds and their habitat. *Alaska Nature Tours, P.O. Box 491, Haines, Alaska, 99827;* telephone *(907) 766-2876,* leads fall eagle-viewing tours from Haines.

At mile 22 you will see a turnoff for the Tlingit village of *Klukwan*. Klukwan, on the bank of the Chilkat River, has always been the principal village of the Chilkat Tlingit. There are two main streets in the village. The lower street at the river edge is lined with weathered frame houses, some of them now abandoned and leaning crazily to one side. The upper street has brand new homes. There is a log tribal house with a painted Eagle and Raven design on the front. I do not encourage you to drive into Klukwan. The community is not equipped for tourists and there is nothing for visitors to see except private residences. While Klukwan is an acknowledged repository of fine Tlingit art, none of it is on public display. There are no totem poles. If you feel you must go, proceed on foot. Klukwan residents object particularly to visitors who roar down the dirt road in their large automobiles or campers and then, deciding there is nothing to see, turn around and roar out again, leaving billowing clouds of dust in their wake. The residents also ask that visitors respect their privacy and not take photos.

Heading back to Haines again on the highway, the *Haines Visitors' Information Center* is located about one mile from town. Drop in for a cup of coffee, and pick up any brochures or maps that you need. The *Welcome poles* on the sign in front were carved by Alaska Indian Arts. The Raven pole on the left features Raven, the creator figure, on top. Whale is beneath him, and then Bear. The pole on the right is the Eagle Council Grounds pole, honoring the eagle and its feeding grounds along the Chilkat River.

Outdoors addicts will find many hiking trails to their liking in Haines (pick up the brochure *Haines is for Hikers* at the visitors' information center or book stands around Haines; it has maps of principal trails). The most strenuous climb takes you to the top of 3,610-foot Mount Ripinsky. As an

The Southeast Alaska State Fair, held the third week of August in Haines every year, draws visitors from all over Southeast.

alternative for those who would rather sit back and let the scenery rush by, Chilkat Guides offers gentle float trips (no white water) down the Chilkat River. You might glimpse eagles, brown and black bears, and moose. (Write *P.O. Box 170, Haines, Alaska, 99827* for reservations and information, or inquire at the *Art Shop* in Port Chilkoot, telephone *(907) 766-2409*.

The list of special events in Haines is topped by the *Southeast Alaska State Fair*, which is held the third week in August of every year. Popular features include the craft exhibits, home-baked and home-canned foods, a horse show, and a parade. Reservations for the ferry are necessary for the week of the fair, even for walk-on passengers. The *Haines King Salmon Derby* takes place in late May or early June. The *Alaska State Community Theatre Festival* is held in Haines in April of odd-numbered years in the Chilkat Center for the Arts. Theater groups from throughout Alaska turn out for workshops and performances. Also in this building, do not miss the *Chilkat Dancers*, and *Lust for Dust* (or *Patience Rewarded*), a lighthearted melodrama based on the Haines story featuring Jack Dalton, Lotta Larue, and Porcupine Pete put on by the Lynn Canal Community Players in the summer. In February, take in the annual *Alcan 200 Snow Machine Race*.

SKAGWAY
Population 700

Everyday is show time in this tiny outpost of the gold rush (1,141 miles from Seattle via the Marine Highway)—in the summer at least. The curtain comes down when the last cruise ship leaves in the fall, and the population dwindles to nearly nothing. Other towns might offer more grandiose scenery, more thought-provoking experiences, or better fishing, but Skagway knows how to entertain.

Skagway is good fun for a day or two, especially if the weather is nice (which it probably will be since the precipitation averages only twenty-six inches a year). You will enjoy the wooden sidewalks, meticulously restored storefronts, old-time hotels, and other trimmings of the Days of '98, topped off with an evening melodrama and a drink at the famous Red Onion Saloon.

BACKGROUND

Skagway is tucked up into the head of Taiya Inlet at the northern extreme of Lynn Canal, ninety air miles northwest of Juneau. The town occupies the level floor of a long, narrow valley at the mouth of the Skagway River. The Coast Mountains rise on every side, a seemingly impenetrable barrier to the gold fields of the Canadian Klondike.

The first recorded settler in Skagway was a farsighted riverboat captain named William Moore. Moore had been in Wrangell during the first

Skagway retains a gold rush image with wooden sidewalks and carefully restored false-fronted buildings.

gold strike to affect Alaska in 1861. He got his share of the bonanza by transporting prospectors by steamer up the Stikine River to the diggings in Canada. He was on the Stikine again in 1873 to move prospectors into the new Cassiar gold fields. By 1887 Moore was helping a survey party determine the boundary line between Alaska and Canada. With his son, he staked a homestead on the flats at the mouth of the Skagway River and began planning a wharf to accommodate the traffic he was sure would come knocking at the back door to the Yukon.

And come they did, ten years later, at a time when the nation was suffering a severe economic depression. When word reached a moody and out-of-work populace in July of 1897 that a "ton of gold" had been brought out of the Klondike, west coast docks groaned under the weight of fortune hunters waiting for steamers to take them north. Six days after the *Portland* docked in Seattle with the first samples of Klondike gold, the *Queen* was bound for Moore's wharf at the head of Lynn Canal with a cargo of impatient prospectors. The stampeders promptly overran Moore's property and set about the business of getting into the Klondike. A tent city sprang into place on the Moore homestead. By October, the new boom-town of Skagway had streets, frame houses, dance halls, and three wharves under construction. The population passed ten thousand and more as wave upon wave of fortune seekers made their way north.

From Skagway, the way to the Klondike led over the Coast Mountains

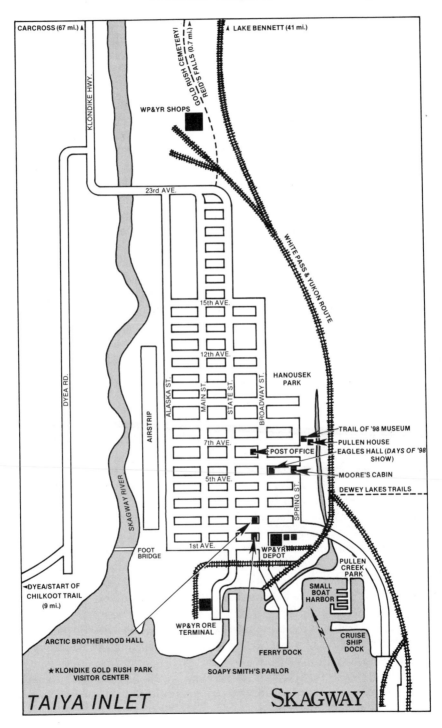

CARCROSS (67 mi.)

LAKE BENNETT (41 mi.)

KLONDIKE HWY.

GOLD RUSH CEMETERY/
REID'S FALLS (0.7 mi.)

WP&YR SHOPS

23rd AVE.

WHITE PASS & YUKON ROUTE

DYEA RD.

15th AVE.

AIRSTRIP

12th AVE.

ALASKA ST.

MAIN ST.

STATE ST.

BROADWAY ST.

HANOUSEK
PARK

SKAGWAY RIVER

7th AVE.

TRAIL OF '98 MUSEUM
PULLEN HOUSE
POST OFFICE
EAGLES HALL (DAYS OF '98
SHOW)

5th AVE.

MOORE'S CABIN

SPRING ST.

DEWEY LAKES TRAILS

1st AVE.

FOOT
BRIDGE

WP&YR
DEPOT

PULLEN
CREEK
PARK

DYEA/START OF
CHILKOOT TRAIL
(9 mi.)

SMALL
BOAT
HARBOR

WP&YR ORE
TERMINAL

ARCTIC BROTHERHOOD HALL

CRUISE
SHIP
DOCK

FERRY DOCK

★ KLONDIKE GOLD RUSH PARK
VISITOR CENTER

SOAPY SMITH'S PARLOR

TAIYA INLET

SKAGWAY

through twenty-nine-hundred-foot White Pass to Lake Bennett in Canada, a trip of approximately forty miles. Lake Bennett was the beginning of a system of interconnecting lakes and rivers that would float the prospectors the rest of the five hundred miles to Dawson on the Yukon River. A more popular alternative was the Chilkoot Trail that followed a parallel course through the mountains from Dyea, an old Indian village and trading post nine miles from Skagway (by today's road) at the extreme northern tip of Taiya Inlet. This trail had long been used by the Chilkat Tlingit as a trading route to the Interior, and hundreds of prospectors had used it to traverse the mountains years before the big strike came. Both trails led to Lake Bennett, but the Chilkoot was shorter at only thirty-two miles.

With shorter came steeper, however; the final half-mile to the thirty-seven-hundred-foot summit of Chilkoot Pass was a tortuous forty-five-degree climb. In the winter, steps were chopped into the snow, and the image of the long, black line of prospectors trudging single file up the "Golden Stairs" of Chilkoot Pass has come to symbolize the sacrifices made in the name of gold. Crossing the pass one time would have been plenty for any man, but the stampeders were forced to assault the summit time and time again, some as many as thirty times, in order to transport their gear and the roughly 1,150 pounds of food (enough for a year's prospecting) that the Canadian government required them to have before crossing the border. At the end of the trail, the stampeders camped beside Lake Bennett where they manufactured crude boats out of the surrounding stands of timber and waited for the spring breakup. When the lake ice broke up on 29 May 1898, more than seven thousand boats charged downriver to Dawson.

Skagway grew in reputation as a hard-bitten, lawless frontier town. Everyone was there for one reason only: to make money—big money—if not in the gold fields then by providing services (some of them of the more reprehensible and unmentionable variety) to those who were on their way to the gold fields, or even by relieving the gold from those on their way back. The most notorious outlaw of the era was Jefferson Randolph "Soapy" Smith, a sleazy, two-bit con artist whose nickname derived from one of his better-known cons, which was to "give away" ordinary bars of soap purportedly wrapped in large denomination bills for the price of a mere five dollars. Soapy enjoyed great success with this and other variations of the standard shell game, but did not hesitate to use more direct methods to unburden prospectors of their grubstakes or their pokes of gold when appropriate. At the same time he was pathetically eager to gain acceptance by the town tradesmen and rode as marshal in Skagway's Fourth of July parade.

The citizens grew increasingly outraged at Smith's brazen lawlessness, however, and in July of 1898, Soapy's luck ran out. Two of his henchmen had robbed a prospector, J. D. Stewart, of twenty-six hundred dollars in gold dust, and Stewart screamed long and loudly for justice. The town citizens gathered down at the docks to discuss the situation. Frank Reid, the town surveyor, stood guard outside. When Soapy learned about the meeting he took his rifle and set off for the dock, but was halted. He struck at Reid with his rifle. Reid pushed it aside and fired his revolver, but missed with the first shot. His second and third shots killed Smith instantly, but Reid took a bullet in the groin and died twelve days later. Both men are buried in Skagway's Gold Rush Cemetery.

During the first year of the rush, an estimated twenty to thirty thousand '98ers crossed the two trails into Canada. It was not long before several enterprising individuals had built crude tramways to help transport goods to the summit. The most sophisticated on the Chilkoot Trail was an aerial tramway completed by the Chilkoot Railroad and Transportation Company in May of 1898. The company charged seven and one-half cents a pound to haul supplies over the pass. In times of such fervor as the gold rush of 1898 though, big dreams are the order of the day, and the man who now stepped onto the stage had the biggest vision of all: to build a railroad over White Pass.

Michael J. Heney, an Irish railroad contractor, was sure that the railway could be built and, after an all-night meeting in Skagway, a group of English financiers agreed. Construction began 27 May 1898, with picks, shovels, and blasting powder. The rails reached to the summit of White Pass by 18 February 1899; to Lake Bennett by 6 July 1899; and to Whitehorse by 29 July 1900: a total distance of 110 miles. Many stories attend the building of the White Pass and Yukon Route (which was quickly nicknamed the "Wait Patiently and You'll Ride") and the superhuman feats of Big Mike Heney, the "Irish Prince." One of them concerns Heney's reaction when his crew reached the summit of White Pass only to be halted by a Canadian border guard. Heney sent up an ambassador with a bottle of scotch in each pocket and a box of cigars under each arm. When the guard woke up a day or so later, so the story goes, Heney's crew was laying track a mile down the other side.

With completion of the railroad, the town of Dyea, which had vied with Skagway for the title of largest town in Alaska, folded. Most of the buildings were torn down for lumber. The White Pass and Yukon Route helped things along by buying up and dismantling the Chilkoot Railroad and Transportation Company tram to eliminate any competition from that direction. Today, the most tangible reminder of the thousands of people who once passed through the town is the Slide Cemetery where victims of an avalanche on the Chilkoot Trail in April of 1898 lie buried.

Although the rush to the Klondike was nearly over by the time the railroad was completed, prospectors having been diverted to the Nome strike in 1899, the White Pass and Yukon operated steadily as a connecting link for passengers and freight between the coast and the head of navigable waters in the Yukon, bringing a sense of stability to the town of Skagway. From its boomtown origins, Skagway steadied to become one of Alaska's first two incorporated cities in 1900 (Juneau was the other). The thousands of occupants turned to hundreds of residents and the population has remained at that level except for a period during World War II when the town swelled again as a supply depot for construction of the Alaska Highway.

Until 1982, the White Pass and Yukon railroad was the focal point of Skagway's economy, operating continuously, winter and summer, as an integrated ship-train-truck transportation system to bring goods into and out of the Yukon. In recent years a major portion of the freight business consisted of hauling mineral concentrates (silver, lead, zinc, copper, and asbestos—not gold) out of Interior mines and shipping them south by water. In 1982, railroad officials announced that the White Pass and Yukon would suspend operations indefinitely: closure of the Anvil Mines near Ross River in the Yukon and the subsequent loss of freight business made the railroad uneconomical. With a majority of permanent residents employed by the railroad, closure of the White Pass and Yukon Route struck at the heart of the community. Plans for reopening the railroad remain uncertain. In the summer, however, Skagway's economy is fueled by more than one-quarter of a million tourists who arrive by cruise ship and highway to relive gold rush history.

And what of Captain Moore, who was unceremoniously pushed aside while his homestead was marked off into city streets? He did not make out too badly after all. After pursuing his claims through the courts, Moore was ultimately awarded one-quarter of the assessed value of all the original town lots in Skagway, and he sold his wharf to the railroad.

Getting There

Skagway is the northernmost stop on the Inside Passage for both cruise ships and Alaska state ferries. Both dock right in town, so you will be able to have a quick look at Skagway even if your ship is in port for only a short time. Your ship will probably be met by one or more of Skagway's horse-drawn wagons offering tours or transportation through town. You can reach Skagway by car from Carcross via the Klondike Highway (connecting with the Alaska Highway at Whitehorse). If traveling this route, you must report to U.S. customs and immigration before entering Skagway. If you are outward-bound, you report to Canadian customs in Fraser. Check ahead for office hours and Canadian regulations concerning firearms, pets, vehicle registration, and cash requirements (and be thankful you do not have to carry a ton of food with you the way the '98ers did!). Scheduled air service (not jet) into Skagway is available from Juneau and Haines. The airstrip is located alongside the Skagway River at the edge of town.

cut into three pieces before it could be moved from its former location on Sixth Avenue. The building was an army barracks prior to the construction of Fort William H. Seward in Port Chilkoot in 1904. When the barracks was installed at the new address, a false front was added to make the building blend in with surrounding facades.

Almost every building in Skagway seems to have played a part in the gold rush, from *Soapy Smith's old parlor house* (Second Avenue and Broadway; not open to the public) to the *Golden North Hotel* (one of Alaska's oldest). The *Red Onion Saloon* dates from 1898 as a saloon and house of prostitution. The saloon, with the original bar, is still popular with local residents. Staff members dress in authentic 1890s attire, and a small collection of bawdy-house miscellany is on display. When the Red Onion was moved to the present location the building was installed backwards; evidently it fit better front-to-back. Farther up Broadway, *Irene's Inn* (Broadway and Sixth), a small hotel and restaurant, dates from 1899 when it was built as The Nome Saloon, one of many saloons and gambling houses then lining Sixth Avenue. The *Skagway Inn Bed & Breakfast* across the street dates from 1898 and is a great place to stay if you do not mind a bath down the hall. Drop in for afternoon tea of homemade decadent desserts, or dinner, too.

The oldest building of all is *Moore's Cabin*, which was built by Captain Moore and his son Ben as part of the Moore homestead in 1888. The tiny house recently has been restored with new exterior logs—the interior newspaper-lined walls remain unchanged. You can peer through the small small window in the front door but will be able to make out little in the gloom. To get to the cabin, walk up Broadway from the waterfront and turn right onto Fifth Avenue at Kirmse's gift shop. The gray frame house beside the cabin is the *Moore House*, later built by Ben Moore to house his family.

Another historical structure houses the Skagway city offices and *Trail of '98 Museum* on Seventh Avenue. The building was constructed in 1899 as McCabe Methodist College, Alaska's first institute of higher learning, but stayed open for only two terms. The building then housed U.S. District Court Number One. In fact, you will see the judge's bench, counsel tables, and jury chairs in the museum upstairs. The Trail of '98 Museum is packed with wonderful relics of the gold rush, from wagon wheels and a pilot's hand-drawn chart of the Yukon River from the stern-wheeler *Klondike*, to games of chance from the Board of Trade saloon, gold scales, rocker boxes, and an early 1900s menu board offering "plain steak" for twenty-five cents, rib steak for thirty-five cents, and sirloin for forty cents. An entire display case is devoted to colorful tobacco and cigarette tins, cigar boxes, and a cigar mold. The museum invites browsing. Treasures are tucked away in every corner: a rusty stove and kettle that crossed the Chilkoot Trail, a well-worn coffee grinder, a black and red one-horse open sleigh, a small organ that was lovingly brought to Skagway in 1897.

Quite a bit of space is devoted to those two famous Skagway characters, Jefferson Randolph Smith and Frank Reid. There are portraits of both men, legal documents pertaining to their estates, the tie Soapy was wearing the day he died, and several gruesome photographs. There is also a 15 July 1898 edition of *The Skaguay News* reporting the events leading up to Soapy's death. You can purchase copies at the front desk for two dollars. They make interesting reading, not just for the details of the story, but for the flamboyant style of writing and the 1890s ads. I get goose bumps reading the steamer ads: "Quick Time. First-Class Accommodations. The Fast and Commodious Steamer 'Farallon,' Makes Regular Trips Between Skaguay, Dyea, Haines' Mission, Juneau, Wrangel and all Puget Sound Ports."

Native artifacts include a high-prowed Tlingit canoe from Klukwan and an Eskimo kayak. There are carved wooden halibut hooks, a valuable Chilkat blanket, baskets, a bentwood box with lid, a potlatch bowl with abalone inlay, and many other fine items. Note the Eskimo snow glasses, one pair carved of wood and another made from bottles.

The museum now has records of persons crossing the Canadian border in either direction during the critical Stampede years. Names are listed alphabetically on index cards, with other information that appeared in the original log books kept by the Royal Canadian Mounted Police. This wonderful data bank enables you to check to see if your ancestor was among

A National Park Service naturalist shows visitors Skagway's first cabin, built in 1888.

those crossing the Chilkoot or White passes. If you find the name, you can then look up the actual microfilmed log entry at the Skagway library. The museum also has passenger lists from the White Pass Steamships and Dawson and Skagway prison files.

Outside the museum, an old White Pass and Yukon steam locomotive rests in the yard. The burned-out shell of a once elegant house to the right of the museum is the *Pullen House*, a former hostelry that gained a wide reputation for fine food and lodgings. Harriet Pullen arrived in Skagway in September of 1897 on the steamer *Rosalie* with seven dollars in her pocket and four children back in Spokane, Washington, to support. She went to work as a cook for a construction outfit and sold home-baked pies on the side. As soon as she could, she bought a house and started her own hotel and went on to become one of Skagway's most prominent citizens. Mrs. Pullen is also remembered in Skagway by the new *Pullen Creek Park* on a little corner of land between the modern White Pass depot and the small boat harbor. A shelter, docks, and walkways make this an appealing spot for a picnic.

Other targets for browsing as you proceed along Broadway in either direction include *Dedman's Photo*, which has an excellent selection of books and other materials pertaining to Skagway and the Chilkoot Trail and a small art gallery upstairs. Some of the paintings are the work of Dedman's owner Barbara Kalen who specializes in original oil paintings depicting scenes along the White Pass and Yukon railroad. Right next door is the *Sweet Tooth Saloon* for sandwiches with homemade bread (try the rye), ice cream confections, and homemade cinnamon rolls and donuts in the morning.

Corrington's Alaskan Ivory, Ltd. is a good place to look for ivory, jade, gold, and other remembrances of Alaska. Watch for the imminent opening of the adjacent *Alaska History Museum*. A local ivory carver with a contemporary style is *David Present*. Stop into his studio on Broadway to view the flowing figures he sculpts from this ancient medium.

For evening entertainment, Skagway puts on a lively melodrama based on the town's early history. *Skaguay in the Days of '98* features the entire roster of Skagway characters, including Captain William Moore, J. D. Stewart, Frank Reid, and Soapy Smith. Some strictly-for-fun gambling (for kids, too) starts the show. The performance takes place in the Eagles Hall at Broadway and Sixth and is amazingly good fun for all. Bring the entire family. You will be surprised how entertaining a little local history can be. Visitors also enjoy the lively 1890s atmosphere of the Klondike Hotel on Third Avenue for cocktails or dinner.

Serious walkers with several hours at their disposal can easily make their way to the *Gold Rush Cemetery*, four miles round trip from downtown Skagway. The excursion covers level ground, and passes a pleasant afternoon, or evening, for that matter, since it is never really dark in Skagway in the summer. You can also take a cab or sign up for an excursion trip on the Skaguay Hack or Skagway Street Car Company. The route lies straight up

State Street from the waterfront. At Twenty-Third Avenue, State Street curves around to the left to cross the Skagway River for the road to Dyea and the Klondike Highway. Your way lies straight ahead and across the railroad tracks, following the sign to Soapy Smith's grave. Continue alongside the tracks. Train buffs and equipment fanciers will have a marvelous time in this stretch because the railroad yard has fascinating piles of spare parts, rusted gear, bits of track, engines and cars on sidings, and so forth. Keep going until you reach the river and the cemetery will be on your right.

There is a sign to the cemetery and a short flight of stairs, at the top of which are two graves and the "largest gold nugget in the world" chained to a tree (Ketchikan makes the same claim about its gold nugget). Walk left on a wooden footbridge beside the railroad tracks to reach the rest of the cemetery. There are many, many graves in the Gold Rush Cemetery, most dating from 1898 to 1904. The two most famous are those of Frank Reid and Jefferson Randolph Smith. Soapy's grave is enclosed within four plain wooden posts with iron pipes strung between and the simple inscription "Jefferson R. Smith, died July 8, 1898, age 38 years." This is not the original tombstone, which disappeared long ago. Reid has been given a massive monument and the words, "He gave his life for the honor of Skagway." Behind the cemetery, a five-minute climb along a marked trail takes you to *Reid's Falls*, a cascading froth of water hidden within the forest.

From Skagway you can embark on a number of interesting excursions. For example, there is a two-hour *cruise on Lynn Canal* aboard the *Glacier Queen* (inquire at the Westmark Hotel). Or, sign up for a *Carcross desert picnic* (that is desert, not dessert). Presented by the Skagway Inn, the package includes a tour of Carcross followed by award-winning smoked-salmon quiche and berry-topped cheesecake in a unique pocket desert off the Klondike Highway. Or, see what it is like to stand high on a cascading river of ice with a Temsco *helicopter glacier tour* (it is really quite a thrill).

For hikers, the *Dewey Lakes trail system* starts across the railroad tracks between Third and Fourth avenues. Signs point the way to several different lakes and falls on trails varying from a half-mile to almost five miles. If you will be in port just for the day or even a few hours, the Dewey Lakes trails provide quick access to the wilderness. A *suspension foot bridge* over the Skagway River at First Avenue gives access to waterfront trails and picnic areas of Yakutania Point. The trail of trails, of course, is the historic *Chilkoot Trail* that leaves from Dyea, nine miles from Skagway via a dirt road (take a cab or scheduled bus). Largely abandoned after the opening of the White Pass railroad, the Chilkoot was reopened for hikers in the 1960s. Today's trail, much improved over the original with footbridges and occasional shelters, measures thirty-three miles from Dyea to Lake Bennett. Although you will be passing through untamed country, the Chilkoot Trail is more of a walk through history than a wilderness adventure. You will encounter many other people along the trail. Camping is allowed in designated areas only; open fires are not allowed. Shelters must be shared and are for drying out only and not overnight use.

All along the trail you will see objects left behind by the thousands of prospectors who traveled the route in 1897 and 1898 and the remains of the sizable communities that sprang up along the way. For example, Sheep Camp at mile 13 at one time had a population of six to eight thousand people waiting out winter storms so they could cross over the pass. There were hotels, saloons, and restaurants to serve them. Lindeman City, over the border almost to Bennett, was a tent town of ten thousand transients in the spring of 1898, but little remains today.

Details of the Chilkoot Trail are considerably beyond the scope of this book, but I will say that I hiked the trail in 1975 with five other women and three dogs. It was quite far along in the season, late September or early October, so we met only one or two other parties along the entire route. The rain pummeled us unpityingly and we holed up at Lake Lindeman for two or three days to dry ourselves out. When the sun finally emerged, we went out and filled our packs with the largest, roundest, sweetest blueberries I have ever seen. Hiking the Chilkoot was one of the unforgettable experiences of my life. I will especially never forget the moment the clouds lifted from The Scales and we got our first look at the pass. I assumed there had been an avalanche or earthquake because the way seemed completely blocked by a mountain of enormous boulders. I had not cottoned to the fact that the 1890s photographs showing stampeders ascending the steep but steady slope to the top of the pass were taken in *winter*. We were crossing Chilkoot Pass in *summer*, without the leveling cloak of snow.

If you contemplate hiking the Chilkoot Trail, plan well in advance. You will need three to five days if it is to be a hike and not a forced march. In former days, hikers used to emerge from the trail at Lake Bennett and take the White Pass and Yukon back to Skagway. With the railroad shut down, the return trip is more complicated. Most hikers take a cut-off trail at Bare Loon Lake (mile 29 on the Chilkoot Trail) that leads to the railroad tracks. From there it's a five-mile trek along the tracks to Log Cabin and the Klondike Highway, where you can catch a bus or hitch a ride back to Skagway or on to Carcross and Whitehorse. In prior years, *Chilkoot Boat Tours* has operated a Zodiac between Bennett and Carcross.

Even if you elect to take the cut-off trail to Log Cabin, you should really hike to the end of the trail at Bennett first. You'll pass the weathered log facade of *Saint Andrews Church*. Prospectors built the church during the winter of 1898–1899 while they were waiting their turn to journey on down to the Yukon. The interior furnishings have been lost to time and souvenir hunters. Across the tracks from the Lake Bennett depot stands the White Pass *snow fleet*. Snow Plow Number One, a 129-ton plow built in 1899, worked the line for sixty-five years, clearing drifts of snow with the ten-

Horse-drawn cabs in Skagway make irresistible photo subjects. The landmark Gold North Hotel dates from 1898.

foot rotary blades.

Before setting out on the trail, check with the National Park Service visitors' center in Skagway for the latest trail information and maps, and get instructions for preclearing Canadian customs.

OFF THE MAIN LINE

Using the *Chilkat, Aurora,* and *LeConte*—the smaller vessels of the Alaska Marine Highway fleet—it is easy to sample some of the fishing towns, vacation retreats, Native villages, and logging communities along the Inside Passage. Away from the bustle of urban centers and tourist crowds, you will have the chance to become acquainted with local residents because people have time to talk with you out in the bush. If you like to fish, hunt, canoe, kayak, watch birds, or photograph the wild, you can use the small port as a base to explore the adjacent country. A few of the destinations (Metlakatla, for instance) make excellent day excursions: over in the morning, a quick look around, and back the same day, with a pleasant cruise in the bargain. Or, you can take the ferry to any of the ports and hop a floatplane back. The possibilities are limitless once you make the commitment to diverge from the established path and experience rural Alaska. All of the following communities are available via the "Blue Canoes," Alaska's grand ladies of the sea.

METLAKATLA
Population 1,270

The Tsimshian community of Metlakatla is located on the west coast of the Annette Island Indian Reserve. The island, approximately twenty miles long and twelve miles across, is at the southern tip of the Southeast island chain, only twenty miles north of the U.S. and Canadian border. Ketchikan is the nearest large port. The M.V. *Aurora* makes the round trip between Ketchikan and Metlakatla on several days of the week. The journey takes approximately one and one-half hours one-way. The current schedule is such that, at least one day a week, you can leave Ketchikan in the morning on one run, spend the day in Metlakatla, and catch a second sailing back to Ketchikan in the late afternoon, arriving in time for dinner. This gives you most of the day to explore the community, plus a beautiful ride coming and going: a perfect excursion for a dry day. Or you *may* be able to spend the night at the Taquan Inn. Write *Taquan Inn, P.O. Box 235, Metlakatla, Alaska, 99926;* telephone *(907) 886-6112.*

Metlakatla was founded by Father William Duncan, a missionary, who led his Tsimshian followers from their former home in British Columbia to establish a model community on this Southeast Alaska island in 1887. The United States government created the Annette Island Indian Reserve in 1891. The community elected not to participate in the Alaska Native Claims Settlement Act of 1971 in favor of retaining their status as a reservation.

Like many other communities in Southeast, Metlakatla is supported by timber and fish. The Annette Hemlock Mill produces cants (squared-off logs with the bark removed) that are later sawn into general construction lumber. Chips and bark are sent to the pulp mill in Ketchikan. Annette Island Packing Company, the community fish-processing plant, operates as both a cold storage and cannery during the six-week summer season. The cannery has been in continuous operation since 1890. Many of the salmon come from Metlakatla's four fish traps, the only such traps allowed in the state. On the journey from Ketchikan you will probably pass at least one of them: a large, floating assembly of heavy-gauge chicken wire and logs. The salmon are guided into the trap through a series of funneling enclosures. Trap-caught salmon are prime fish because they are kept alive until they are harvested. Traps used to be the primary means of harvesting salmon, but the method proved too efficient and the salmon stocks were depleted. The traps were outlawed when Alaska became a state in 1959.

When you exit from the ferry, bear right along Walden Point Road. After a pleasant walk past some stunted trees and muskeg, you will come to the Annette Hemlock Mill and then the cannery (no tours, alas). Continue down the road to the center of town. There is a good camera view of the entire cannery complex from the floatplane dock. Sights around town include a new Indian longhouse with a canoe and Tsimshian arts and crafts on display (open weekdays); and the white, twin-steepled William Duncan Memorial Church (not the original, which burned down in 1948). Father Duncan is buried beside the church. His cottage is still standing and available for viewing on weekdays, and weekends by appointment. The missionary lived in the house until his death in 1918.

Metlakatla has two grocery stores, a small cafe, and several snack bars, so you should be able to put together some lunch if you have not brought it with you (no liquor is available, though, as Metlakatla is dry). There is a grassy bank overlooking the harbor where you can sit and enjoy your meal while watching the bald eagles fish for theirs. But do go into the store because you may be surprised at the selection of foods that are stocked in a small, community store in rural Alaska. Some of the items I noted were microwave popcorn, tortillas (both flour and corn), and frozen Chinese dinners. The *Taquan Inn Cafe* serves a mean fried bread (an Indian specialty) with a paper cup of syrup for 75 cents. If you return to the ferry landing ahead of schedule, there is a pebble beach off to the side where you can plant yourself to watch the ship come in.

PRINCE OF WALES ISLAND

Prince of Wales is the largest island in Southeast, measuring 135 miles long by 45 miles wide. The island lies 45 miles west of Ketchikan, an approximate three and one-half hour ride on the *Aurora* or *Chilkat*. The ferry, which makes the trip several times a week, docks at *Hollis*, a former gold-mining town and logging camp that is now limited to the ferry terminal and a small float. Prince of Wales has been logged extensively and is undergoing further timber harvest by several Alaska Native corporations, but the island still offers opportunities for travelers that are not available elsewhere. Because of the logging, the island has the most extensive road system in Southeast (more than seven hundred miles of road), which means that you can drive in virtually any direction to camp, fish, or be by yourself. Fishing is excellent for Dolly Varden, rainbow, steelhead, and cutthroat trout and several types of salmon. Besides the 990 miles of saltwater coast, there are many interior lakes and streams, most of which have seen few

Metlakatla's four floating fish traps are the only ones allowed in the state. You can also tour a cannery there.

fishermen as yet.

From Hollis, the road leads westward to connect with a network of old and new logging roads. A turnoff to the south leads to the village of *Hydaburg* (population 475), the principal community of Haida Indians in Southeast. The village was established in 1911–1912 when several Haida villages in the vicinity joined together to form a school. At Hydaburg you will find a warm welcome, a wonderful collection of old totem poles, a new cold storage plant, and a good hamburger at the *Tides Inn* on the waterfront.

Craig (population 1,170), thirty-one miles from Hollis, is situated on a tiny island connected by a short causeway to Prince of Wales. Craig is a lively community. Loggers and fishermen come together to blow off steam at the Craig Inn on Saturday nights. The community was formerly the site of several fish salteries, followed by canneries, and a sizable seine fleet still ties up at the dock. Craig has grocery stores, hotels, bars, a library, and a bank. There are three restaurants. At the *Captain's Table,* the Pan-abode log cabin, the conversation turns on riggin' slingin', choker settin', and other logger concerns over burgers, fries, and shakes. Hang around long enough and you will pick up the lingo. *Ruth Ann's Restaurant* on the water serves fancier fare. The *Haida-Way Lodge* has surprisingly pleasant rooms that are furnished in natural woods and comfortable earth colors (ask for the room farthest from the restaurant and lounge). Write *P.O. Box 90, Craig, Alaska, 99921*; telephone *(907) 826-3268.*

The nearby community of *Klawock* (population 700) is a Tlingit Indian village, twenty-four miles from Hollis. Klawock was the site of the first

The Annette Island Packing Company operates a cold storage and cannery during a six-week summer season.

salmon cannery in Alaska in 1878, which operated for fifty-one years. Klawock has a remarkable collection of memorial and mortuary poles, replicas and restored originals, that were gathered from abandoned sites farther north on the island, from the village of Tuxekan in particular. The poles are arranged in a park overlooking the town. One of the most striking has a twelve-foot Killer Whale mounted crosswise atop the figure of Brown Bear. Another unusual pole recalls Raven's efforts to destroy a giant clam that was threatening the people. The clam is shown halfway up the pole.

Klawock has a small boat harbor, grocery stores, and a cafe, but no bars or liquor stores (the community is dry). The town is blessed with two nearby lodges, however, with good food and comfortable furnishings. The *Prince of Wales Lodge* specializes in fishing vacations with a complete package of meals, lodging, boats, guides, the works. The restaurant is open to the public as well. Prince of Wales Lodge also operates the Rent-A-Dent agency on the island. Write *Prince of Wales Lodge, P.O. Box 72, Klawock, Alaska, 99925*; telephone *(907) 755-2227*. The *Fireweed Lodge*, overlooking Klawock Lagoon, is popular with local residents for family style dinners. Fishing is available here, too, practically from the front deck. Write *Fireweed Lodge, P.O. Box 116, Klawock, Alaska, 99925*; telephone *(907) 755-2930*. The lodge handles Budget car rentals. Clean but small and spartan beach cabins (skiffs, too) can be rented from *Log Cabin Resort and Campground, P.O. Box 54, Klawock, Alaska, 99925*; telephone *(907) 755-2205.*

Klawock is a place for standing and watching. At the time of our visit, in late July, subsistence fishing for sockeye was in progress, so we watched the fishermen embark in small skiffs and set their nets, like miniature purse seines, to bring in their haul of salmon. Then there were home-canning operations under way on various front porches, and strips of bright red sockeye draped over the railings in preparation for smoking.

The road to *Thorne Bay* (population 475) winds northwest from Klawock for thirty-five miles (fifty-nine miles from Hollis) through the spectacular interior forest. You will see many signs of logging and wild flowers rimming the road, especially Alaska cotton, fireweed, and bunch-berry. Thorne Bay used to be the largest logging camp in Alaska, with a school, church, post office, and shops. Louisiana-Pacific has since packed up most of the logging operation, but the community voted in 1982 to become a third-class city. Area residents hope Thorne Bay will expand into a new recreation center for Southeast. There is a grocery store and a small restaurant. Overnight accommodations in town are on a bed-and-breakfast basis. Contact the city of Thorne Bay for referrals. Or, spend a night moored in a quiet cove at *McFarland's Floatel,* a floating bed and breakfast operated by Jim McFarland, a forester, and Jeannie McFarland, an artist who teaches pine needle raffia basketry. Write *P.O. Box 159, Thorne Bay, Alaska, 99919;* telephone *(907) 828-3335.*

The town, composed largely of mobile homes, still has a temporary look, but this is sure to change as southeasterners take advantage of the

· *Float houses near the fishing town of Craig are left high on the flats when the tide goes out.*

Memorial and mortuary poles were brought to Klawock from several abandoned villages on Prince of Wales Island.

superb water setting. A short drive out of Thorne Bay takes you to a picnic beach overlooking Clarence Strait; you can sometimes spot cruise ships steaming past in the distance.

North of Thorne Bay, you will find prime wilderness fishing and camping in and around intense logging activity. Facilities are few up here. *Coffman Cove, Whale Pass,* and *Labouchere Bay* are logging camp communities in various stages of evolution. (Like Thorne Bay, Coffman Cove has put down permanent roots—there is a school, store, and cafe.) At the extreme northern tip of the island, the fishing villages of *Port Protection* and *Point Baker*—by choice unconnected to and thus unreachable by the island road system—look toward the sea, straining to preserve their privacy and independence.

At present the roads on Prince of Wales Island are not paved and some, especially on the north end, are extremely rough. Be sure you have at least one spare tire and ascertain in advance the availability of fuel along your route. As you tour the island, bear in mind that these are logging roads; you have to share the right-of-way with trucks that will not slow down for long. Be prepared to give way. Also, road signs are scarce, so you may have to rely on a map to find your way around the island (see below). Taking your car or camper on the ferry from Ketchikan is probably the

Float houses bob in the sunset at Thorne Bay, a former Louisiana-Pacific logging camp.

simplest way to explore Prince of Wales. There are alternatives. You can rent a car in Ketchikan and take it on the ferry with you. (Rent-a-Dent on Tongass Avenue has some Prince of Wales specials they reserve for use on the island.) You can also rent a vehicle in Klawock, but you may have to find a ride from the ferry terminal at Hollis to pick it up. There are no buses, but some sort of shuttle service usually operates between Hollis, Craig, and Klawock.

Prince of Wales Island is a special place to experience undeveloped Southeast. There is lots of room to fish and camp and plenty of animal life to observe. Black bears are commonly sighted. It is one of the greenest places around because so much of the island is second-growth timber. If you intend to camp, check with the U.S. Forest Service office in Craig to see which lands have been declared off limits by the Native corporations: the rest is Tongass National Forest and yours to enjoy. There are a few forest service recreational cabins and campsites. If Prince of Wales sounds appealing, write for Leaflet Number 180, *Prince of Wales Island Road Guide*, from the *Forest Supervisor, Tongass National Forest, Federal Building, Ketchikan, Alaska, 99901*; telephone *(907) 225-3101*. Enclose $2.00. Besides mapping the road system, the pamphlet spells out details about wildlife, fishing, communities, and camping.

KAKE
Population 665

The Tlingit community of Kake lies on the northwest corner of Kupreanof Island. The Alaska ferry stops once a week en route between Petersburg and Sitka. Kake has always relied on fishing to fuel the economy, first as a cannery site and lately with a cold storage plant. The community depends heavily on logging, too.

Kake is a handy place to stop for a few hours or overnight if you are touring Southeast by private boat and need to refuel and replenish supplies. There are two grocery stores, a restaurant, and a place to lay your head at the *New Town Inn*, providing there is room. The beds are frequently taken by visiting construction crews or businessmen. Write *New Town Inn, P.O. Box 222, Kake, Alaska, 99830*; telephone *(907) 785-3472*.

Kake is the home of Alaska's tallest totem pole (132.5 feet), which was carved by Alaska Indian Arts in Haines for Expo 70 in Osaka, Japan. The pole is anchored with guy wires to the top of a bluff overlooking the town. The village of Kake is arranged in traditional Native style along a gently sloping beach. These days the boats drawn up on shore are aluminum Lunds

Kake lies on a gentle curve of beach as did Tlingit villages of old. Aluminum skiffs are drawn up on shore.

and not cedar canoes, but the effect is the same. The fishing is good for salmon, halibut, and trout, but do not expect to find any special facilities or activities for visitors. You will be on your own. Several logging roads provide access to forest, beaches, and picnic sites. There is scheduled air service to Kake from both Petersburg and Sitka on floatplanes.

ANGOON
Population 640

Angoon is the sole permanent community on 1,709-square-mile Admiralty Island southwest of Juneau. The village straddles a finger of land on the west coast of the island, fronting on a crescent of beach on Chatham Strait while turbulent Kootznahoo Inlet rushes past the back door. Angoon remains a stronghold of Tlingit culture within the unspoiled wilderness of Admiralty Island National Monument, where the villagers coexist with the island bear and bald eagles as they have for centuries.

Industry came to Angoon in the nineteenth century with the Northwest Trading Company of Portland, Oregon, which built a shore-based whaling station on Killisnoo Island, three miles to the south of Angoon. The whale carcasses were processed into oil, bone meal, and fertilizer. Later a herring reduction plant operated on the same site. A second whaling station was established on the southeast tip of Admiralty in 1907. While both ventures were short-lived, the whaling industry brought disaster to the village of Angoon in an incident that is remembered with bitterness today. In 1882, a Tlingit shaman was killed accidentally when a harpoon gun exploded aboard a Northwest Trading Company vessel. The Tlingit community demanded that the trading company compensate for the life of the shaman with a payment of two hundred blankets. When the company refused, the situation escalated, and ended with navy vessels coming from Sitka to shell and burn the village houses and canoes. Angoon was rebuilt gradually over the next decade.

The people of Angoon did obtain ninety thousand dollars in reparations from the government in 1973. In 1982, one hundred years after the shelling, a memorial potlatch was held to commemorate the unfortunate event and to dedicate three new totem poles, the first steps in what villagers hope will be a major restoration of the community housefronts to a semblance of their 1882 appearance.

Today Angoon's economy is based primarily upon fishing. The fishermen, most of them hand-trollers, go out in the morning and sell their catch in the evening to a cash buyer in the harbor. Many of the rhythms of the old life-style are still apparent in this isolated community. Subsistence fishing takes precedence in August and September when villagers move up Kootznahoo Inlet into Mitchell Bay to set their beach seines and take the salmon the state allows them to catch for personal use.

With the regular service provided by the state ferry system—usually the *LeConte*, which arrives some three times a week on the run between Juneau and Sitka—Angoon is slowly and carefully entering the tourist trade. The attractions are primarily the wilderness experience in and around Angoon and the access the community provides to the rest of the island. Admiralty has the highest brown bear population in Southeast (the Tlingit name for Admiralty, Kootznahoo, is translated to mean "bear fort," or "fortress of the bears"). Estimates suggest one brown bear for every square mile. Bald eagles are another Admiralty specialty. An average of two eagle-nesting trees per mile along the 678 miles of shoreline gives Admiralty Island the highest known concentration of bald eagles on the continent. Humpback whales are commonly seen in Mitchell Bay at the upper reaches of Kootznahoo Inlet.

Angoon is also the terminus for the Cross-Admiralty Canoe Route from Mole Harbor on Seymour Canal on the eastern shore of the island. The thirty-two-mile route bisects the island via a series of midland lakes and short portages, with Forest Service cabins strategically placed along the way. Allow six to ten days for a leisurely trip. Consult Margaret Piggott's *Discover Southeast Alaska with Pack and Paddle* (The Mountaineers) for a thorough description of this route. *Alaska Discovery* offers guided canoe and camping trips on the Cross-Admiralty route. Write *Alaska Discovery, 369 South Franklin Street, Juneau, Alaska, 99801*; telephone *(907) 586-1911*. Alaska Discovery will also rent you a canoe in Angoon for use in Mitchell Bay—write to the address above or inquire at the Angoon Trading Co. store in Angoon. The tidal rip causes very fast currents in Kootznahoo Inlet and Mitchell Bay that are hazardous for the unwary.

Angoon is well prepared to accommodate visitors. The waterfront *Favorite Bay Inn Bed & Breakfast,* near the boat harbor and floatplane docks, offers personable lodging in a 1930s-era home that once served as a general store. Write *P.O. Box 101, Angoon, Alaska, 99820;* telephone *(907) 788-3123.* The *Kootznahoo Lodge* has rooms for daily rentals or longer and *Demmert's Restaurant.* Write *Kootznahoo Lodge, P.O. Box 134, Angoon, Alaska, 99820;* telephone *(907) 788-3501.* The lodge overlooks the old floatplane dock on Kootznahoo Inlet. Small boats are moored there, too, and you can usually find someone willing to take you out fishing or sightseeing up into Mitchell Bay. At any hour, there always seems to be somebody bringing in a load of salmon, halibut, octopus, or other bounty from the sea. If you walk out on the dock and look down into the clear water, you will see some beautiful examples of *metridium*, a large, white sea anemone that clings to the pilings. Prod it gently with a stick and the petals will close up tight.

In the village there are a couple of grocery stores but no bars or liquor stores; Angoon is dry. A fifteen-minute walk along a well-maintained forest path will take you to the cemetery (go up the hill past the Salvation

Army building at the north end of town); or you can follow along the shingle beach. You will see Orthodox crosses side by side with cherubic angels and totemic carvings. The beach lends itself to tide pool investigations and a leisurely picnic lunch.

South of the village on Kootznahoo Inlet you will come to the small boat harbor where the commercial fishing boats tie up. A cash buyer for Petersburg Fisheries is moored in the harbor. Walk down in the evening when the fleet is coming in and watch them unload the day's catch.

You will find the people of Angoon cautiously friendly, if you respect their community and their love for their island wilderness. Angoon has few of the amenities that accompany development and the experience is not for everyone, but it is for those who take pleasure in enjoying the quieter country on their own. The wildlife quotient is truly spectacular. There is a particular spot on the road between the floatplane dock and the village where there never fails to be something to watch. Once when we looked over the edge of the road onto Kootznahoo Inlet, a school of herring flashed in the sunlight. Another day we walked along and a pair of tiny harbor porpoises coursed along the shore. The next time we passed the spot, a bald eagle burst into view like a conjurer's pigeon, then settled heavily into the branches below.

The ferry docks at Killisnoo Harbor opposite Killisnoo Island, approximately three miles south of Angoon. You will have to hitch a ride into town if

The water boils past the floatplane dock on turbulent Kootznahoo Inlet. Small boats that moor at the dock may offer fishing trips.

you are carrying too much to walk. There is an old graveyard with some impressive carvings above the beach to the right of the dock (as you face the water). There is a Beaver totem near the beach and others up a small knoll. One in particular has three faces and a salmon carved in low relief. Killisnoo Island has several summer homes, and a homey sportfishing lodge with restaurant and private cabins right on the beach. Write *Whalers Cove Lodge, P.O. Box 101, Angoon, Alaska, 99820*; telephone *(907) 788-3123*.

HOONAH
Population 905

Hoonah is one of three communities on Chichagof Island that can be reached by Alaska state ferry (there are no road connections between them). Hoonah, the largest Tlingit settlement in Southeast, lies on the northeast corner of the island in Icy Strait, just twenty miles from Glacier Bay. In fact, Hoonah legends indicate that their people migrated from Glacier Bay to the present site long ago. Like so many traditional Indian villages that were located near the resources of the sea, Hoonah became a cannery center in the early part of the century. Hoonah Cold Storage continues to be an economic force in the community, but logging is now the primary industry. Huna Totem Corporation, formed under the Alaska Native Claims Settlement Act of 1971, is logging the surrounding lands and exporting timber to Japan.

Hoonah has something to offer the visitor who is looking for an out-of-the-way experience. Comfortable lodging is available at the *Totem Lodge*. The rooms are attractively furnished in rustic decor, and the restaurant and lounge are lively with loggers, fishermen, and most everyone else in the evening. Fishing charters are available through the lodge as well. Write *Totem Lodge, P.O. Box 320, Hoonah, Alaska, 99829*; telephone *(907) 945-3636*.

The ferry docks about a mile northwest of the town center. As you stroll down the dirt road toward town you will pass identical wooden frame houses in weathered pastels. The structures were put up under a government housing program after a fire devastated the old village in 1944. Canoes, totem poles, and many valuable pieces of art were destroyed as well. Newer housing developments are on the south side of town. You will pass Thompson Dock where *Hoonah Cold Storage* buys and processes salmon, halibut, and crab. The cold storage has operated on this site for at least twenty years. You are welcome to look around if they are not too busy and have a quick education in the mechanics of cold storage. (Stop in at the office first and ask permission.) When we were there in July, troll-caught salmon were being unloaded from the boats onto the dock where they were washed, trimmed, glazed with a solution of water and corn syrup to prevent dehydration, frozen, and shipped to a broker in Bellingham,

Three stone faces and a salmon mark a grave near the Angoon ferry terminal, where ferries stop twice a week.

Washington, in 750-pound totes. The salmon roe are brined and packed in special wooden boxes for export to Japan. You can buy fresh fish from the cold storage, too.

Opposite Thompson Dock on the uphill side you will see the *L. Kane Store*, which has been in business since 1893. The storefront is decorated with colorful Eagle and Raven designs. The store carries everything from rubber boots to frozen chocolate éclairs. The Hoonah city offices are right here, too, and will provide you with any information you need. Farther along Front Street to the south is the *Glacier Winds* gift shop. Check here for local artwork, silver jewelry, and craft items such as beaded moccasins and Tlingit dolls. Farther south there is the new George Hall Jr. Memorial Boat Harbor with first-class docking and repair facilities.

Hoonah has a new *cultural center* operated by the Hoonah Indian Association. The address is on Roosevelt Drive, but street signs are not evident. To get to the center, you have to turn uphill from the water. Your best bet is to ask directions from the city offices or a passerby. The center is open every weekday. Many of the exhibit items are on loan from local residents, and displays change periodically. On my last visit I saw a couple of totem poles and a painted wall screen commemorating the ancestral homelands of the Eagle and Raven clans. Among the other items were a magnificent beaded Thunderbird blanket, a Chilkat blanket, and a beaded

Government frame houses were constructed after a fire destroyed the old village of Hoonah.

octopus bag and other costume regalia that has been passed down through at least three generations.

If you have time for more walking (or you can take a taxi), proceed north past the ferry terminal. You will pass a graveyard on the right side of the road with old Orthodox crosses and at least one large carved totem among the berry bushes and evergreens. In approximately two miles you will come to the old Hoonah Packing cannery that processed salmon until 1944. The complex of buildings is used by Columbia Wards Fisheries to outfit their seine fleet. When we happened by in early July, the fleet was just getting ready to put to sea. The big seiners, with names like the *Mary Joanne*, *Western Queen*, *Karen Jean*, and *Sea Ranger*, were all lined up, testing gear and taking on supplies. There are established hiking trails east of town. Five miles west of town, at Game Creek, is Mount Bether Bible Center, a Christian agricultural settlement of about one hundred residents, which is accessible by boat only.

Hoonah is a destination to consider for a one- or two-day excursion

Seine fishermen hoist the net aboard for the start of the fishing season at Columbia Wards Fisheries at Hoonah.

from Juneau. Like other villages off the main line, Hoonah is not for the luxury-minded or faint of heart, but for the adventuresome and self-sufficient. The town is only three hours by ferry from Juneau.

TENAKEE SPRINGS
Population 100

Tenakee Inlet, which cleaves Chichagof Island from the northeast shore, was once the site of both crab and salmon canneries. The hamlet of Tenakee Springs, at the north shore of the inlet, developed as a winter retreat for fishermen and prospectors who had discovered that hot sulfur springs bubble out of the earth there at temperatures of 106 to 108 degrees. By 1900, small, hand-hewn cabins had sprouted along the beach. Today Tenakee Springs provides a relaxed alternative lifestyle for approximately one hundred southeasterners who flee the confines of city life for this haven of genteel rusticity. Some full-time residents are retirement age, while others are raising families and working the land. Many homeowners live in Juneau and use Tenakee for a weekend and vacation retreat.

From shipboard—Alaska state ferries make the eight-hour trip from Juneau a couple times a week—Tenakee appears as a long row of dollhouses on stilts along the water. The cabins are arranged along a dirt and gravel path that reaches nearly eight miles in either direction from the center of town, but most fall within a two-mile stretch. No vehicles are allowed in the community except an ancient and decrepit oil truck and a fire truck, although there is an increasing preponderance—some say an alarming preponderance—of three- and four-wheel ATVs.

The atmosphere in Tenakee is one of studied neglect. Overalls and comfortable surroundings set the tone and no one is too keen on development. Tenakee has electricity and telephones but no city water or sewer system. Outhouses are stationed out over the tide. A walk on the path in either direction yields many arresting images for the camera or canvas: rusted oil drums perched outside each cabin on special wooden platforms, old-fashioned wringer washing machines out on the porch, luxurious flower and vegetable gardens, piles of crab pots, hand-hewn and notched log cabins, and various contraptions for hauling things from the ferry or floatplane dock or buckets of water from the creek or cold spring.

Tenakee is not without commercial enterprise. *Snyder Mercantile*, at the entrance to the ferry dock, carries all necessary provisions, including marine fuels (hours vary). Sometimes you can buy fresh Tenakee-grown vegetables and day-old eggs. The *Shamrock* is a senior citizens center, coffee club, and bingo parlor. There is a library, post office, and city hall. The *Blue Moon Cafe* gives you a meal if Rosie feels like cooking. Farther down the path toward the boat harbor, the *Tenakee Tavern* is a cozy corner that frequently turns rowdy at night.

More important than any of these is the *bathhouse*, which is the focal point of Tenakee. The painted concrete bathhouse at the end of the ferry dock opposite Snyder Mercantile was built to enclose the principal spring in 1940. The water flows into the natural rock bath at the rate of seven gallons per minute. Bath hours are posted: men from 2 to 6 P.M. and 10 P.M. to 9 A.M.; women 6 to 10 P.M. and 9 A.M. to 2 P.M. These hours are strictly adhered to; mixed bathing is but a wishful dream on the part of the more forward-thinking residents. Life in Tenakee revolves around the bath. It is customary to bathe at least once every day and twice is preferred. Women bring the children and bathe them, too; sometimes they bring the laundry as well. There is an outer dressing room (with a stove for winter use) with hooks for your clothes and benches where you can lie down and cool off when you emerge from the bath. A short flight of steps leads down to an inner door opening onto the steamy interior of the bath. The bath itself is a small, deep, rectangular pool. A concrete floor surrounds the bath and channels the overflow to the outside of the bathhouse. The rules are the same as in a Japanese bath: no soap in the water and wash yourself *before* getting in to soak. You start by sitting on the concrete floor. Pick up one of

Tenakee Springs offers a relaxed and alternative lifestyle. Life centers around the hot sulfur bath.

A stroll along the Tenakee path leads past hand-notched cabins and luxurious gardens.

the plastic jugs you will see lying around (currently old Wesson Oil bottles). Dip the jug in the bath and pour the hot water over your body. After you have scrubbed, shampooed, and rinsed via the jug, lower yourself gingerly into the bath for a good soak. (Be sure to remove your silver jewelry before bathing because the water will turn it black.) Before you leave Tenakee, a small donation to the bathhouse fund at Snyder Mercantile is appropriate to help with the upkeep.

Other recreational activities in Tenakee include walking up and down the path; fishing for crab, salmon, halibut, and trout; picking salmonberries, raspberries, and thimbleberries; cooking; watching bald eagles and humpback whales cavort off the front deck; and reading an armload of trashy novels brought for the purpose. Tenakee is a form of therapy.

Tenakee-style rental cabins with cooking facilities are available through *Snyder Mercantile* at very reasonable prices (especially the big one, which has a fireplace and sleeps six). Reservations are essential during summer and the fall hunting season. Write *Snyder Mercantile, P.O. Box 505, Tenakee Springs, Alaska, 99841;* telephone *(907) 736-2205.* The

Tenakee Inn and Tavern, telephone *(907) 736-9238,* has rooms with private baths and kitchenettes, rental kayaks and skiffs, a laundromat, small restaurant, and wonderful outside deck. But call ahead—they are not always open in the off-season.

PELICAN
Population 215

Pelican is the third Chichagof Island community on the Alaska Marine Highway System. The ferry pulls into this small fishing town on Lisianski Inlet, on the northwest corner of the island, about twice a month on a special run from Juneau—less frequently in winter. If the schedule is suitable, you can make a fun (and very long) day of it by catching the ferry out in the morning for the trip to Pelican, looking around during the two-hour stopover, and returning to Juneau. Or, you can take the ferry out and charter a plane back. The ferry trip takes approximately seven hours in each direction.

Pelican hums during the fishing season with the comings and goings of the commercial fleet and the activity of Pelican Cold Storage. Stores, cafes, and even a steambath line the wide wooden boardwalk, but the focus in Pelican is on *Rose's Bar and Grill* where fisherfolk gather at night. Pelican is not an old community; it dates from the early 1940s when the processing plant was built.

HYDER
Population 75

Way up at the end of the Portland Canal, the skinny waterway that marks the southern border between Southeast Alaska and Canada, lies a tiny rural village named Hyder and its Canadian neighbor, Stewart. Publicized as the "friendliest ghost town in Alaska," Hyder counted ten thousand residents in the days when gold and silver flowed from the hills. Nowadays Hyder is virtually an American extension of Stewart. Townspeople live on Canadian time, share a Canadian area code (604 instead of 907 like the rest of Alaska), send their children to a Canadian school, and pay their bills in Canadian dollars.

There is not a lot to the town—a triplet of bars, a couple of gift shops and places to eat, a monument or two. What they have in spades is fantastic glacier scenery, tremendous fishing, enormous good will, and easy access. You can reach Hyder both by road (from the Cassiar Highway 37 in British Columbia, connecting with the Alaska Highway) and Alaska ferry from Ketchikan (summer only, once a week—the ferry actually docks in Stewart). Lodging is at the *Sealaska Inn,* a mile from the ferry dock. Write *Sealaska Inn, Hyder, Alaska, 99923;* telephone *(604) 636-2486.*

Pelican's wide wooden boardwalk is an expressway for every sort of two- and three-wheeled vehicle. (Scott Foster)

Sixteen separate glaciers flow from the mountains into the twin arms of Glacier Bay. (Alaska Division of Tourism)

GLACIER BAY NATIONAL PARK AND PRESERVE

Sixteen separate glaciers flow out of the Saint Elias Mountains into the two arms of Glacier Bay. Here, amid the ice-locked upper reaches of the bay, visitors confront the mysterious antecedents of the modern era. Those privileged to look upon this icy wilderness journey back to an age when the present Southeast rain forests were not yet established, and the simplest form of vegetation strove for a tentative hold on the denuded land.

Most cruise ships include Glacier Bay in the Inside Passage itinerary so their passengers can enjoy the splendor of the ice blue glaciers, the fantastically shaped icebergs, the humpback whales that frequent the inlet, and some of the two hundred-plus species of birds that have been recorded within the park. Alaska state ferries do not travel into the bay, but other alternatives include day trips and overnight excursions with local charter operators. You can even kayak through Glacier Bay with one of the kayak and camping package trips offered by Alaska Discovery. For more information about guided kayaking in Glacier Bay, write *Alaska Discovery, 369 South Franklin Street, Juneau, Alaska, 99801*; telephone *(907) 586-1911*. For kayak rentals in Glacier Bay contact *Glacier Bay Sea Kayaks, P.O. Box 26, Gustavus, Alaska, 99826;* telephone *(907) 697-2257.*

The headquarters for the park is at Bartlett Cove, on the east side of the entrance to the bay. For the last few years, the park has limited the number of motorized boats entering the bay in order to minimize the disturbance to the humpback whales that feed there in the summer. If you wish to take your own boat into the bay, you may need to write ahead for a free seven-day permit. Most requests for permits are usually for the first two weeks in July, so you would be wise to schedule your trip for a different period. Write *Glacier Bay National Park and Preserve, Gustavus, Alaska, 99826.* Telephone reservations are possible by calling the park information station "whale phone" at Bartlett Cove at *(907) 697-2268* (summer only). You can also try radioing Bartlett Cove (*KWM 20 Bartlett Cove*) on *VHF Channel 16* when you are in the area to see if there have been any last-minute cancellations. You can also fly into the area by small airplane or by scheduled jet service from Juneau (summer only). The airport is in the rural community of Gustavus, nine miles from Bartlett Cove. Or you can take the *Glacier Express,* a high-speed catamaran that makes the trip between Juneau and Gustavus in just three and one-half smooth hours. There is no road access into Glacier Bay or Gustavus from other Southeast communities. You must arrive by boat or plane.

The *Glacier Bay Lodge* at Bartlett Cove has comfortable rooms and a restaurant in an appropriately rustic building. It is open from mid-May through the end of September. Write *Glacier Bay Lodge, Gustavus, Alaska, 99826;* telephone *(907) 697-2225* in summer, and *1620 Metropolitan Park Building, Seattle, Washington, 98101;* telephone *(206) 623-2417* the rest of the year. From the lodge, you can catch the daily excursion cruise leaving in the morning. For details concerning sight-seeing, camping, fishing, boating, and other aspects of the park, contact the *Superintendent, Glacier Bay National Park and Preserve, Gustavus, Alaska, 99826;* telephone *(907) 697-2230.*

Gustavus has a year-round population of approximately two hundred. Many Juneau residents have summer cabins there. The land is flat and gardening is a treat; in fact the area provided meat and garden produce for nearby canneries in the early part of the century. Strawberries—both wild and cultivated—are a Gustavus specialty.

One of the most celebrated kitchens in Alaska is in Gustavus. The *Gustavus Inn* has been operated by various members of the Lesh family since the mid-1960s. When we first went there, in 1969, Jack and Sally Lesh were running the old homestead, raising a family, reporting the weather, driving the school bus, operating the single telephone in the community, and preparing the finest meals in Southeast Alaska for a grateful and loyal clientele, some of whom would fly over from Juneau on a summer evening solely for the pleasure of sitting at Sally's table. The family lived in the big farmhouse, and a Quonset hut at the rear provided quarters for summer guests and the occasional winter road crew. The old house over-flowed with warmth, only part of which was attributable to the big oil stove in the kitchen.

In the years since our first visit, the inn has passed into the capable hands of several Lesh children. Changes have been made (for a time the big house sheltered the guests and the hosts lived in the Quonset) but the kitch-en is still renowned for the produce picked from the inn's own gardens, the fresh-caught bounty from the sea, the home-baked bread and wild-berry desserts, the tried-and-true family recipes (some of which have been col-lected into a cookbook published by the inn), and the kelp pickles and other local specialties. The meals are served family-style, giving you an oppor-tunity to get acquainted with your neighbors and hosts. The inn has bicycles, fishing gear, and most other items you might need to enjoy your stay. Hike over to the Salmon River and try your luck catching something for dinner. Your hosts can also arrange for your boat excursion into Glacier Bay, and match you up with an expert local fishing guide. Write *Gustavus Inn, P.O. Box 60, Gustavus, Alaska, 99826;* telephone *(907) 697-2254.*

Many other accommodations are available in Gustavus, from fishing lodges to rental cabins and bed and breakfasts. A new rustic-style hostelry, the *Glacier Bay Country Inn,* stands on 160-acres of trees, hayfields, and potato gardens, one and one-half miles off the main road. Annie and Al Unrein have taken as much care with the pleasant rooms (all with private bath) as they do with your sight-seeing and travel arrangements and the three home-cooked meals a day. It is very peaceful here. Write *Glacier Bay Country Inn, P.O. Box 5, Gustavus, Alaska, 99826;* telephone *(907) 697-2288.*

THE REMOTE INNS

In addition to the communities available to the visitor via the Alaska Marine Highway System, there are dozens of remote lodges *that require a floatplane or private boat for access.* They are not reachable by cruise ship, ferry, or road. While a more expensive proposition, these secluded inns of-fer the traveler a uniquely Southeast experience. Situated on freshwater lakes or saltwater shores, the wilderness resorts offer outstanding fishing, hunting, and photography together with good food and superlative Alaskan hospitality. Most are closed over the winter; write for details. Here are some to consider.

Yes Bay Lodge is a family resort, catering equally to local residents, private boaters, and visitors from afar, on an inlet on the mainland fifty miles northwest of Ketchikan. Meals are served family-style and the emphasis is on Alaska seafood. Both saltwater and freshwater fishing are amply available, and the lodge smokes and packages your fish. Write *Hack Family, Yes Bay Lodge, Yes Bay via Ketchikan, Alaska, 99950*; radiophone *Ketchikan KOJ 89*.

The most elaborate resort in the Ketchikan area is *Waterfall Resort*, sixty-two miles west of Ketchikan on the outer coast of Prince of Wales Island (but not on the road system). Waterfall has been built out of what was one of the largest canneries in Southeast Alaska. Accommodations include twenty-six cabins that have been transformed from cannery workers' housing into luxurious guest quarters. Each cabin is equipped with a full bath, wet bar, and refrigerator. Family-style meals served in the former mess hall capitalize on the abundant local seafood. (Two-hundred-pound halibut have been caught off the dock.)

For entertainment, there is first-class fishing for salmon, halibut, and steelhead; hikes to the waterfall (one and one-half miles on a cedar boardwalk); large-screen television; billiards; and photographing old cannery buildings. Meals, guide service, speedboats, lodging, and round-trip floatplane transportation from Ketchikan are all included in the per person rate. For nonfishermen, Waterfall's nature tour packages include guided whalewatching excursions, eagle observations, and trips to nearby bird colonies, Indian villages, and petroglyph beaches. A small store carries fishing gear, groceries, and a modest collection of Native artifacts. Private boaters can run

Waterfall Resort is located at a former cannery site. Cannery workers' cottages are now luxurious guest quarters.

Bob and Edith Nelson have been welcoming guests to their Thayer Lake wilderness lodge for more than thirty summers.

into the protected harbor for fuel, stock up on groceries, and, if the lodge is not too busy, buy meals, too. The bar is a comfortable place to swap tales with the locals. Write *Waterfall Resort, P.O. Box 6440, Ketchikan, Alaska, 99901*; telephone *(907) 225-9461* or *toll free (800) 544-5125*.

   Thayer Lake Lodge is tucked onto the shore of a freshwater lake in the middle of Admiralty Island National Monument Wilderness. Bob and Edith Nelson of Ketchikan began constructing the lodge in 1947 and have hosted summertime guests there every year but one since 1952. Facilities consist of a comfortable main lodge with two upstairs guest rooms plus two independent lakefront cabins. You choose between the Nelson family's cooking at the lodge or self-service in the cabins.

Cutthroat in nine-mile Thayer Lake are not trophy-sized but are plentiful with spinning gear or fly rod. Thayer Lake Lodge is less strictly a fishing resort, however, than a contemplative wilderness experience. The acres of forest surrounding the lodge have heard few human voices. Canoes and aluminum skiffs are at your disposal for exploring the lake: paddle gently about, investigate muskeg meadows, amble along six miles of gentle, maintained forest trails, drop a line into the water, listen to the call of the loons. Then, settle back and enjoy the company of your hosts. After thirty summers on the lake, the Nelsons have achieved a singular peace with their primitive wilderness surroundings. Ask Bob to explain the workings of his handmade wooden waterwheel.

Lodge and cabins are comfortably rustic, with hand-built spruce bunks, rock fireplaces, and full bath facilities. Float trips down Thayer Creek to Chatham Strait are available. Thayer Lake Lodge is reached by floatplane from Juneau or Angoon. There is also a trail from the vicinity of Angoon. Many guests fly in to the lodge and top off their wilderness adventure with a guided walk/float trip back to Angoon. Write *Thayer Lake Lodge, P.O. Box 5416, Ketchikan, Alaska, 99901*; telephone *(907) 789-5646.*

The *Admiralty Inn* at Funter Bay, on the northwest corner of Admiralty Island, promises a "personalized" wilderness adventure built around a showcase pioneer cabin, which was hand-built by meticulous Swedish woodcraftsman Gunnar Ohman. Ohman trapped and fished for a living and began building his Funter Bay dream cabin in 1949. He and his wife Lazzette lived there year-round.

Gunnar's spruce log cabin is smoothed and hand-fitted together like a giant wooden puzzle. Windows and doorways are lovingly trimmed with polished yellow cedar inlays. Hand-built tables and cabinets, bookshelves, and secret nooks are testimony to years of long winter nights. Not satisfied with just the main cabin, Gunnar built outbuildings for every conceivable purpose. There's a smokehouse for fish and another for game, a boathouse, butcher house and root cellar, shop, and steambath.

Lodge owners Dale Anderson and Ford Horst, both pilots, acquired the four-acre homestead in 1983 and opened the lodge to a limited number of visitors in the summer of 1984. Overnight guests arrive after a ten-minute floatplane ride from the Juneau airport (piloted by one of their hosts) and are lodged in either the old cabin or the rebuilt bunkhouse—all modernized with private baths. The lodge staff and boats are at your disposal to make your wilderness dreams a reality: you can fish for salmon, halibut, or snapper; pull up a crab pot; go on a photo safari for brown bear, bald eagles, and other wild creatures; enjoy a scuba-diving expedition; or canoe quietly around Funter Bay. The bay is the site of a former cannery. The old cannery buildings across the water are a picturesque backdrop to the wilderness. In the morning you'll wake to see deer browsing at the

The cornerstone of the Admiralty Inn is a showcase spruce log cabin built by Swedish woodcraftsman Gunnar Ohman.

water's edge. At night cruise ships pass on the horizon on their way out of Glacier Bay. Write *Admiralty Inn, P.O. Box 32239, Juneau, Alaska, 99803*; telephone *(907) 789-3263*.

Taku Glacier Lodge, 30 air miles from Juneau, has one of the most dramatic wilderness settings in Alaska. Situated on the Taku River at the head of Taku Inlet, the traditional log lodge is a stone's throw away from two spectacular glaciers. The site was developed as a private hunting lodge in 1923. In the 1930s, the lodge was opened commercially by the famous adventuress Mary Joyce, who journeyed one thousand miles by dogsled, pulled by her Taku River Huskies, to attend the 1936 Fairbanks Ice Carnival.

Owner Ron Maas acquired the property in 1971 and, with his wife, Kathy, set out to restore the lodge and outbuildings for summer guests. Standing on a grassy bluff above the riverbank, the single-story lodge is the epitome of the Alaskan bush cabin, complete with moose rack and massive granite fireplace. Interior walls are hung with fur pelts, showshoes, traps, and dog harnesses.

In summer, Taku Glacier Lodge puts on an organized fly-in salmon bake that is prepurchased by many cruise ship passengers as a Juneau excursion. You leave by floatplane from the Seadrome on the Juneau waterfront (noncruise ship passengers buy tickets there) and are treated to a twenty-minute flyover of the Juneau Ice Cap on your way to the lodge.

Anchored on a grassy bluff above the Taku River, Taku Glacier Lodge commands one of the most impressive views in wilderness Alaska.

Then sit down to a meal of grilled salmon, homemade sourdough rolls, beans, coleslaw, and possibly the best oatmeal-raisin cookies in America, before making the return flight to Juneau.

Taku Glacier Lodge also has overnight accommodations. Guests are housed in separate quarters, which are simple but comfortable, with full baths. For overnight lodgers, recreational activities include guided trips to nearby glaciers, river fishing for Dolly Varden and cutthroat trout, hiking, and canoeing. Meals are all home-cooked; Kathy Maas presides in the kitchen. Write *Taku Glacier Lodge, Number 2 Marine Way, Suite 228, Juneau, Alaska, 99801*; telephone *(907) 586-1362* or *586-1282*; or contact the lodge office at the Seadrome at Merchant's Wharf in Juneau.

Baranof Wilderness Lodge at Warm Springs Bay, on the east coast of Baranof Island, just opened its doors in 1984. Owners Clark and Melinda Gruening of Juneau acquired the property two years previously, however, and their patient, deliberate planning shows in the finished quality of the operation. Warm Springs Bay was a rest-and-recreation center for the canned salmon industry in the 1930s and a small community grew up around the hot mineral springs at the head of the bay. Today the settlement consists of a few cabins, general store, bathhouse, and state float frequented by commercial fishermen and recreational boaters. With most of the canneries long gone, the bay generally sees no more strenuous activity than the hooking of a giant halibut or a soak in the mineral baths.

The Gruenings' lodge lies on six acres of wilderness, fronting on the bay. Facilities include a main lodge where guests gather to socialize and sit down for meals at a hand-hewn table for twelve. Guests are billeted in new, private, pine-finished cabins with electric baseboard heat. Showers are available, but soaking in the wood-fired redwood hot tub in the woods beside Sadie Creek is much more fun. During August, you can watch from your bath as pink salmon surge up the creek to spawn.

The Gruenings have designed their lodge as an all-around wilderness experience. There is excellent salmon (all species) and halibut fishing in Warm Springs Bay, but the locale offers much more. You can hike the three-quarter-mile boardwalk trail to freshwater Baranof Lake. Take the lodge canoe and explore the lake or fish for cutthroat. Intermediate hiking trails lead through Southeast rain forest to alpine meadows and high ridge walks. The Gruenings will guide you to secluded sand beaches, seal-covered rocks, brown bear haunts, and salt lagoons. Then, hike the trail or canoe into "town." Visit Wally Sonnenberg's old store and try a hot mineral bath. Back at the lodge, you'll forget you're in wilderness with Melinda Gruening's four-course dinners. Drawing upon the abundant seafood, fresh produce from the lodge garden, and her practiced baking skills, Melinda spares nothing to make your mealtime moments as un-camplike as possible. Baranof Wilderness Lodge is reached by floatplane

Baranof Wilderness Lodge lies on six acres of wilderness at Warm Springs Bay. Guest quarters are in private waterfront cabins.

from Sitka. Write *Baranof Wilderness Lodge, P.O. Box 210022, Auke Bay, Alaska, 99821*; telephone *(907) 586-8110* (1 October through 31 May); *747-8636* (1 June through 30 September).

Elfin Cove, a fishing hamlet with a resident population of around fifty, is located on the northwest corner of Chichagof Island, on Cross Sound. Like Pelican, also on Chichagof, the community is close to the Fairweather fishing grounds on the outside coast. There are two harbors. The outer harbor, with a view of Brady Glacier across Cross Sound, contains the floatplane dock, fuel dock, and the cash buyers that purchase fish from incoming fishermen. The inner harbor, connected to the outer by a narrow channel called The Gut, is edged with a wooden boardwalk lined with tiny cabins and, increasingly, larger vacation homes. Fishing and pleasure boats can tie up at either of two protected floats.

Rooms are available at the *Elf Inn* (three upstairs, plus a rental cabin) where the restaurant serves good, hearty, home-cooked meals. Sit at the

The serene hamlet of Elfin Cove is a fishing center in summer and lapses into snowy silence in winter.

Visitors go ashore at Elfin Cove to pick up some of Augusta Clements's home-baked bread.

U-shaped counter and hobnob with the fishermen, or retreat to the dining room. Write *Elf Inn, P.O. Box 22, Elfin Cove, Alaska, 99825*; telephone *(907) 239-2204.* Fishing and sight-seeing charters are available. The *Elfin Cove Sportfishing Lodge* has quarters for a limited number of guests with a full package of fishing charters and guide service. Write *Elfin Cove Sportfishing Lodge, P.O. Box 4839, Federal Way, WA, 98063;* telephone *(206) 228-7092* or toll free *(800) 422-2824* (winter) or *c/o Elfin Cove, Alaska, 99825;* telephone *(907) 239-2212* (summer).

Elfin Cove is home port for many fishermen in the summer fishing season. At night the inner harbor fills with fishing boats, sailboats, and private cruisers from Southeast ports and elsewhere. In the winter, the town quiets. If you are stocking up in Elfin Cove, be sure to ask at the store for Augusta Clements's home-baked bread.

Information Sources

Alaska State Division of Tourism
P.O. Box E
Juneau, Alaska, 99811
(907) 465-2010

Southeast Alaska Tourism Council
P.O. Box 20710
Juneau, Alaska, 99802

Alaska Marine Highway System
P.O. Box R
Juneau, Alaska, 99811
(907) 465-3941/42; or toll free
   (800) 642-0066

Alaska Department of Fish
   and Game
Public Communications Section
P.O. Box 3-2000
Juneau, Alaska, 99802-2000
(907) 465-4112

U.S. Forest Service
Public Affairs Office
P.O. Box 21628
Juneau, Alaska, 99802
(907) 586-8806

Alaska Bed & Breakfast
   Association—
   Southeastern Alaska
P.O. Box 3-6500, Suite 169
Juneau, Alaska, 99802
(907) 586-2959

Haines Visitors' Bureau
P.O. Box 518
Haines, Alaska, 99827
(907) 766-2234

Juneau Convention and Visitors'
   Bureau
76 Egan Drive, Suite 140
Juneau, Alaska, 99801
(907) 586-1737

Ketchikan Visitors' Bureau
131 Front Street
Ketchikan, Alaska, 99901
(907) 225-6166

Petersburg Chamber of Commerce
P.O. Box 649
Petersburg, Alaska, 99833
(907) 772-3646

Prince Rupert Convention and
   Visitors' Bureau
P.O. Box 669
Prince Rupert, British Columbia,
   Canada, V8J 3S1
(604) 624-5637

Sitka Visitors' Bureau
P.O. Box 1226
Sitka, Alaska, 99835
(907) 747-5940

Sitka National Historical Park
P.O. Box 738
Sitka, Alaska, 99835
(907) 747-6281

Skagway Convention and Visitors'
  Bureau
P.O. Box 415
Skagway, Alaska, 99840
(907) 983-2854

Klondike Gold Rush National
  Historical Park
P.O. Box 517
Skagway, Alaska, 99840
(907) 983-2921

Wrangell Visitors' Bureau
P.O. Box 1078
Wrangell, Alaska, 99929
(907) 874-3770

Glacier Bay National Park and
  Preserve
Gustavus, Alaska, 99826
(907) 697-2230

Misty Fiords National Monument
3031 Tongass Avenue
Ketchikan, Alaska, 99901
(907) 225-2148

Selected Reading

PLANNING YOUR TRIP

The Milepost: Mile-By-Mile Logs of the Alaska Highway, All Highways in Alaska and Major Travel Routes Through Western Canada. Anchorage: Alaska Northwest Publishing Company, 1988.

Searby, Ellen. *The Inside Passage Traveler: Getting Around in Southeastern Alaska.* Juneau: Windham Bay Press, 1988.

HISTORY

De Armond, R. N., ed. *Early Visitors to Southeastern Alaska: Nine Accounts.* Anchorage: Alaska Northwest Publishing Company, 1978.

Muir, John. *Travels in Alaska.* Boston: Houghton Mifflin Company, 1979, ed.

NATIVE ART AND CULTURE

Garfield, Viola E., and Forrest, Lynn A. *The Wolf and the Raven: Totem Poles of Southeastern Alaska*, 2nd ed. Seattle and London: University of Washington Press, 1961.

Holm, Bill. *Northwest Coast Indian Art: An Analysis of Form.* Seattle and London: University of Washington Press, 1965.

Stewart, Hilary. *Indian Fishing: Early Methods on the Northwest Coast.* Seattle and London: University of Washington Press, 1977.

Stewart, Hilary. *Looking at Indian Art of the Northwest Coast.* Seattle and London: University of Washington Press, 1979.

THE OUTDOORS

Armstrong, Robert H., and the editors of *Alaska* magazine. *A New, Expanded Guide to the Birds of Alaska*. Anchorage: Alaska Northwest Publishing Company, 1983.

Piggott, Margaret H. *Discover Southeast Alaska with Pack and Paddle*. Seattle: The Mountaineers, 1974.

White, Helen A., ed. *The Alaska-Yukon Wild Flowers Guide*. Anchorage: Alaska Northwest Publishing Company, 1974.

COMMERCIAL FISHING

Caldwell, Francis E. *Pacific Troller: Life on the Northwest Fishing Grounds*. Anchorage: Alaska Northwest Publishing Company, 1978.

Upton, Joe. *Alaska Blues: A Fisherman's Journal*. Anchorage: Alaska Northwest Publishing Company, 1977.

Index